'Into Africa'

by

Sam Manicom

Channel Islands to Cape Town by Motorcycle

'*One of the gladdest moments of human life, methinks, is the departure upon a distant journey into unknown lands. Shaking off with one mighty effort the fetters of habit, the leaden weight of routine, the cloak of many cares and the slavery of home, man feels once more happy.*'

Sir Richard Burton.

A CIP catalogue record for this title is available from the British Library.

First edition November 2005. Second edition May 2008

ISBN 978-0-9556573-1-3

Edited by Paul Blezard, Nikki Madan Schiannini and Peter Henshaw
Cover design by Fil Schiannini and Chris Woodman
Page layout by Fil Schiannini and Birgit Schuenemann
Motorcycle Line Art by Jez Cooper
Line Art by Sam Manicom and Francis Matta

Printed and bound in Great Britain by CPI Mackays
Although every effort has been made to trace the present copyright holders, we apologise in advance for any unintentional omission or neglect and will be pleased to insert appropriate acknowledgement to individuals in any subsequent edition of this publication.

www.sam-manicom.com

Contents

Prologue

I see myself as a pretty ordinary bloke and when I sat down to write this book, it all felt a bit of a cheek. I mean, who was I to think I had the right to write? I wasn't sure, but the itch in the back of my mind came from people I've met over the past years. Many said to me, 'You're incredibly lucky to have been able to travel the world, I wish I could'. At first when people said that, my self-centred attitude was 'if I can so can you'. I believed that people generally have the ability to make their lives head in the direction they wish; I was wrong.

The first person to make me ponder this properly was Charley. He looked and sounded desperate to get out on the road. He'd read travel books and lived the world from those pages, but wanted to get out and taste the wealth of experiences for himself. "I simply can't", he told me. Charley was an only child, his father was dead and his mother was heavily disabled. "I'm all she's got," he said. "I can't leave her. All I can do at the moment is live my dream through others; you are incredibly lucky." I was humbled by his acceptance of his situation, his loyalty to his mother and the fact that he hadn't allowed his dream to die.

I heard stories of situations and priorities in other peoples' lives that made me realise how fortunate I was. I learnt from the people I met on the road that we don't all have the ability to make dreams a reality. We can enjoy the high points we do make happen and value them for what they are, but we can also taste and develop our dreams through the adventures of others. What sort of humans would we be if we didn't dream?

'Into Africa' is written for those of you fortunate enough to know that you can go out and live the dream. Value that, and just do it; you'll never regret it. I hope that the book will be an encouragement.

It's also written for those who love the sound of travelling but are quite happy with adventure from the pages. I too am drawn by tales of the road, and know the value of a comfy armchair at the end of a long day. I hope you will enjoy the mad, the scary, the beautiful, and the surprises. There were days that my traveller's guardian angel took time off without warning me - I managed to get myself arrested, jailed, and shot at. I also cost my medical insurance company a fortune! When my angel was there, the journey was a combination of fascination and adrenaline burning fun.

In particular though, this book is written for those of you who, like Charley, live in circumstances that may never allow you to ride two wheels into adventure. I write with full appreciation of exactly how fortunate I really am. If you can't do it, then live the dream with me. This is the story of a yearlong trip through one of the most fascinating continents on earth – Africa.

Pre Africa, my life was as ordinary as life can get, but something wasn't quite right. I had a reasonable education, a job, and I was healthy. I was a shop manager on Jersey; the work was manic and decidedly full time. This didn't leave much freedom to enjoy the money I was earning, and I never managed to see my family in England as often as I ought. The long hours meant that I was beginning to lose touch with friends too, but my sights were set on promotion and a fat pay cheque; they had been for too many years and I'd almost made it. I never had the time to feel properly dissatisfied, but I was beginning to wonder what it was all for. Could I really see myself doing the same thing forever? Then, fears of a recession began to creep into the world of retail and I saw my hard earned future disappearing. This look into the future set me dreaming of the road and taking a close look at my life as a whole. I knew that I wasn't the first person to do this and that encouraged me to think outside the boundaries.

I'm not sure exactly when the motorcycle idea started, but it must have been when I'd realised that I could actually do anything I wanted – if I put my mind to it. At the time that was an inspirational feeling. There really was nothing to stop me but I did try to find excuses not to go; after all, the dream wasn't ordinary even if I was.

There was something really rather nice about the notion of riding a motor bike the length of Africa; the idea appealed to the romantic in me. I'd backpacked in different parts of the world and particularly liked the idea of the freedom a bike could give me, especially after being stuck indoors for so many years. The lazy side of me rather liked the thought of not having to carry a rucksack!

It also felt like I'd be taking my life and turning it inside out. The more I thought about it, the more I came to the conclusion that my life needed a damn good shaking – what better way to do it than this. On top of those thoughts, there'd been a niggling voice in the back of my mind which had popped up far too often for safety. It kept spouting the words, 'A challenge like this will be fun!' A bike would be the perfect way to get into adventures, but there was a lot to learn – not least of which was that I didn't know how to ride a motorbike.

As the plans came together I began to feel a tad guilty about the concept of being a relatively rich tourist riding through some of the most poverty stricken areas in the world. I tried the argument with myself that by going on this trip, my experiences and the knowledge gained might help in some way, but I wasn't very convincing.

I decided that it might just be possible to raise money for a couple of relevant charities. I chose Mission Aviation Fellowship because I wanted to do something to help the countries I would be seeing, and even perhaps help some of the people I might meet.

The second charity was Children in Need; helping those at home is important too. I also hoped that by following my trip, the children in the schools on Jersey who were collecting money might glean value from their vicarious contact with the countries I would be travelling through. The children liked the idea that I would be sponsored by the number of countries I managed to make it across; after all, I was still learning to ride a bike. One of the children asked me how many times I was going to fall off. I lost count!

'Into Africa' is written for all of the children, teachers, parents and friends who became involved.

The last group the book is written for, are the people I met along the way who showed me, through acts of great generosity and simple kindness alike, that this world of ours is a fantastic place to live. I don't really know how to thank Peter and Edith, without whom at worst I'd be dead, and at best I'd be blind. You are both amazing.

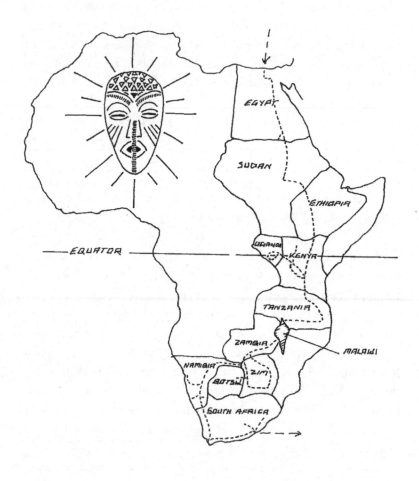

Alexandria to Durban - 22.000 miles - as the crow doesn't fly

Chapter One

"Captain Joseph"

'A man never goes so far as when he does not know where he is going.'

Oliver Cromwell.

I felt as if John and I were almost floating over the perfect asphalt. The ride was wonderfully smooth and there were none of the usual rattling 'bike-on-a-rough-road' sounds. We clicked along comfortably at ninety kilometres an hour. Not too fast to miss the scenery and not too fast to deal with the ever present risk of a dashing animal, but fast enough to feel that we were getting somewhere. The day was slightly over-cast with clouds that were tinged only with silver-grey and not the menacing purple-grey of a coming storm.

Rising gently, the road no longer shimmered with heat and for once we didn't feel overdressed. As we drew closer to the last major town on the road to the Malawi border, huts and mud brick shops began to appear along the roadside. Hand painted signs advertised fruits and vegetables alongside garish posters for Omo washing powder, flour and cigarettes. We slowed down for each cluster of buildings, nervous of dogs, goats and children. The traffic thickened rapidly and the little clusters of buildings merged into continuous outskirts. A few hundred metres in front, a bus was pulling over to the side – I slowed right down.

When a bus pulls to a halt in Africa, life explodes. There's a mad rush to get off, to drag belongings off the giant roof rack and to search out friends in the milling confusion. There never seem to be any toilets so there is always a dash for the bushes as well. Travelling by bike I at least had a chance to pee in sweet smelling peace and quiet, but bus riders don't have that luxury. What they do get is a full choice of refreshments whenever the bus stops. Street vendors selling fruit, soft drinks, skewered goat meat, samosas or plastic bags full of fresh pineapple cubes, all rush into the chaos with the hope that the passengers leaning out of the windows would buy something for the journey. I'd seen enough African bus stops by the time I made it to Tanzania to know that no one would be looking out for a passing motorcycle. Slowing even more, the worst of the rush had pretty much cleared from the road by the time we got close. With the headlight on full beam and my thumb on the horn I felt sure that as usual we'd make it through the chaos.

We didn't. There on the right stood an Mzee who was carefully looking both ways before stepping out into the road. I'd never seen anyone do that before in Africa. Normally the inevitable potholes, the condition of the vehicles or the enthusiastic yells of the conductors meant that a pedestrian could hear something coming, and they wouldn't need to look. The old man stared straight at us, and hesitated before trying to make it across, but try he did.

With just two steps he was in front of us; there was no time to react as the front wheel hit him with a sickening thump. As we hit the road, I saw him somersault almost in slow motion over to the rubbish-strewn roadside.

Somehow, I ended up on my feet with just the sleeve of my jacket scratched, but John was rolling in agony in the middle of the road. Seeing that there wasn't a lot to do for him, I rushed over to the bike where petrol was spewing over the hot engine. A passer-by helped me pick it up from where it had landed almost upside down in the ditch. Another spectator yelled in Swahili, "You must not move your machine, the police will be coming!" After squatting down to turn the petrol off, I looked up to see that I was surrounded. Above me, all except for a small oval of blue grey, shadowy black faces had closed off the sky. I was scared. There were many stories about what had happened to other bikers who'd been unlucky enough to hit someone in Africa. Some had only just escaped with their lives, and some hadn't escaped at all.

John lay hunched on the road holding his knees and I could even see the tears on his shocked face. What had I done? Even if it had felt the right thing to do, John's agony meant that making a run for it on the bike wasn't an option. I decided to stay crouching down by the bike, and tried to look as pathetic as possible in the hope that if I looked a complete wimp they wouldn't string me up. In the meantime the police had been summoned, and with no police cars available, they were hitch hiking their way out to us.

My oval of blue-grey sky had all but disappeared when a man pushed through the crowd. In really good English he asked, "Mister, are you OK?" He'd seen the accident happen and said that it wasn't my fault. In fact our bright clothes, headlight and horn had made a lot of people see what had happened. He apologised for not getting to me sooner but explained, "I have been talking to the other people who saw the accident. I have been collecting names and addresses for when you go to court." Court? I hadn't even got close to thinking about that far ahead! He shook me by the hand and introduced himself as Joseph. He was a retired Captain from the Tanzanian army and lived close by. He told me that I shouldn't be afraid of the people, that they were just concerned that I was OK. All the faces instantly began to look less threatening and more sympathetic. "You will have to stay to deal with the police," he said. "But your friend looks as if he needs medical attention."

The crowd had already commandeered a passing Land Rover pick-up truck to take the man I'd hit to the hospital, and Joseph suggested that we should put John in to go too. In my shocked state, I told Joseph that we shouldn't move John until the ambulance came. He looked at me and quietly said, "No ambulance, this is Tanzania you know."

Over with the silent John, I told him that we would have to move him, that it was bound to hurt but that we had to get him to hospital. Joseph and I picked him up, and carried him as gently as we could over to the Land Rover. He'd landed hard on his knees; the only parts of his body that we hadn't made a big effort to protect when we'd been kitting him out to ride with me for a few weeks. Sod's law.

The crowd stood watching silently as we eased him into the back of the pick-up, and there I got my first proper sight of the man who'd been knocked over. He sat leaning against the back of the cab and to my complete horror, a part of his leg stood foot to the floor in a growing pool of dark red blood. I'd somehow managed to take it off below the knee, and his stump was spurting regular jets of blood. I was stunned for a moment, and then yelled at them to get him to hospital quickly. I'd no idea how long he'd been sitting there in that state but they shouldn't have waited for John. Putting a tourniquet on him never even entered my mind.

The police arrived with an air of considerable authority and with a flourish of self-importance they set about making notes and drawing diagrams. An old-fashioned tape measure in a circular wooden case was produced and they made me show them where the impact had been. They looked down the road to where the bike was and shaking their heads, measured the distance. I asked Joseph what the problem was. "They say that your machine has slid a long way." It had. Even at a touch less than twenty kilometres per hour, the brand new smooth asphalt, smooth luggage and the long sloping camber had carried the heavy bike at least twenty-five feet. Beginning to shake and with a queasy stomach, the feeling that it was all a dream washed over me. While the police measured, I found the point where the man had landed and the large red stain in the dust told it all. To the left of the stain, a three-foot spike of angle iron was sticking out of the ground. At some time in the past there had been a sign here, but when it was taken down removing the spike had presumably been too much effort. The man had hit the spike on his fall; if it hadn't been there, he would almost certainly still have had his leg.

The bike was virtually undamaged. It had broken mirrors, the rack on one side had cracked through, there were scratches down the panniers and the handlebars were twisted slightly out of position. The indicator I'd broken in Sudan was dangling again, but other than that she was fine. There didn't even seem to be any marks where I'd hit the man. "Can you ride the bike?" the police asked me via Joseph. I could, and with Joseph offering his services as interpreter, they flagged down a car for the ride to the police station. Joseph's final post in the army had been in this town and he told me that he knew some of the senior police officers that would be dealing with me. His offer of help gave an instant feeling of relief. My Swahili was good enough for bargaining in the market, but no way was it good enough to deal with this.

After following them to the police station, the bike, my keys, carnet, licence, passport and money were all confiscated. I wondered if I'd ever see any of them again. The booking-in room was a mass of yelling, arguing people and to top it all after just moments of being in the chaos, a badly beaten up man was thrown to the floor inside the room. His ears and nose had blood pouring from them and he looked no more than semi-conscious. They thrust me into a cell, and it was like being shoved onto the set of movie.

The concrete cell reeked of urine and a bucket in the corner stunk of faeces. The room was lit only by a small barred window that was set high into the wall. A single dust filled shaft of light cut into the dank darkness. As my eyes got used to the gloom I realised that there was a group of men already there; all of their eyes were on me. The hair on the back of my neck moved under the collar of my leather jacket and trying to look taller than my six one, I leant against the wall and stared back. I was scared again, but had the feeling that if I didn't look tough there'd be trouble. Almost everywhere on the trip so far there had been a sort of guarded respect towards me. I'd never been sure if it was the colour of my skin, my comparative wealth or what I was doing that engendered this respect, but there wasn't a trace of it now. Time passed in slow motion and my mouth went dry. I couldn't stop trembling and all I wanted to do was sit down. Then, the largest man opened his flies and took out his erect penis. With a touch of the bizarre, as he took his first step towards me the shaft of light from the window hit him and made him centre stage. Masturbating as he came closer, I suddenly knew what an animal felt like when rooted to the spot by zooming headlights in the dark. There was no mistaking what was in this guy's mind. Tanzania has a major Aids problem, and besides that...

A self-preservation instinct took over and without thinking I behaved totally out of character. I thrashed out at the two nearest men with all the strength that fear and frustration could muster. Whilst pounding at them for those few moments I was yelling "Guard,

guard!" and he came running. The door swung open; the beam of light stayed right on the big man who stood with his erect penis still in his hand. The guard dragged me out and angrily thrust me into an empty room. I sat and shook. I felt disgust and wanted to vomit.

Not long afterwards they took me back to the original booking-in room which by now was much quieter. John was sitting there looking in pain, and rather shocked; to our relief though nothing seemed to be broken.

"They cleaned the gravel out of my knees with a scrubbing brush," he said wincing at the memory. But he then said something even scarier, "The Land Rover drove to the police station first, and they made us wait for nearly twenty minutes while a report was made. I had to yell and shout to get them to take the man to the hospital; it's only just over the road too!"

John's knees hadn't been X-rayed, which concerned us, and we were chewing over what to do about it when an Aid worker walked in. Christine took control, got John straight back to the hospital and into x-ray. John said that she'd been a gem. The x-ray happily had shown no fractures.

All this time Joseph was there. He argued with the desk sergeant who was taking the same line as his constables. "The Muzungu (White man or foreigner) must have been speeding", said the desk sergeant as he stabbed his finger in my direction. I tried arguing, "20 ks wasn't speeding." But he wasn't listening.

Though I felt extremely uncomfortable about the injured man, I knew that it hadn't been my fault. Short of not being there at all, just about everything had been done right. After writing out and signing a statement to that effect, they left me to worry about what would happen next.

At that moment, the representative of the British Embassy turned up. It had never entered my mind that there would even be one out here. By sheer fluke, Con had driven past the crowds on the road and had seen my Jersey number plate. Past experience had told him that it would be better to let things calm down a little before getting involved, and his timing was perfect. After some persuasive conversation, the police released us into his custody to be booked into a local hotel while further investigations were made. In the St. Joseph Hotel we lay exhausted, stunned and, in John's case, hurting. That evening, Con turned up and took us through into the bar. He proceeded to get us very drunk and bought us an excellent meal. Over the next days he was to be very kind, and kept us with one foot in reality. I tossed and turned with dreams that kept waking me through that first night and at five in the morning I had to make a rush for the toilet. I'd either picked up a stomach bug, or all the tension and the shock was getting to me.

The police had told me to report to the station at eight o'clock for the bike to be inspected for roadworthiness. Arriving in plenty of time, I was shown through to wait in a courtyard for the inspector. I was relieved when Joseph arrived soon after. Within minutes, the Chief Inspector had filled in a form, had a brief look at the bike and that was that. Next we had to go to the traffic chief's office. He told me via Joseph that I was going to have to appear in court for speeding; they were sure that the bike had slid too far. Arguing as best I could that they had no experience of how far a bike of this size would slide on a brand new road surface that didn't even have a gravel coating, made no difference. The road had been severely potholed for the previous ten years and most of the local bikes were much lighter 125cc trail bikes. They did give my bike back, but kept most of my papers.

John and I spent the rest of the day quietly exploring and finding a welder to fix the broken rack. We were used to being stared at but now we couldn't help feeling that they were accusing stares. The reality of course was that the town was big enough for most people to have heard nothing about the accident. To my delight, the welder we found also managed to make a functional mirror out of the two broken ones. I hit the sack early that night and slept much better, the squits had gone and things were moving, albeit slowly. The news from the hospital was that the man was still alive and the police told me that there was only going to be a speeding charge. If that was the case, it made sense to pay the fine and say no more, but I couldn't help feelings of guilt.

We were kept waiting for four hours at the police station the next day. Then we were told when I had to be in court, and what the 'charges' were going to be. The charges were 'speeding', 'driving without due care and attention', and 'attempt to commit grievous bodily harm'! I was stunned - not only two traffic violations, but a criminal charge as well. They were saying that I had driven at the man on purpose! Joseph was as amazed as we were; he'd had little inkling that this was going to happen. If I was found guilty I'd be back in jail and properly this time. The prosecuting officer worked hard at trying to persuade me to plead guilty. "If you do", she said. "You'll be on your way in no time." This seemed an odd prediction after pleading guilty to serious charges so I refused. I wasn't guilty and common sense pointed out that promises of freedom could easily be broken, and pleading guilty could open a whole can of worms.

On the day of the hearing I was made to stand out in the dusty high walled courtyard with the other rogues and villains. The smooth rendered walls made the yard feel like an open-air cell, and naturally John and I were the centre of attention. Eventually my name was called; John, Con and Joseph were allowed into the courtroom too. The charges were read and everyone seemed amazed at my firm "Not guilty." response. The black robed magistrate looked across at the prosecuting officer with a question mark on his face. She just shrugged her shoulders and sat down. There was silence in the room and then the magistrate, shuffling his papers with a sharp tap onto the bench said,

"The police must have time to collect evidence and therefore the case will go up to the regional court in one month." My jaw must have dropped open. One month! "Please sir, that's an awfully long time", I said to the magistrate who looked at me in surprise. "Oh, well", he said. "How about two weeks?" I thought quickly and decided not to push my luck any further. "Thank you sir." Two whole weeks and John needed to head back to Kenya for his flight home, but there was really no choice but to accept it. Then another surprise, the magistrate asked if there was someone who would stand bail for me. I looked to Con who shocked me by shaking his head. I didn't know then that you have to be a Tanzanian citizen to stand bail for anyone in Tanzania. Joseph, a man who had known me for just a few days, stood and agreed to put his farm up as bail. His farm was a house he'd built himself, a shed, an acre of land, two cows and half a dozen chickens. That was just about all he had to feed himself and his family. His pension from the Tanzanian army was just twenty pounds sterling per year. I was stunned at his selfless generosity.

While we were waiting for the bail officer to turn up, Joseph disappeared for 45 long minutes. I have to admit that I thought he'd suddenly realised the enormity of his commitment and had disappeared for good before the papers could be signed. But, before we'd gone into the court I'd told him that whatever happened in there I was going to do my best for the injured man. I'd buy a wooden leg and give him enough money to keep him and his family going for two years. At least that way he had a chance to get as well as possible, and no one was going to suffer further than was unavoidable because of my holiday. I'd told Joseph that he should tell no one about this before the trial was over, in case someone took it as an admission of guilt. He'd told me that the man was a shoe repairer and that a wooden leg would not stop him earning a living once he was well again. At least that was something.

Joseph had broken his promise of sealed lips. He'd just been to the man's family and told them what I'd said. Hospital treatment is free in Tanzania, but there is no compensation system and no real aftercare. He told the family that if I went to jail they'd get nothing from the government and that I would need all I had to survive. The family happily agreed to the charges being dropped; one of them had seen the accident and knew that it hadn't been my fault anyway. Then, with one of the brothers, Joseph went to talk to the magistrate - who just happened to have been at school with him. The magistrate had listened to the plan, and had said that as far as he was concerned the charges could be dropped. "In the end though", he said. "It's down to the police, particularly the Criminal Investigations Department."

We hurried down to the police station and with some effort eventually persuaded the senior officers that the plan was best for all involved. I still had to go to the regional court the next day for the charges to be officially dropped, but it now looked as if there was a way out.

We had to be at the main court for eight thirty. I shot out to collect Joseph who I'd discovered by now had been walking all the way into town to help me every day. Not a thing had got done on his farm for all this time and he hadn't been able to afford to get in by minibus. I was annoyed with myself for not even thinking about it, but Joseph just seemed to think that it was normal to walk. At the courthouse, there wasn't a soul to be seen. Joseph said that this was pretty much the way of things, so we went down to the bus station to book John his ticket. We were in luck. For four thousand five hundred Tanzanian shillings, he could have seat number two. This was the only seat on the bus with legroom for beanpoles with damaged knees.

Confusion, waiting and general lack of activity was the rule for much of the rest of the day, but a crowd was starting to collect and there were a lot of sideways looks in our direction. It wasn't until after two that we were told to go through the crowds into the courthouse. The building was set in a shallow amphitheatre where spectators sat watching through the windows and listening to the relayed reports from inside. A small boy stood listening from the doorway and periodically he would rush out to shout what was happening. Men with trays walked through the people selling oranges and boiled sweets. Boys with old galvanised buckets hawked unshelled peanuts and iced soft drinks – the carnival was in town. I suspected that the fact that a Muzungu was on trial was added spice.

Finally, at three o'clock, I was called to the stand, and the court fell completely silent. "Mr Sam, under the Tanzanian law code No 4783, you are advised that all charges against you have been withdrawn." The curiosity filled silence turned into a stunned silence. Then a combination of a groan and a buzz of comment burst from the lips of those who'd come to watch the show. From outside came the sound of the boy relaying the news and then, for a moment or two, there was another small groan that seemed to echo around the building. I waited to smile until well away from the court. Yes! I thought. 'Free, though I'd lost a little skin from my teeth.'

There were final statements to sign at the police station and then I was able to look after the injured man, Mr Sanga. A Danish aid worker was running the prosthesis department in the hospital and he willingly took the cost of making a leg. "But", he told me. "I can't make the leg until the stump has shrunk." This would be quite a while so I decided to pay for it up front and to give Mr Sanga the receipt along with his living money. I was a bit worried that if I'd given him the whole lot in cash then he might not have got a properly made prosthesis at all.

Now to face seeing Mr Sanga, it didn't feel right to leave without visiting him. I found him lying on sweat stained sheets on a paint chipped iron bed in a ward with at least thirty occupants. I'd never seen a black man look grey before. The surgeon had told me that if they had got Mr Sanga to the hospital just five minutes later, it would have been too late. If he had died, then perhaps the charges against me would have included murder. It seemed politic not to tell John at the time that I was thankful he'd hurt his knees. Without him being in the Land Rover, Mr Sanga wouldn't have made it.

In many Tanzanian hospitals, trained doctors and nurses carry out medical care but the family washes the sheets and provides food. If the patient isn't local, then often the family will camp outside and one member at a time will sleep under the hospital bed to provide instant care when needed. When we arrived on the ward a large part of the family was there to greet us. I was nervous and a little voice was telling me that I didn't need to be there at all. But I did, and on being introduced I shook the weak hand that was held in my direction. To my amazement Mr Sanga said sorry, to me! I don't remember what I said to him at first, but gave him the money and the receipt for the wooden leg, and told him that I hoped he would get fit soon. It was soon clear

21

that he was exhausted so we headed for the door. His older brothers came with us to deliver the punch line.

They shook me by the hand and thanked me for what I was doing. They told us that they hoped the incident hadn't spoiled our visit to Tanzania too much, and that we'd still be able to leave with good memories of the country and its people. "And anyway", the oldest brother said. "He always had one leg shorter than the other. Now he can have two the same length!"

Chapter Two
"The Point of No Return"
What he didn't know would make a library anyone would be proud of.

Anon

Before leaving the Channel Islands, the thought of almost killing someone and the possibility of being raped hadn't entered my mind. Perhaps I'd been incredibly naïve or, quite simply ignorant of what I was facing when I made the decision to learn to ride a bike, chuck in my job and ride the length of Africa. The romance of the idea, the preparation, winding up my job and the challenge of the time schedule I'd set myself had been both the spur and enough to occupy my mind. I've got to be honest though; there was a certain element of not wanting to think too hard about what might go wrong. If I'd thought about the risks too much then I'd almost certainly have let the dream remain just that.

The open roads of Italy allowed for more thinking time but thankfully my imagination didn't stretch as far as perhaps it ought. Even so, the further south I headed and the closer I got to the Greek port of Piraeus, my personal point of no return, the more I began to worry that I'd made a big mistake about the whole idea. Thoughts edged nastily into my mind whenever they could and I was getting scared. There were so many things that could go wrong. Would I be quick thinking enough when faced with dodgy officials? Would I get ripped off? Would I have enough money? Would I be able to get the visas I'd need? What would it be like in the politically sensitive sections? Were my maps any good? How would I cope if I fell off the bike in a remote place and broke something? My imagination conjured up all sorts of visions of me in pain, alone and helpless. I also wondered how my family would feel if I snuffed it 'out there'. I just hoped that they would feel happy that I'd been doing something I really wanted to do. But now I was on the way I wasn't so sure that I wanted to do it any more.

Along with my thoughts I was battling with the bike I'd bought. The BMW R80 GS was far too big for me, and because I'd tried to plan for everything it was overloaded to a ridiculous extent. The selling point of the beast had been that the famous BMW boxer engine was supposed to be bullet-proof and simple enough for idiots to deal with. That had sounded about right, but I felt as if I was riding a drunken pig!

When I wasn't scaring myself with thoughts or by doing something stupid with the bike, I was revelling in the sensation of being free from the normality of every day life. Being a tourist again was fun; Europe was a good winding-down stage from deadlines and the need to

 try to get everything done yesterday. I had an instinct that told me I'd cope with whatever Africa was going to throw at me, if I calmed down and became more patient. My instinct said that I'd have to take on board the 'chameleon factor'; take it slow and adapt to every situation I found myself in. When I wasn't thinking dire thoughts it was almost as if I could persuade myself that I was just on holiday. So far I hadn't done anything really daft and with each mile there was always plenty to keep me busy.

Pompeii was firmly on the list of places I wanted to visit on the way south, or so I thought until just before I had my first crash. I'd managed to get lost again and found myself in the crowded streets of a strange town; I don't mind getting lost because some of the best adventures in my life have begun in a place I wasn't supposed to be. People in fancy dress, carnival floats and excited, running children surrounded me and though it was all rather manic I had the feeling that I'd ended up getting lost in the right place. Fireworks popped adding to the people noise and filling the air with the acrid smell of gunpowder.

Before me, two cars had also got caught in the excitement and I let them make a path through the crowds for me. Then the red Fiat indicated to go right through a gap and as he turned I sped up a bit not wanting to lose the other car. The next thing I knew was that the Fiat driver had changed his mind and was heading almost sideways towards me. Life turned into slow motion, and the inevitable happened. With a loud crunch the car collected a deep pannier shaped dent. The crush of the crowd stopped me falling over but within seconds I was faced by four arm-waving, decidedly angry men. The crowd stepped back a pace, and everyone turned to watch the new entertainment.

There was no escape. I'd learned enough arm waving and shoulder shrugging to plead innocence but it wasn't working. The situation started to turn really ugly and I thought I was about to get thumped. Then from above, a stern voice rapped out at the men and several hundred eyes swivelled upwards in unison. There on a wrought iron balcony stood an old man dressed as if he had just stepped off the set of a gangster movie. Clad in a double-breasted pin stripe suit, he'd seen the whole thing and after a few moments of firm talking, the crowd parted and I climbed onto the bike not quite able to believe that I was free. I had a moment of electric-start bliss, and we left before the spell was broken. Pompeii could wait for another trip.

My narrow escape changed my mood and I decided to chase across to the east coast port of Brindisi. If quick enough, I'd make it in time for the evening ferry across the Adriatic to Greece. This far south, the late afternoon was gently warm and arriving in plenty of time allowed me to settle down under the palm trees of the harbour square to watch life go by. With the bike ticking as it cooled, my mind buzzed with the thought that, except for the last few metres I now had my first two countries under my wheels.

There was still lots to do though, and the man in the booking office gave me a warning that took away some of my buzz. "You musta not leavea your bike unattended", he said. "There are many bada people in Brindisi." As a backpacker I'd heard these sorts of dire warnings many times before but usually they had been about the people in the next town or region. This clerk had to know his own doorstep though, so I had a problem. Before the ferry could leave at 8 pm, he instructed that I'd need to confirm my ticket at 5pm, then go to the police, on to immigration and finally to customs. All my locked boxes and panniers were just going to have to earn their keep. One way or another this was going to be the first time I'd have to leave the bike unattended in a border situation and as it wouldn't be the last, it was time to be philosophical. All would be OK, or it wouldn't, and I'd have to deal with it.

Brindisi's ferry square filled up as the hours went by and it turned out to be a great meeting place. Everyone had a story to tell; some were told with long faces and others with full-on exuberance. Jean and Betty, two Aussies in a camper van had had hard times and their tale served as a good warning. The camper had just been broken into and their cameras and stereo were long gone, but robbery also happens to the experienced. Allan said, "Yeah, they got me too. I was sitting on the train minding my own business and a couple of guys pulled a knife on me." All the cash he had left was the money he'd had stashed in his shoes. Another lesson learned and I thought about how I too could distribute my Traveller's cheques and cash. Some of my stash was already up inside the tube of the main frame on the bike. The rest I split between my money belt, my boots, a split in the shoulder pad of my bike jacket and I tucked a little more into a plastic bag with my spare parts for the bike. I kept walk-around money in my wallet and a back-up wedge in my daypack, but I kept the travellers cheques handy in case I was required to show that I wasn't skint.

The dusty, rather beat up port of Igoumentisa welcomed me the next day but I only stayed long enough to stock up on freshly baked bread, Feta cheese, huge olives and a bottle of retsina wine. This stuff is reputedly flavoured with pine resin to get its decidedly unique taste and the first glass I'd ever had of the stuff was quite revolting. The second glass hadn't tasted quite so bad and by the third glass, it was actually pretty good! Now though, I wanted a beach and trundled along the coast looking down over little sandy coves. The road took me through the shade of olive groves and past blossom laden almond trees. Rush hour was a couple of battered pickup trucks and a pair of donkeys. I found my campsite on the beach and pitched the tent under a bougainvillaea's purple blossoms. The sea was warm and as I sat in the gentle breeze I felt at peace with the world. This was what it was all about.

The camping site I'd found was actually another of Europe's 'closed for the winter' sites, but Yorgos the very amiable manager greeted me with a wide grin and a "Yassou Kalimera." 'Hello, good morning' in Greek has a nice ring to it. He stood before me dressed in typical Greek working clothes. His scruffy boots were lacking more than a couple of layers of polish. He wore dark trousers that had dust patches on the knees and an old blue shirt whose collar had needed turning months before; he had to be a bachelor. His hands were rough and his chin hadn't seen a razor for several days. I wondered what sort of picture he was forming of me as he, still grinning, stared back. Yorgos turned out to be a real character. I could use the campsite but on one condition, I had to drink wine with him in the evening.

Yorgos had lived in the States for eight years and his English was excellent. Though it didn't help my Greek to improve, it helped considerably as the evening's wine began to flow. "I really enjoyed the US and it was a great experience but I came back to see my family and I realised what I was missing", Yorgos said. He agreed that the States were in fact the land of opportunity but said, "The price is a crazy pace of life and I don't always agree with how Americans think. Here I can use all I learned in America but still live the life of a Greek." His plans for the campsite, surrounded by ancient olive trees and shady bougainvillaea, sounded perhaps a little too grand. But if anyone could succeed I suspected that Yorgos could, if he didn't settle in to the way of life too much.

Back at my brand new tent I'd had a visitor and I learned another simple lesson the hard way. Yani the campsite cat had smelt the last of my Italian salami and had decided that the walls of my home were not a problem. He kindly left me the salami wrapper, and a series of seven inch rips in the tent inner.

The next day could easily have been very lazy but the itch to keep moving was there. African rains were on my mind; if I was late I'd cop it on some of the worst dirt roads. But first, a good breakfast was needed to get rid of some of my hangover. Yorgos could really drink and I, like a prat, had tried to keep up with him. Several cups of hot coffee would go down well but I still hadn't managed to get my new cooker working properly. Half the time all it wanted to do was to gush clouds of thick black, petrol-laden fumes which though warm, coated everything with soot. Even a simple cup of tea ended up flavoured with a foul gasoline tang. So far, it seemed that the only thing it would be good for was if I got stuck in the desert and needed to send up a smoke signal to a passing aeroplane!

Whilst loading the bike, I noticed a tiny oil leak from the front cover of the engine, but it was only tiny so working on the 'if it ain't broke, don't fix it' theory, I carried on loading. The day's ride took me looping and curling along the coast road. The bike hummed and I sang. Sadly for the villagers along the road, the tune 'The House of the Rising Sun' got stuck in my head that day.

My search for an open campsite caused me problems once more but yet again, luck was with me. This time, my Yorgos was called Thomas. With a cracked grin from above a grizzled, stubbly chin, Thomas told me that he owned a holiday village not far away. Though closed for the season it was definitely open to a mad man on his way to ride through Africa – so long as I didn't mind the cold showers.

Over an inevitable bottle of wine that night, Thomas told me a little about himself. I guessed that he was probably in his early fifties. A short and stocky man, he looked tremendously fit and tough, rather like a dormant paratrooper. I suspected that he wasn't a good man to upset. His usual expression was off-puttingly stern and an artist friend of his had captured it perfectly in a pencil drawing. He did have a wonderful smile though, and when he got enthused about things it would transform his face.

We'd started our conversation in Greek but soon switched to English and his was surprisingly accented with an enthusiastic Scottish burr. "I managed to get into the UK to study, but I couldn't speak English", he said. Fairly quickly, he sorted out a job up in Scotland on one of the new dams that were being built. "It was a good job", Thomas told me. "There was plenty to paint and I didn't need English for that. But I decided to teach myself anyway and some of my first words were learnt by finding out what the sentences on the toilet walls meant!" At a click of his amber worry beads, he could turn on a very fluent, very blue stream of sentences.

That night we sat up on the balcony of one of the holiday apartments. It looked down onto the small fishing village, and out over the coast where the main road snaked its way along the dips and curves of the shoreline. In the still, deep blue of the night, the heavy trucks that were thundering along it looked like dragons in a Chinese parade. Greek lorry drivers love to decorate their trucks with all sorts of coloured lights so the effect was quite spectacular. Thomas told me that every night the parade would go on for hour after hour. It was hypnotically similar to watching the flames of a campfire.

He also told me that the effect was heightened that night because the morning would bring a general strike across Greece. "The drivers are all rushing to beat the strike", he said. By not reading the papers, nor listening to the radio, this was news to me - bad news at that. "There will be no electricity", Thomas warned. "That means no banks, no petrol and even worse for you, the ports could close." Having discussed this weighty matter, Thomas in true Greek style advised, "As there's nothing you can do, you should have some more wine."

Dawn came as Friday the 13th. I'd lost touch with the days and hadn't realised until Thomas pointed it out. What a good day for a strike, but there were 'up' sides. The road to the ruins of the ancient city of Delphi was blissfully quiet.

The early morning sky was exactly the same colour as the sea. There didn't even seem to be a horizon, no dividing line at all. The only break in the pure 'forget-me-not' blue was the land. It seemed to float as if hanging unconnected to anything in a pool of blue space. This was an absolute first for me and if I'd seen it on a painting, I would probably have made some sort of remark about the artist having lost touch with reality, but here spread before me was reality. With this one view, doing the trip by bike had suddenly made complete sense. The bike had allowed me to stop at the perfect point to take in the magical scene. I couldn't have stopped a car on the narrow road, I'd have just had a detached glimpse

29

through the tinted windows of a bus, and a train wouldn't have taken me anywhere near it.

Making its way inland, the Delphi road lifted itself through a series of tortuous curves and bends. The only person I saw was an old man plodding peacefully along on a donkey. The old city sat quiet and majestic on an olive green mountainside that was tinted with the pastel pink of blossoming almond trees. I'd had no idea that this was how I would find Delphi but it seemed that I'd arrived at the perfect time to see the city at its best. The still early hour meant that the ruins were pretty much deserted. With the sunlight low and a little hazy over the mountains it felt like I'd found another stroke of perfection. Perhaps Friday the 13th was going to turn out to be a lucky day on the trip?

It wasn't hard to imagine what the city would be like in full summer swing. By the time I'd climbed up the long curving stone terraces of the stadium, the sun had cleared away the haze and it had changed from comfortably cool, to hot. For the first time on the trip my feet were baking in my bike boots and I wondered what they would be like to wear in the desert. The city moved from dozing in gentle rays to full on activity in the day's heat. The first tourist coaches began to arrive and from my perch high up in the city I could see the spread and flow of the lines of people. I settled down to watch. Faint jumbles of accents drifted up towards me from overweight and red faced, but enthusiastic visitors. Admiring them for getting out to see some of the world, I sat and played mind games. For a while it was fun to dress them all in robes, togas and ancient Greek uniforms. I wondered how much their movements differed from those of visitors to the city when it was in its glory. We humans are such funny creatures, predictable in so many ways and really, people are just the same whatever race or time they may be from. Things beautiful astound us all, and expressions of awe are the same tone in any language. I rather liked the eerie sense that the ghosts were still there watching us wandering their city, and I wondered what they were thinking about us all as we trod their familiar paths.

For a moment up there on the terrace I felt lonely. The day was beautiful and it seemed wrong not to be sharing it with someone special.

I tried hard not to let the feeling spoil the day. If there had been someone else with me, perhaps I wouldn't have had the time to recognise the beauty or feel the freedom to fantasise about the city, and these special moments might not have been there at all. It seemed very healthy to be thinking these thoughts as I was on my own, and the situation was unlikely to change. The bonuses of solo travel were obvious to me once more and Friday the 13th continued to be a good day.

The real Friday the 13th started on Saturday the 14th. In the morning, the Peloponese ferry left without me. When setting my watch by Yorgos's clock, there'd been nothing to warn me that it had been an hour out. After moments of irritation I suddenly realised that in the grand scheme of things, missing the boat didn't matter a jot. Settling into 'Greek time' wasn't hard to do and down at the jetty there were plenty of people to watch. Baskets of fish were unloaded by raucous men who called to passers by with witty remarks. Tiny cups of thick, syrupy coffee were sipped at cafe tables and just about every man I could see was smoking grim smelling cigarettes. White walls, terracotta roofs, the deep blue of the sea and olive tree slopes made the backdrop. Fishing boats painted blue, black and white bobbed against the jetty, and sea gulls circled overhead as sea gulls are supposed to do. Time almost stood still for a moment and it seemed absolutely right that it should, and even more right that I should too.

The ferry eased towards the ramp with a last minute swirling flair and its landing craft bows dropped open with a thud. There was a pause before well-filled cars, strikebreaking trucks and noisy smoking mopeds streamed up onto the jetty. Old men dressed in black and blue, wheeled off ancient battered bicycles with well-loaded wicker baskets. Dumpy women shrouded from head to toe in black shoes, black stockings, black dresses and black headscarves, walked tiredly off the ferry, as if they were carrying the woes of the world on their shoulders. Almost shadow like, they stubbornly heaved at cantankerous donkeys that were pulling carts loaded with vegetables. A couple of brightly clad tourists on chunky, gleaming, neatly loaded bicycles eased through the rush - they passed me with a wave.

31

Then the tide of people turned and a new set of look-alikes rushed up the ramp for the twenty-minute return journey. The Captain, whose rich curling moustache made him look like one of the heroes from a Sinbad movie, casually guided the boat across the Straits with the practised ease of a bus driver. Somehow I'd ended up second in line to be off the boat, but in front of me was a flashy white Mercedes whose driver seemed to come from a different world from the rest of us. As soon as the ferry hit the other side, he switched on his engine and revved the Mercedes to a roar whilst bumping irritably at the exit ramp. With the ramp down, he sped off leaving a shower of sparks from his exhaust.

The road from Patras to Corinth split into two directions - to the left, a motorway over which hung a large toll sign and to the right, the old road and no toll. The old road won the toss - more interesting but also rather sad. Village after village lined its sides, linking and blending together in a never-ending dusty sprawl of unattractive, dying structures. Each one seemed to have more than its fair share of missing tiles, cracked walls and peeling paint. I guessed that the motorway had sucked away passing trade and that this had been like the loss of water to a struggling plant. I splashed out on a coke at a tumbledown roadside stall, paying my toll for the old road.

A glance down at my boots snapped me out of these musings. My right foot was wet and glistening with oil. A greasy black smear of an oil leak had spread its way from the front of the engine, over the casing and onto my boot. 'Brilliant, haven't even left Europe yet', I grumbled to myself. Of course I'd no idea what the problem might be but decided that it looked worse than it really was, so rode on to Corinth. I could check it out when I stopped for the night. And, I reasoned, if it looked to be a problem, then in Europe at least I could get help with it. I'd rather have my warning signs now, but then again, maybe the Greek garages were on strike too. I was already happy that I carried so much fuel, 53 litres in total, though I'd never dreamt of being so glad of it so soon - the ferry had worked, but the fuel pumps for the past day had not.

Ancient Corinth brought me a new character. There on Old Corinth's town square, which also doubled as a free campsite, was a dilapidated camper van. John, the van's owner had a travelling style that was 'wing and a prayer' and he was having a ball. When I first saw him I thought 'fat and fit'. He could also talk the hind leg off a donkey; I feared for the local steeds. I soon picked up that he was a fatalist, a Ju Jitsu instructor, a believer in the Labour movement, had sold everything at home to travel, was on his way to India, had almost no money left, and was trying to get a job locally to teach English (phew). He also had a washing machine in his van and offered, "Would you like to use it?" Half of this was said whilst standing on a carved stone plinth pretending to be an ancient Greek statue, with one leg missing!

I took him up on the offer and also the chance to sleep in his van. No tent to battle with sounded like a pleasant change, but I was quick to sleep in the tent the next night. Not only did John toss and turn in his sleep which made the whole van rock furiously, but he snored as hard and as fast as he talked. My socks came up a treat though.

Mad John was on an even steeper learning curve than I was. With total confidence in his ability to sort things out as they happened, he'd set off from home having done very little research. His dream was still India; did I know what paperwork he'd need for the trip? Passport, OK. "Carnet, what on earth is that?" he asked. "A carnet is a temporary import guarantee for your van when you cross into each new country outside Europe, costs a bit though", I told him. John was undaunted, as a 'citizen of the world' he was sure that he could go anywhere, and do anything.

After Rome I had no fear of Athens or Piraeus, but my confidence was premature. The road signs were awful, the traffic the densest in Europe and by the time I reached the docks it was dark. If things went wrong now, I'd miss the boat to Egypt and the next one would be days away. I plunged into my first taste of the world of international Customs and Immigration, and felt under pressure for the first time in days. Brindisi's set up had been child's play, but this time I was leaving a continent. The next four hours were spent with lots of contradicting directions, no signposts and grumpy port officials, most of whom didn't seem to know what they were doing. Thankfully my little bit of Greek was a big help and the officials who did know what they were doing pushed me through what seemed to have no right to be called a system. When eventually standing with the bike in front of the ship, I was tired, thirsty and yes, a bit scared. This was it, I was about to leave Europe.

I rode down the ramp and stopped, stunned. There before me were fifty enduro motorcycles: Germans, French, Swiss, Italians, Dutch and a solitary British bike. Could they all be going through Africa? I couldn't understand it. Wasn't my trip supposed to be something unusual? Behind me the giant doors closed on Greece, and the ship's engines vibrated the deck under my feet. Sweating in the muggy enclosed air, I strapped the bike down as best I could and thought that maybe my worries about the trip had been a bit stupid.

My cabin was a shared one and Willie from Switzerland was a biker too. "The other bikes belong to guys on shorter holidays," he told me. Nearly everyone was heading for the Sahara, and for a cruise around the pyramids, tombs and temples. Another odd look was added to my collection when I told him where I was going. Leaving me to shower, he told me where the bar was and we arranged to meet up. The shower was bliss and my socks enjoyed being washed in hot water again; I seemed to be developing a clean sock fetish.

With the 'Eggitto's' engines throbbing under me, the thoughts came rolling back. What was I doing? Had I turned nuts, or was an amazing adventure just beginning? Whilst researching the trip, I'd looked at the eastern route, but the wars in Sudan and Ethiopia had effectively blocked the way for the last two decades. So, I'd concentrated on the Western route. Suddenly that route had closed too. Rioting and killings in Algeria caused southern neighbour Niger to shut its border. This was a real disaster because there just didn't seem to be another way to go. Further west was closed as well - rebel problems in Spanish Sahara. Libya and Chad looked impassable too.

Faced with the end of the trip before it had started, I'd made tentative enquiries at the Sudanese and Ethiopian embassies in London anyway. Sudan said, "Overland from Egypt, no visa possible", but the Ethiopians had a surprise for me. "Sure", the official said. "A visa is not a problem; we are at peace now you know." I'd kept quiet about the gossip I'd heard to the effect that the visa was valid for entry by air only.

Three days later impressive visas for Egypt and Ethiopia sat in my brand new ninety-page passport. Two things were lacking though, a visa for Sudan, and an entry by air only stamp on the Ethiopian visa. If the latter was a mistake, I was happy to say nothing. As for the Sudanese visa, I'd just have to chance it.

I set off for the bar; never having had much contact with bikers, this seemed the ideal opportunity to talk and learn. The word had got out and some of the other riders knew who I was already and I collected nods as I walked in. It felt pretty good, though I was feeling a bit of a fake amongst all these real bikers. Hay and his wife Jose from Holland then told me who the other British bike belonged to. The bike, an older BMW R80GS than mine, had stood out like a sore thumb amongst all the other sleek hi-tech machinery down below. It already looked well worn and as if its gear had been put together on the cheap. Strapped on the back were old style Craven panniers and army surplus knapsacks hung over the tank. Mike and his wife Sally were heading south, all the way south. I liked them both immediately. Mike, lean, broad shouldered with a shock of black hair and a steady handshake, gave me a measured look. Sally, a bubbly friendly girl, gave me a beaming smile. Around us, the rest of the bikers were getting stuck in to the ale. There'd be a few headaches in the morning but for now, no one cared. We'd left mainland Europe – only a brief stop on the island of Crete to go, and then Africa. My butterflies fluttered again but sleep came with a grin. I was heading from Greece – the cradle of civilisation, to Africa – the cradle of mankind.

Chapter Three

"Tail End Charlie"

'There are incompetent enthusiasts and they are a mighty dangerous lot.'

G.C.Lichtenburg

The 'Eggitto' is a lifeline to the island of Crete. For three seasons of the year, the ship brought supplies, tourists and money to bolster this rocky island's economy. The normal four-hour stop at Heraklion, the capital city and main port, gives enough time for business to be conducted and for the ship's passengers to have a leg stretch on dry land. We arrived two and a half hours late which, the Captain informed everyone, he wanted to try to make back by cutting the visit short. In spite of this and the teeming rain, most of us two wheelers decided that a leg stretch and a look-see was worth a quick soaking.

Inevitably, time slipped by too fast and some of us had to make a mad dash back to the ship. We all made it, except for one poor Egyptian who was still on 'Greek time'. He arrived a couple of minutes after the last ropes were thrown ashore. While he stood on the jetty looking damply forlorn, aboard ship his wife was screaming and shouting to anyone who would listen. Her husband had no money, no luggage and worst of all he'd left his passport on board.

Outside the harbour, a large swell soon reached nausea levels. I was glad that I'd strapped the bike down, in spite of the Piraeus customs officer's weather forecast of calm. By dinnertime, the decks were pretty much deserted and the air in the walkways was revoltingly tainted by an acrid scent that seemed to have an infectious effect on many of those who were still up and about. In the bar though, a large group of German bikers were still drinking enthusiastically. I found Mike sitting in the cafeteria happily tucking into a small mountain of food. As all food was included in the price of the passage I was tempted too, but my stomach was wobbling on the borderline. However, knowing that this might be the last chance of a familiar meal for some time, I joined the small queue at the counter. I'd risk it but positive thinking didn't take into account a drunken biker who pulled up in the queue behind me. As he breathed fumes and spittle at me from a rocking six inches away, my stomach heaved.

In the morning, a hot breeze full of unfamiliar scents wafted over us as we stood at the railings watching Africa get closer. Garbage, diesel and spices were stirred into a greasy, sweaty assault on the senses that made me wonder once again if I was mad. Sally was obviously having the same sort of thoughts; I couldn't tell what Mike was thinking.

In the clammy stale air down below, trucks idled their engines, car drivers organised their passengers, and bikers milled around nervously making last minute adjustments to their gear. More than a few were paying a sweaty price for the previous night's enthusiasm in the bar but I felt excited, and surprised myself at how my fear seemed to have disappeared. Fifty bikes stood with engines running, the ramp went down and minutes later we were riding off into chaos. At a row of small green painted wooden offices, a round little Egyptian official flagged us down shouting, "Come quickly, in a moment many people, much trouble!" He knew what was coming next; customs, registration documents, insurance, immigration, temporary importation papers and total confusion. No one knew what to do. One official was at lunch, another hadn't turned up for work that day, and no one seemed sure where the rest were, or to care. The officials who had turned up seemed to treat the chaos as normal. They were also able to combine indifference, indolence and pure arrogance into a power game that added an edge of tension to the uncertainty. Minutes stretched into sweaty hours, frustration levels grew and hangovers throbbed. Tales were told by old hands about people's paperwork going missing, of bribes and of last minute refusals for no reason at all.

A biker's information underground developed as doors were finally being opened and rubber stamps were brought out. Each little scrap of passed on news broke down the confusion piece by piece. Sweat trickled down my neck, and my leather jacket became a real hindrance as I tried to keep track of the various bits of paperwork. But perversely, as the hours ticked by I started to enjoy the 'hurry up and wait' pace. I felt that the adventure really had begun when the djelalaba clad motor tax official said "Oh yes Misters, you must pay money (a ridiculous amount) for you to have your rubber stamp". We gently but firmly declined and told him that there must be another official who could clarify the situation.

Sitting down to see what would happen next gave me the time to admire his djelalaba. This cotton, neck to ankle, robe seemed a perfect breezy solution to the muggy humid air, but I wouldn't have swapped it for my bike gear for a minute. Eventually our patience paid off and the taxman gave up; after five sweaty, tense hours we were done. All there was left for us to do was to bolt on our impressive temporary Egyptian number plates. Mine had a bright yellow but very battered background, and I'd no idea what the bright red Arabic slashes said. Then we hit the road and with dual-lane highway for most of the way, there was just still time to make it to Cairo before dark; Alexandria's grime held no attractions for us.

Grubby, long-robed, brown-faced kids ran out waving and yelling excitedly as our little convoy sped past. Irrigated fields, mud brick houses and palm trees lined the road. I couldn't help grinning as my sweat evaporated in the slipstream. I'd never ridden with other bikers before so this was fun, and tagging on as 'tail-end-Charlie' meant that if I did something dumb then maybe no one would notice. The quality of the road encouraged us to go faster but as the daylight began to end, common sense slowed us down. The sun was slipping lower as a flaming edged orange red ball that seemed in its dying moments to hang just above the horizon for a few bonus minutes.

Common sense had done us well because as the sun finally disappeared, our headlights lit up the first of the sand dunes across the road. The desert winds had blown ripple-topped banks of sand as a trap to the unwary. As we neared Cairo, the road also became a sort of dog graveyard. Pathetic mound after pathetic mound lay sprawled on the litter-strewn verges or bloody and mangled in the road itself. It was a sobering sight and I rode on wondering how they had all managed to get killed. The roads were open with clear verges and not particularly fast; perhaps life for the dogs was so miserable that this was a traditional suicide site. But perhaps the simple fact was that the dogs were totally lacking in road sense.

We were heading for the camping site in Cairo's suburb of Giza. The last few kilometres are through lumpy darkened back streets that are lined with the houses of people who are a long way from the top of the wealth scale. Our headlights lit up the square, flat roofed, smooth-rendered 'boxes' that were huddled together in rows of uneven terraces. In the darkness, they looked like an old man's decaying teeth. Rubbish filled ditches lined our way where stagnant water lay in mosquito-infested pools. Sometimes the terraces were broken by stretches of wasteland that over the years had turned into rubbish dumps. Even though the scene contained the shadowy almost biblical outline of a donkey or a camel here and there, it wasn't very welcoming after the relative luxury of the ship, but the campsite was a little oasis. Tall fences, lush grass, palm trees for shade, and a security guard. Just three Egyptian pounds or fifty pence a night made it a touch of perfection in comparison to the outside world. Dogs barked and mosquitoes buzzed as I drifted off to sleep in the cool of my first night in Africa.

The next days were a whirl of organising the necessities of life and sight-seeing. Food, money, visas, washing, bike maintenance, the pyramids, the fabulous Cairo museum, the City of the Dead where people live amongst the tombs and of course, our first sight of the Nile – the longest river in the world. We rode all over the city from one office or sight to the next. The GS felt amazingly light with the gear stripped off and I was surprised at how courteous most of the other traffic was. The Cairo metro area, the largest in Africa, is fed by a series of multi-lane highways. Inevitably we found ourselves in the wrong lane for where we wanted to go but the traffic always allowed us to slip through; even the police seemed to enjoy our being there. One bored, solar topee'd policeman on a stand in the middle of eight lanes of organised chaos, actually stopped the traffic just for us to go through. He threw a salute as we passed, and then his white-gloved hands got the traffic going again.

In 969, Cairo was actually founded by a Sicilian General called Gawhar. He'd originally named the city, Al Mansureya but this was later changed to Al Qahira, the Triumphant City, hence 'Cairo'. Over history the city has been influenced by every foreign power that has ruled Egypt, and there have been many of those including the British, the Greeks and the Romans, old and new. All have left their mark and it makes sense that this is why the city is so cosmopolitan. In fact Careans don't consider themselves to be Africans at all. Part of this cosmopolitan air comes, I think, from it being placed at a sort of axis point for land and sea transport from the Middle East, Africa and Europe. Its religions must play a part too. Without doubt this is an Islamic city, but the Coptic Christians and Jews are still visible strengths.

At the pyramids, a dusty car pulled alongside me and stopped. The driver leaned out and said, "Welcome to Egypt. Where are you from?" This was the first time of many that this question would be asked, but with nothing to lose I replied, "Jersey", partly thinking 'this'll fox him'. "Ahh yes," the young man returned. "A fine place, my father is a banker there." Small world, and so for that matter were the pyramids. All

the photos and films I'd seen over the years had made me think that they would be enormous. Not so with the vastness of the open desert as backdrop, but I did marvel at how they were made. Each block weighs about two tons and had been carried for hundreds of miles. I thought that the Sphinx looked as if he was totally out of place amidst the tourist stalls and touts. Rather like a man who turns up to a black tie dinner wearing fancy dress. It didn't help that some thoughtless person, with no respect for history and fine lines, had stuck an antenna of some sort onto the Sphinx's bottom.

The shops in the villages around the camping site were hole-in-the-wall affairs and each seemed to specialise in just five or six items. The washing shop stocked long bars of nicotine-coloured, waxy soap. They wouldn't make your washing soft or smell good - just clean.

The vegetable stalls were made up of any old junk that could be scavenged and cobbled together to make a waist-high roadside counter for the produce to collect dust on. Again, the selection was limited. Oranges, tomatoes, potatoes and onions were about it, but we were learning fast how many culinary variations of those ingredients there were, so long as we had our supplies of mixed herbs, garlic, curry powder and chilli.

My favourite was the Kornafa stall. The cook stood under a faded and patched blue awning with the tools of his trade surrounding him. As we watched he swung into action. Inside his large oil barrel he lit a wood fire. When the flames were high, he placed a greasy disc of steel plate over the top. This looked like an extra thick wok that had been run over and unevenly flattened. Having placed the 'wok', the cook fastidiously wiped his hands on his equally greasy apron before picking up what looked like a round-bottomed funnel. Into this he poured a thick mixture of grease, flour and water, which immediately dribbled out onto the disc in a collection of cream swirls. The swirls quickly joined together and inflated into a sort of pastry that could be eaten savoury or as a sweet. The smell was delicious and the sweet version was very popular, particularly with the local kids.

Having risked the potential results of the cooks greasy fingers and filthy apron, we wandered back through the villages to the campsite. It was rather like playing hopscotch as we tried to dodge the puddles, rubbish and piles of animal shit. We also had to keep an eye open for the seemingly fearless rats.

Over the days rushing around the city centre, I'd grown to like the scents that emanated from the many street food stalls. But my 'fresh from Europe' mind didn't like the look of the food that created those tantalising smells. However delicious it smelt, slime green did not look appetising and my pre-trip decision to try as many local foods as possible wobbled badly in those first few days.

In spite of all the rubbish and open sewers, people's spirits seemed in no way dampened. For them it was normal and they just got on with life. As I began to realise this over those first days, I started to look past the squalor to the people themselves.

The lady in the bread shop was a sweetheart. She didn't speak any English though, and her sign language was shy. We didn't speak much Arabic so her daughter, who was learning English in school, was always summoned to deal with us. It was obviously a matter of pride that her daughter could speak English as well as she could. She was probably ten or eleven years old but had the confidence and manner of someone much older. The girl had a cheeky face, which she seemed to battle with to keep under control.

With us late out of our sleeping bags one morning, the lady had sold out of bread, but with a scolding waggle of her finger, the girl shot off over the street debris to return moments later with still warm loaves for us. The flat, golden-coloured, air filled bread tastes wonderful when eaten fresh, but left until lunchtime it would taste like cardboard. She presented the loaves to us with a little curtsey, another cheeky grin and another finger waggle.

Mike, Sally and I talked carefully about the route south, and we decided to travel together for a while. They'd also planned to go the Western Sahara route and had ended up with the same last minute hassles that I'd had. To my surprise they'd organised a visa for Sudan; it only needed picking up from the embassy. We decided that I should go along with them and with luck I'd be able to find an official who thought that two bikes travelling together would be safer, and therefore would give me a visa too.

I knew from backpacking trips that the solo traveller is often treated in a completely different way from a group. I suppose that people together always seem to be self-sufficient, but a traveller on their own is more vulnerable. When travelling alone, I'd always get more invitations and offers of hospitality from the local people. I guessed that my apparent vulnerability made me more approachable. Just being a stranger had often been enough of an icebreaker for conversation to start. A new adventure would begin right there and I'd never had a bad time by going with the flow. By moving on with Mike and Sally I knew that I'd be losing this facet of travel, but the more I thought about it the more it seemed that meeting the two of them had been meant to happen. It felt like it would be good for all of us and if it ceased to be so, we could part.

We walked into the Sudanese Embassy and past the rows of backpackers that were lining the lobby walls. Each, for want of something better to do, watched us as if to see what new faces had come to join the ranks of the hopeful. Some of these guys had been waiting for weeks for their visas; each day they would come and queue for hours only to be told, 'no news yet'.

It had taken longer than we'd hoped to get our letters of recommendation from the British Embassy so as we arrived the visa clerk was just closing up, but he seemed to like the look of us and showed us into a back office. With Mike and Sally telling their story the 'door' opened a touch further for me too. "Yes possible," he said to me. "But it will take three weeks." I cajoled a bit and he came down to two weeks. A bit more persuasion brought it down to a week but this time he added, "There's no guarantee."

Impressed at how quickly he'd dropped from three weeks to one, I encouraged him a little more. "Ok, Ok," he said. "Three days, but still no guarantee." While he turned back to Mike and Sally, I pondered the waiting rows outside and wondered how much value his 'three days' actually had.

In the upper offices, after some initial confusion, all seemed well for Mike and Sally and I could sense their relief. This had to be my moment as well. To the side of the office sat a wizened older man who had no obvious official capacity, but he had been nodding to us in a friendly fashion. With fingers crossed I started to present my case to him.

Just as I was beginning to feel that he either had a nodding disorder and understood not a jot of English, or that I was definitely out of luck and that he was just being polite, a very dark skinned, immaculately dressed man came storming in. He carried an air of complete authority and was shouting furiously. The nodding man pointed over and said quietly in excellent English, "Talk to him."

The Vice Consul's stony face regarded me from the other side of his desk. I was glad that I'd put on the best and cleanest clothes I'd got, but his stern look wasn't in the least encouraging. In fact it was completely unfathomable with not a twitch to indicate yes or no. Once again I started on my story but this time I had help in Arabic from the office staff. I brought out all the official looking paperwork I could find; including the articles the Jersey Evening Post had done before I'd set off. As we all talked, the V.C. wrote on each of my papers. Then, without a word he pointed to the door; I was sure that I was out of luck.

Just a few minutes later, a minion came out of the V.C's office and hurried past me with my papers in his hand. I wondered which dusty backwater they were bound for. Moments later he came back again and presented them to the manager who said "No" in no uncertain terms. Around me, no one would meet my eyes. Once again, the assistant ducked back into the office where the manager was doing a perfect stony impersonation of his dark skinned boss. Then to my amazement he said, "OK," and grinned as if the whole procedure had been quite normal. The office staff shared conspiratorial, friendly smiles with me and it began to sink in that we'd all achieved something quite special.

Mike and Sally were equally surprised that I'd got a visa for Ethiopia. They'd been told it wasn't possible. Maybe in Sudan they could come with me to the Ethiopian Embassy and the same plan would work again, but in reverse.

Hay, Jose, Mike, Sally, Deit and I linked up again to head south down the banks of the Nile. It's a bizarre ride. You can see desert on both sides of the valley. There's a lush green strip of land that's bordered by cream-coloured sandy desolation. In the middle of the day the heat becomes intense and the only way we found to keep cool was to keep riding, with stops only in deep shade. These bum rests were always an adventure as five bikes stopping on a seemingly deserted section of road always attracted a crowd of spectators from thin air. Orange sellers, old men on donkeys, mischievous kids and the inevitable mangy dogs would descend upon us. It was never very restful, but always an event.

Pulling away from one such rest, the bike felt wrong, sluggish. Kids would often try to hang on the bikes as we rode away so I checked my mirror. There were no uninvited passengers, but behind me billowed a large umbrella. Some cheeky child had hooked it to my luggage and fifty faces behind us were split with broad grins.

The Moslem time of Ramadan was upon us. I was already used to the muezzin wailing cries of "Allah o Akbar"(God is great) from the mosques, and didn't even mind that the first of the day happened at four am. But, the month-long fast made riding a dangerous business. The Ramadan rules stipulate no cigarettes and no food in daylight hours. This made the other road users a menace, especially towards the end of the day when everyone was grouchy and just wanted to get home. Most days we found a place to stay before the clock ticked round into the danger zone, but when we didn't nerves tingled.

The other menaces of the road were running kids, dogs, brainless goats, taxis and 'one eyed monsters'. Trucks in Egypt have to be treated with respect by a lowly biker. Size matters and the trucks are wrecks. They go too fast, and in the dusk their solitary working headlight gives you little warning. Only one headlight because, we were told, their drivers are afraid of wearing out their batteries if they use both! Smashes are common.

Egypt, like France, Italy and Greece, had its own set of overtaking rules. The main rule seemed to be – if there is another vehicle in the way; expect them to pull over for you! This didn't always happen so we were riding with our headlights on full beam. That made infinite sense to us but seemed to be a source of total irritation to the local truck drivers. "Don't these **** tourists know anything?"

Fuel was incredibly cheap at eighty pence a gallon but it was pretty grim stuff. A combination of low octane petrol, heat, and stop-go traffic soon had my bike too hot and 'pinking' like mad. I didn't know what this nasty pinging, ticking noise was; just that it sounded awful. Was the engine going wrong already, why was there no power when opening the throttle? I could ignore it and hope that it would go away, or bite the bullet and try to fix whatever was wrong before it got out of hand. Mike and Hay put my mind at rest though; their bikes had been doing the same. "Just ease off on the throttle when it happens and don't try to pull away so hard", Mike advised. Mostly it worked, though I began to think about the fact that my bike had no oil cooler and everyone else's did. The boxer's fins had been great to warm my hands on when it had been cold on the way across Europe but now they were working overtime to cool the engine. The foot pegs were right underneath those fins and that meant that each day my feet were sitting in boot-sized pools of sweat.

Periodically, we'd come across a police checkpoint. These were ramshackle affairs made of rusty old oil drums filled with cement and straddled by a few warped wooden poles. For padding, the police had used any other debris that had been lying around. They were usually manned by a dapper, khaki-clad policeman, whose dual reason for being there seemed to be to smile and salute tourist motor bikers, and hassle everyone else. We were later told that in times of strife these roadblocks are particularly nasty affairs.

Each day I was surprised and enthralled. Most of the time my education was of the enthralled kind but every now and then, we'd see something that would underline how lucky we were to be Europeans.

Once, just when I was looking forward to the end of the day, a cool beer and some peace and quiet, Jose and I got cut off from the others. Right in front of us a blue pick-up truck knocked down and killed a horse that was pulling a cart. Before our eyes, complete misery unfolded across the horse owner's face. In one short moment his life's savings, income and future were gone. The pick-up truck had kept on going, as in fact we had been warned to do should we ever hit anything, or even anybody. I'd been struggling with the thought of doing that, but seeing misery in front of us turn rapidly into anguished rage and frustration, I suspected that the driver would have been strung up from the nearest lamppost if he'd stayed. The temper of the inevitable crowd was sympathetically hot and Jose and I were happy to sneak away as quietly as possible.

Riding 'tail-end-Charlie' held other problems for me. When you are at the back, you are reacting to what all the other riders in front of you are doing. It means that easy gaps in the traffic for them to slip into are closing fast by the time you get there. That means there is always the risk of losing the rest, or worse, making a bad decision and coming a cropper. As I also discovered, it gives others a chance to react to you. As the road led south the attitude of the children changed and in many places, it seemed downright mean. The kids would see the first rider coming, would pick up stones and by the time I got there the stones would be flying across the road. My bike gear saved me from the worst but I never knew when a large chunk would cause real problems. Until then, the kids had just wanted to wave and to touch the bikes. Their excitement had been fun and I for one hadn't minded them touching the bike so long as they didn't try to pinch anything.

Sally, as pillion rider with hands potentially free, was designated the task of chief waver. A couple of times she'd managed to wave us all out of a potentially nasty situation. Trying her technique I was rather chuffed to find that if I waved just before they threw their stones, the kids would look momentarily confused, drop the stones and wave back. Then I'd be past them.

Tombs, temples and pyramids. Rice paddies, donkey-powered milling stones, water buffalo and date palms. The Valley of the Kings by day and Luxor at night. Felucca sailboats, floating tourist hotels, Nile perch and the water-borne disease bilharzia. Snowy white egrets, elegant storks and ever-active weaverbirds. Heat, mosquitoes, cheap hotels, bed-bug hunts and a never-ending thirst. Icy-cold litres of beer, long days of riding, shared meals and a wonderful sense of freedom kept us enthralled all the way down to Aswan. Here a huge dam blocks the Nile to form Lake Nasser. This bizarre mass of water in the middle of the desert stretches right over the border and down into the Sudan.

Aswan itself seemed quite different from anywhere else we'd been in Egypt. The desert comes much closer to the road, as if the money ran out, not the water. The vegetation is sparser and the houses

 poorer, but the people were incredibly friendly. The crowded night time souk was excellent and the feeling within the market walls was safe, and fun. People laughed, joked and called out greetings to each other. The French promenade along their main streets, but here the wealthy Egyptians promenade in their market. The air in the souk was filled with the heady aroma of spices, people, fruit and baking bread. Around us were the dramatic sounds of hard and fast bargaining, a game of Egyptian life that everyone seemed to be enjoying in the cool of the evening.

To one side of the souk, a bakery was going at full tilt. The daylight hours are so hot in this part of the country that the main meal of the day is inevitably eaten in the evening and Ramadan was just adding to the demand. A man, clad only in a loincloth, rushed out to us as we strolled on by. He'd popped out of a glowing hole in the wall to invite us to come and see the bread being made. Inside, rows of semi clad, sweating men fed flat cakes of dough into rounded slots in the clay walls and stoked the wood burning furnaces; I wondered where all the wood came from. In spite of the incredible heat, the men working in the flickering orange light were full of good humour; cheerful banter zapped back and forth across the room. The smells from the ovens were delicious and we left feeling almost full on the scent alone.

My first taste of pure desert riding was on asphalt and the road down to the border was superb. I'd read other people's descriptions about roads that seem to go on forever until they drop as a dot over the horizon. This one did just that as it stretched out across a landscape of pink, dirty yellow, beige and grey desert undulations. I'd also read about the deafening silence of the desert; it's really true, but you have to be there. At rest breaks once the hot ticking from our engines had stopped, there wasn't a sound to be heard. No wind, no cars, no people, no birds, just the sort of silence that makes you want to hold your breath. To the sides, mile after mile of beautiful rolling sand dunes stretched as far as we could see. I felt like I was riding across the set for 'Lawrence of Arabia', a phenomenal experience and the perfect build up to Abu Simbel.

Our guidebooks said that the temple was a must and that it was just north of the border with Sudan. Abu Simbel had been transported block-by-block to its current home overlooking Lake Nasser. If the temple had been left where it was, the new lake behind the dam would

have drowned it. It seemed an admirable piece of conservation — nothing like it had ever been done before. The rumour we'd heard all the way through Egypt was that the Sudanese land border was closed, but while down looking at the temple, we wanted to check out the crossing point for ourselves, just in case. Our only other choice to get into Sudan was by the passenger ferry down the length of the lake.

Abu Simbel instantly became my favourite of the wonders of Egypt. In spite of all the World War II Italian squaddies' graffiti, the temple is in superb condition. There's a rather spooky, mysterious air to it and the giant statues are majestic. Both the engineering that went into building it in the first place, and the engineering that went into moving it to its new home made it special. For me it was a kind of exclamation mark at the end of the country. However, at the border the road was strung with rolls of barbed wire. Concrete tank obstacles, and old oil drums with skull and cross bone decoration gave us a pretty obvious message; the border was definitely closed.

With no way to get across the land border we decided to make the long dash back to Aswan on the same day, and that dropped us right in it. The wind was getting up and we desert ignoramuses didn't realise that this heralded a sand storm. Off we set, running north. Riding the undulating road at speed was rather like riding a roller coaster, but this time fierce side winds made life hard. As the only obstacles for miles, the wind seemed to be enjoying a vicious game of skittles with us. Sand drifted across the road and our spinning wheels caused little whirl wind cones to zip out across the desert. Fine gritty dust worked its way through our face scarves as we fought to keep the bikes upright. Each time I bit down with the effort of doing so, my teeth crunched on the collecting sand that I no longer had the spit to get rid of. The air was so hot and dry that it literally burned the insides of our nostrils as we breathed. On a brief stop, within seconds our sweat soaked heads and shirts were bone dry. I started to feel like a sheet of human sandpaper. Finally the sun dropped down into the blowing storm, setting a raging orange glow to the world. As darkness came we thankfully slipped into a bunkered down city full of people who had known better than to be out and about.

Next day, down at the Nile Navigation Company offices, the slow chase with officials began once more. Tickets had to be bought, and we needed to find out where number plates could be returned, and carnets exit stamped. If they weren't, then at some time in the future we'd end up having to pay importation tax and fines for bikes that we'd already taken out. The offices reminded me of India. Dusty tomes of ledgers lined the shelves. Men sat waiting patiently in the corridors whilst other men sat officiously in the cubby-hole interiors. The ticket officer said, "You want to go to Wadi Halfa! Why? It was my home, I live here now, and this is much better. Africa starts at Wadi Halfa. Not nice at all!"

We chased around erratically for an hour before a guard helped us out. Until then I'd felt that I was some sort of overgrown fly trapped and bouncing off the inside walls of a glass jar – loads of noise, but painfully not getting anywhere. The guard took us through a maze of white-washed corridors until he stopped almost reverently outside one of the offices. After a couple of moments he pulled himself erect, saluted, and stamped his feet together. We were ushered in, and then carefully ignored for a few minutes. But the Port Commander's eyes were twinkling. "Ahh yes", he said. "You are needing Mr Suleman."

Down by the waters edge we found Mr Suleman and his cronies under a corrugated tin roofed lean-to. Queues of respectful Egyptian and Sudanese men stretched away from his desk and out into the heat. Mr Suleman was obviously the king pin of the docks and as he seemed to like the look of us everything went amazingly smoothly.

Ramadan ended at three thirty am on our last day in Egypt with the honking of horns, the rejuvenated yelling 'song' from the muezzin, and people rushing through the streets calling and shouting to each other.

Having had this early start to the day we were up packed and ready to head for the docks in good time. Goodbyes to the others were hard, especially as it felt like the end of an era. Mike, Sally and I were also conscious that heading for the Sudan was even more like stepping out into the unknown than Egypt had been. The only thing to do was to get on with it.

With the weight of extra desert supplies strapped onto the bike, it felt like I was riding a drunken pig again and if Mike hadn't been around I'd probably have been riding with a broken shaft drive. "With the first set of potholes, you'll be in big trouble, you haven't wound the suspension hard enough", he said. This lucky escape meant that the day started well, but then it slipped into a scene from the script of a farce. As the play unfolded around us, baksheesh (bribe money) was demanded, fees were suddenly inflated and the rushing confusion felt like it was being orchestrated to make life more difficult for everyone.

For hour after hour, white and blue clad porters poured past us with incredible loads of luggage. As the bikes would have to go in the entrance corridor, we were destined to be last aboard and that gave us plenty of time to sit and watch. Pick up trucks rolled by, straining with loads twice as high as their cabs. Orders were shouted, a lost child cried, a donkey brayed frantically, a boat's horn tooted somewhere and I began to wonder where on earth everything was going to fit, and how they were possibly going to unravel what belonged to whom.

When our turn came, we managed to recruit five of the porters to help heave the bikes over the plank and down the two four-foot drops from the dock pontoons into the entrance gangway of the ferry. The gangway was filling up fast; soon there wouldn't be two BMW sized spaces left, but with Sally watching the pile of our unloaded gear all was going well until suddenly there were just two helpers instead of five. My bike was left teetering on the edge of the drop over the lake! With calm from Mike, curses from me and indifference from our helpers, both bikes eventually nestled safely amongst the sacks of rice, trusses of chickens, goats, bags of beans and rusty black bicycles that looked as if they had been around since colonial days.

The inside of the boat was filthy and the constant spitting on anything that stayed still long enough to be spat on, just added a 'lovely' patina to the mess. The men's toilet floor floated with two inches of urine, old newspapers, and cigarette butts which clustered in little bobbing islands. Sally said that the ladies toilet was just as bad.

In the cafeteria, stainless steel trays were full of brown crusty sludge and our tuna sandwiches seemed like a 'cordon bleu' delicacy in comparison. With nowhere else remotely clean to sit, we climbed over the roof's chain railings and onto a baking hot but empty space. In the clear air the stark view was amazing; nothing but three clear lines of water, sand and sky. Next stop, real Africa!

Chapter Four
"Hookahs and Forgeries"
'A tourist sees what he went to see, a traveller sees what he sees.'

Anon

Leaning over the railings watching the final departure moves, I met Bob or rather, he met me. A jet black Ghanaian whose face had been scarred with the swirling lines of tribal markings, he told me that he had travelled overland by truck from Ghana. He was on his way to Athens to get a job on a ship.

"In twelve months on a ship", he said, "I can earn more than a top civil servant back home."

It was a good incentive to make the long hard journey, but he'd only made it as far as Egypt. The border officials had refused him entry, thrown him in jail for a week and had that day ejected him from the country. "No one had said that the visa was for use by air only", said Bob.

At this point I got the nasty feeling that a request for money was about to follow. What a suspicious mind I'd got. No, he had friends in Khartoum and was on the way there to try to borrow some money from them. Then he'd fly to Greece, via Egypt to make a point, if only a pride point to himself. Bob seemed to have calmed down to a state of mild annoyance, but he really didn't like Egyptians at all.

The old ferry tugged itself away from the pontoon with surprising agility and the breeze took away the worst of the heat. As it did so we decided that we'd got the best spot on the boat, but every so often the heat, noise and stench of packed-in life would waft up from down below. We were heading for the new town of Wadi Halfa. Its old namesake, a palm tree lined border town, was now under several feet of Lake Nasser. Mike took a look at the bikes to find that their GS now had a sack of carrots and a baby goat loaded on top of it. Mine was snuggled down below a load of hay.

Our roof-top spot was right next to the prayer area. Every now and then a crowd of white robed men, never women, would troop up and face east. They'd unroll their prayer mats and then, after a moment's hush, the mullah would start the prayers. Bottoms up! I was impressed with their dedication to their religion and felt honoured to be a front row witness to the display of faith, but I didn't know enough about Islam to decide if I should be impressed with the religion as a whole, or not. The next weeks would be a good opportunity to learn.

Mike and I were summoned to fill in landing cards and it was a nice surprise that the task wasn't being left until the last minute. But besides that I was really happy to get in the shade for a while. A coke would have gone down very well too; up on the exposed roof area we'd been sweating hard. The air up there in the breeze was so dry that if it hadn't been for damp patches left on the deck when one or the other of us moved, we wouldn't have been aware of sweating at all. My skin never felt wet, but I felt thirsty all the time and that, I'd read, was a big warning of dehydration. Sally stayed with the bags and the sun; as a woman, local culture said she wasn't expected to deal with any of the paperwork. The landing card process was carried out from briefcases on old trestle tables in a sweaty, smoke filled compartment. I didn't envy the officials their task as they too were obviously feeling the heat. But they were calm, pleasant and mild mannered with everybody, and we passed through the queue quickly.

Our ferry tickets had come with food coupons, but having already seen what was on offer we weren't in a hurry to use them. At one of the other tables in the compartment, a man had the job of handing out plastic discs in return for the coupons. For five green ones you could get five teas. For one green and two pink you'd get a tea and two plates of congealed stodge. We chose the strong black very sweet tea that was served with a large tannin stained green plastic jug. This was dipped into a great steaming vat of tea and its contents slopped into finger marked glasses. The glasses were dipped and rinsed in a bowl of water that by the time we got to it had a film of grease floating on top. The tea was delicious but we decided that our carefully filtered water from Aswan was probably much safer, so gave away the extra green discs.

Mike's thirty-second birthday started at three thirty in the morning with prayers. Those early hours of cool were important, as by seven thirty it had warmed up to the same temperature as midday in a brilliant English summer. With the dawn, the sun rose up over the ragged pencil line of land that split the sky and the lake. Sitting up there on the roof of the ferry I felt marvellously happy. I had good friends, my bike and I was already surrounded by the sands of Sudan.

The ferry Captain had started a three-month relief contract six years before, and had never left. I heard that he'd trained on the ferries in the English Channel. He seemed to see the Aswan ferry as cruising in comparison. "It's become too easy over the years, I go back and forth and maybe I will until the lake silts up."

He was the first person who had voiced the fears that we'd read about. The Nile valley had been a fertile place and stayed that way over  the centuries because of the annual floods. These would bring nutrient-rich silt from the lush plains of southern Sudan and Uganda. When the dam had been built to provide hydroelectric power, and to allow year round water supplies, the yearly rush of goodness ceased and had began to back up in the lake itself. Bets were already being taken on how long it would be before the lake became an incredibly fertile marsh. The Captain remained philosophical about it all. "It's good for everybody now."

Eventually the ferry arrived at a couple of old barges, two squat concrete buildings, a bunch of ramshackle wooden huts, a truck stop and a lot of sand. Enthusiastic helpers heaved the bikes off the ferry and to our surprise, asked for nothing except a smile and a handshake in return. One of them looked a bit sheepish though. Moments before he'd pulled an indicator off my bike as he tugged it ashore. But I couldn't blame him; I should have shown everyone where they could grab hold.

Around us the other passengers were throwing sacks, bundles and chickens onto the trucks.

"Hurry, hurry", we were told. "If you do not go quickly there will be nowhere left to stay in the city."

City, what city? All we could see were tracks in the sand that seemed to lead off in all directions.

While Mike and I had dealt with getting the bikes off, Sally had stayed with our bags. With the mass of people and luggage moving through the exits, we decided to pass our kit through a window. I balanced on the railings below and could just reach the bags from Sally. Mike then took them from me. It was a great system until a very angry man saw us and started to shout, "This is a window, not a door! This is a window, not a door! Window! Not Door!" It seemed a good idea to stop. At customs our luggage was checked very thoroughly for booze. Sudan, being strongly Moslem, meant that our next beer would be in Ethiopia.

An old Bedford truck, axles sagging, belched a cloud of dense black smoke and set off across the sand. We decided to follow and suddenly I was astride a bike that felt like an upside-down pendulum. Too much luggage, soft deep sand and total ignorance made the ride one of the maddest things I'd ever done. As the back end of the bike swung madly from side to side I hung on tight, amazed that Mike and Sally were staying upright at all. It's called 'fish tailing' and there's no choice but to go faster and hang on. Slow down and there isn't enough momentum to push through the sand. Go too fast and you either make it, or fall off big time. We made it, but looked at each other with consternation as the reality of the ride across the Sahara dawned upon us. Soft sand, 'two up' and two peoples luggage was going to push Mike, Sally and their bike to their limits. I'd no idea where my limits were, but I did know that the ride hadn't been fun. There wasn't any asphalt across this part of the desert, and the tracks we'd been told about didn't sound as if they even remotely lived up to their name. I went to sleep that night thinking, 'you idiot, accept it, you don't know what you are doing!'

New Wadi Halfa is a collection of mud brick and concrete houses that sit defying the intense desert climate. The uneven streets are dusty and the blistering heat doesn't allow for any trees. The dogs look starved and the people look beaten; even the flies look exhausted. A few stringy tomato plants were the only sign that anything could grow in this grim town.

The grandly named Nile Hotel was the only hotel with somewhere to park the bikes off the road, and with at least the possibility of water to drink. Hidden behind four high walls, it was a sleepy world of its own. Water dripped sporadically from the communal  tap, the beds had thirsty bugs, and what little shade there was had its own collection of flies that buzzed drunkenly off the walls. The Hotel had in fact once been a grand affair. In the old Whadi Halfa it had had river views, whitewashed walls, palm trees had surrounded it and such dignitaries as the Emperor of Ethiopia, Haille Sellassi, had stayed there. Drowning the town had obviously been the short end of the stick for some.

The manager of the hotel had a drooping left eyelid and wildly staring right eye that made him look like a scurvy villain from a 'B' movie. He insisted that it was impossible for anyone to stay in his hotel without a passport. Customs had been just as adamant that they had to keep them to process our bike papers, so we'd obtained receipts, and had nervously left them. But now with no choice, I went back to get them. The ride to the port was a playtime blast. I knew where to go and this time I had no luggage. The sand was pure adrenaline fun and I zipped across it with a huge grin.

At the hotel the manager grudgingly gave us a couple of the rooms on the barrack-like courtyard. They cost forty-five Sudanese pounds each, which was about thirty pence and would do very nicely.

As the end of day cool approached, Matthew the urbane Nigerian army officer from the room next to ours told us that there would be Nubian wrestling out at the edge of the town. I wasn't sure what to make of Matthew. He was a real character with a great sense of humour, but there was something clandestine about him that made me feel wary. Grabbing cameras and water we set off for the desert where, in the middle of nothing, a large square of people had formed. Excitement hung in the air. The men were all dressed in white Djelalabas and most wore the turban like cream crepe head dresses of northern Sudan. I was surprised to see so many women there. They added a bright, vivid splash of colour to the ranks of white and cream. Everyone carried a large stick which they waved madly in the air at every point of triumph, or beat the ground with in enthusiastic hefty thumps. Each time a point was scored by the tall, fit, dust-covered wrestlers, the crowd would break away from the fight to dance with elbows, knees and robes flying wildly in all directions. The Nubians had once used these wrestling matches to strike fear and terror into the hearts of their Egyptian enemies. I could see how it had worked.

The bare-chested fighters sported a wild collection of brightly coloured shorts that would have been more at home on an Australian surfer's beach. With regular dips down to dust their hands in the fine sand, they would circle each other, bobbing and weaving like cobras looking for the moment to strike. Like lightning, one of them would dart forward and group mayhem would start. Fast and furious they fought with dust rising from their swirling stamping feet as each tried to throw his opponent onto the sand. Great shouts and cheers would go up from the crowd as a team finally won. The winners were then carried shoulder high around the madly celebrating throng.

In between bouts of fighting, the opposing teams strutted and danced out into the arena to taunt their opposites with silly walks, dog barking impersonations, stick waving and bottom pointing. The best fools always got the loudest jeers and cheers. Every so often the women would rush out, robes flowing behind them as bright streaks. They'd bash the ground around a hero's feet with their sticks and then dart back from the arena into the approving crowd.

As the tournament ended, the dancing began. By this time it was almost dusk and the sun was lowering itself into the wrestler's dust cloud. For the women in particular, the wrestling appeared to be of great value. They had seemed to lose a lot of inhibitions and I suspected that we'd been treated to a rare sight in Sudan's male dominated world.

Back at the hotel we brewed up. Bob, Matthew, Jeroun (a backpacker from Holland), Sally and I toasted Mike a 'Happy Birthday', and for a birthday dinner we set off for one of the 'Ful and fish' stalls we'd seen on the way back from the wrestling. Ful is a green bean dish that's heavy with tomatoes and is steeped in olive oil. It's as greasy as it sounds and with no cutlery on offer you eat it with your fingers. We didn't try the fish; it looked a bit of a risk.

The next stall served glasses of hot very sweet tea which is drunk black and teeth coatingly strong. The stall itself was almost medieval and I had the delightful feeling that I'd stepped back in time. As the power had been off in Wadi Halfa for about an hour by this time, we sat drinking the tea in almost total darkness, but we didn't care. The semi-darkness allowed us to have the stars as our ceiling and as the rare candles lighted only the people's faces the whole scene was eerie and intimate.

'Africa time' at least started in Wadi Halfa. The bank was open but until someone bothered to send the rate of exchange up from Khartoum, we couldn't change money. We had fees to pay so searched out the very efficient black money market instead. Once we had some cash there were a lot of things to do. Customs, alien registration, route information, and we were now interested in anything we could find out about the weekly train to Khartoum. We were also on the hunt for fresh food, but that seemed a bit of a lost cause. The more we saw of Whaddi Halfa, the more it seemed to exist in this desolate place only as a railhead for the line to Sudan's capital city, and as a statement of ownership of this part of the Sahara. Though Sudan means 'Land of the Blacks', people of Arab descent were the ones making the statement.

Obtaining our Alien Registration Cards was an unbelievable chore. The officials were all very nice, but handshakes and smiles were the only things that seemed to happen with smooth efficiency. Mostly they didn't seem to know what they were doing. It was almost as if the environment had shrivelled and dried their brains. They were the most helpful people I'd ever come across who didn't actually help to get anything done. After three hours we were half way through the procedure. Then we were told to wait for half an hour for a particular official to come. After the half an hour, I was told 'just another fifteen minutes', then another fifteen minutes. By this time Mike had taken Sally back to the hotel. She wasn't feeling well and we wondered if the heat was getting too much for her. Trying not to antagonise anyone, I asked for our man again. "Sorry mister, he's gone for breakfast." Breakfast? It was the middle of the day! "Come back at one o'clock", the officer said.

I just couldn't be angry; they were all so polite and friendly. It would have been far too hard work to be angry in that heat anyway.

The hotel manager didn't like me at all; perhaps he'd sensed how I'd characterised him. After two days of queuing in offices I needed a shower, badly. I'd been sweating so fast at least I didn't smell. Any poisons had long since been diluted and sweated out, but I felt unclean. Not a drop of water came out of the efficient looking showerhead and when the manager said, "No problem, wait five minutes", so quickly, I knew in fact there was a problem. I decided to think positive and undressed, but nothing happened. 'Be patient you are on Africa time', I told myself. Five more minutes of standing sweating furiously in the rough concrete, open-to-the-sun cubicle proved a point to me. Positive thought waves don't make it through air that's wobbling into the atmosphere at forty-five degrees in the shade. I tried again and this time, with a sigh, the manager pulled himself out of his chair as if I'd just asked him to go out and run a half marathon. Still no water and by now I was beginning to get a bit pissed off. Then, from the other side of the wall came the sound of a tap being turned. Water drizzled out and I quickly shampooed, just in time to hear the sound of that same tap turning off the flow. It took me half an hour to rinse the soap out of my hair and off my body but only because, this time, Africa had worked for me. Someone hadn't got round to fixing a leaky washer on the shower tap and the resulting leak gave me enough water to finish the job. I stepped out a clean winner and gave the manager a thumb's up on the way past. Hopefully, we wouldn't be there long enough for me to need another shower; he'd probably keep me waiting hours for the next one.

By the end of day two we'd completed all the formalities but Sally had started running a fever and was looking very pale. Filtering our water and mostly being careful with what we ate just hadn't been enough for her. Faced with the choice of sitting the fever out, hoping that she'd soon be fit enough to ride the desert, or trying to get tickets for the train, Mike, Bob and I set off for the station. Bob led us to a group of people who were crowding around an unmarked office. Another lesson learned. Just look for the crowd, queue up and with luck it's where you want to be. The man at the desk scribbled on a piece of paper, ripped it off the page and thrust it at us saying, "Tomorrow."

The freight office was sign posted, and almost deserted. Its interior was dark and dingy, but cool. Mice crawled playfully on the floor while two men sat inside a wire cage. I couldn't help but grin at the apparent reversal of roles. The younger of the two adjusted his crochet skullcap while his colleague stroked his greying goatee beard, and a price for the bikes was worked out. This took a lot of head scratching, mutual consultation, and a grease-stained piece of cardboard upon which where a series of ball-penned Arabic etchings. The critical factors seemed to be those etchings, and the weight of the motorcycles. After several efforts to get it right, Mike's lighter bike was going to cost just over nine English pounds, and mine eleven pounds. This, I thought was a fair price for over two hundred miles of pure desert.

The proceedings were tinged with a touch of disappointment but also with a sense of relief. If we could get on the train with the bikes then we could get Sally to hospital if it came to that. She wasn't well and seemed to be getting worse. I was feeling a little relieved too because with just over three months biking experience, I was sure that I hadn't learned enough to ride across the Sahara. The only information we could get was that there are two ways to ride across the desert here. One is to follow the soft sands along the river Nile and the other is to run alongside the railway line. The giant gullies across the desert - wadis - are the price you pay for this much shorter but equally soft route. Our bikes would have made hard work of either way. For me, this section was only a small part of the whole trip and I wanted to experience all of it - if some was to be done by train, why not?

Trying to secure those train tickets pushed our patience to its limit. 'Africa time' played more games with us. Everything happened incredibly slowly, but our luck was in and we finally bagged some of the last tickets, with confirmed seats too. The perspiring railway officers said that there would be room for the bikes in the cargo cars if we could get them up the six feet from the sand.

This train ride used to be one of the 'seven great train journeys of the world'. General Gordon's men laid down the track when the Sudan had been under British control. But since the country had gained independence in 1956, nature had taken its course with the line, and the equipment. When the train eventually pulled in, inevitably late, we bundled Sally into our six-seater compartment. It was embarrassing to have to kick those without tickets out first. As we hurried off to load the bikes I noticed that there wasn't any glass in many of the trains' windows. Loading the bikes went much more smoothly than I'd thought, though we did make the mistake of not tying them down. With everything else that had to be dealt with, it didn't occur to either of us that it should be done.

The twenty-three-car train was made up of cargo to the rear, then the open windows and hard bench seats of third class, just spit and grit on the floor. Next came second-class with cracked and split padded seats, some window glass and eight people to a compartment. Along the line were the dusty, dingy sleeper cars with two bunks to a compartment. The mattresses that we could see were filthy and holed, and the mirrors were fly-blown, chipped and peeling. Finally came first class. It was one of these that we'd booked and though not much better, with just six people to a compartment, it would do nicely. Up in front, a dilapidated diesel engine squatted on the track already looking as if just the thought of having to pull this lot across the desert was far too much for it.

Sally was in the middle of a battle which was made worse by the general confusion. It seemed that the officials had 'forgotten' to reserve our seats. Now it was our turn to be kicked out and it took two hours of chasing around, arguing and haggling before we finally wangled ourselves seats in a second-class compartment. The ticket man was a chap called Osman. He looked rather like an overgrown gargoyle. On his head he wore a neat white skullcap and in a crowd all you could see of him was this white disc bobbing around at chest height. He was a man of infinite patience, and needed to be, as crowds of passengers constantly mobbed him, all of whom had a problem that apparently only he could sort out.

Everyone in our compartment looked slightly stunned and dazed as we snaked out across the sands; it had only taken nine hours to get the train loaded and ready to go, but the women in the carriage next door were in party mood. The sun went down to the sounds of a beating drum and the women singing. The songs were sometimes sad, sometimes happy and sometimes amazingly raucous, but always with an evocative beat. Now we really felt that we'd arrived in Africa.

The corridors were packed with the by now familiar collection of bundles, humans, goods and livestock. Tarzan type lianas from the ceiling would have been very useful. The toilets were also full of passengers, their packages and bundles. As Sally needed to make some desperate toilet dashes through this melee, it turned out to be a really rough ride for her. The fever had turned into violent diarrhoea and the journey was going to take three days. That meant an average speed of about 15 mph. In Gordon's day the journey had taken just twenty-seven hours.

When the train began to roll, Sally whispered to Mike, "Look down." The walls of the carriage didn't appear to be fastened to the floor! With each bump, they moved one way and the floor another. Through this gap we could see the flickering track and sleepers. The train moved further out into the desert and a hot dusty wind blew in through the glassless windows. We'd heard that it was possible to ride the roof and sure enough it was packed. Some people ride up there

63

because it's a little less crowded, some because it's cheap, and some because they'd jumped on board at the last minute for a free ride. Security guards with big sticks roam the train ready to throw these people overboard if they can catch them. They do it literally and we saw several bodies hit the sand as the train trundled along.

The night passed tortuously. The compartment was designed for just eight people and we were eleven adults. Some compartments had more and I dreaded to think what third class was like. I'd never spent such an uncomfortable night before, but all the same, a lot happened. For example, at two am the train pulled into a way station with a jolt that probably woke everyone on board; the cynic in me thought that the driver was probably in league with the locals. Out of the darkness, stalls appeared as their proprietor's lit hurricane lamps. "Ful Aishe, Fuuul Aiiishe", was the call as people leapt off the train and within seconds were squatting on the ground eating their beans and tomatoes. With business in full swing, the lamps lit up the village behind. The white conical buildings looked rather like bread ovens or upturned funnels. They were, I supposed, made this way to reflect away the worst of the day's heat. I was glad that I didn't have to call it home.

When the train jolted to a stop next, we were in the middle of nowhere. Men, long white robes flowing, were piling off the train and running out into the desert; it was prayer time. The men knelt backsides towards the train, their faces in the direction of Mecca; the women prayed quietly inside the train. When prayers had finished, robes were rustled and prayer sites became impromptu urinals. Inside the train, the women presumably 'crossed their legs'! Sally took another Immodium.

The next morning, a hot wind blasted into the compartment. Sweat was quickly sucked dry leaving only my backside and contact points with my neighbours damp. By the wayside were sun bleached camel bones that warned that even the most resilient of beasts could come a cropper. The locals in Wadi Halfa had warned us to take plenty of drinking water, but with only way stations for most of the ride water was still going to be a problem. Station No.6 had its own supply; the rest had to wait for the train to deliver supplies. We did have plenty of food though. Bread, dates, tinned sardines, tomatoes and some horribly sour lemon drops. For most of the time none of us felt hungry, but we still found meal times interesting. The other people in the compartment, though they didn't know each other before the journey, began to cut whatever they had into a communal bowl - dried fish, tomatoes, onions, rice, peanuts, herbs and lemon juice. Right hands dipped into the bowl holding wedges of flat unleavened bread to act as scoops for the liquid at the bottom. I really liked the look of this, but did wonder what bugs must be passing from unwashed hand to unwashed hand.

It took nearly forty-eight hours of hot stop-and-go days, chilly stop-and-go nights, and lots of smile exchanging and cramped manoeuvring, before we were invited to join the meals. I felt that the offer to join in was an honour, but I also felt a touch guilty at the little food we had left by that time to go in the pot as our share. No one seemed to mind though, and once the ice was firmly broken the questions began to flow back and forth. One of our new friends was a schoolteacher and could speak good English. He worked quite happily as translator between us all. "Is it true that our robes are ridiculed in your country?" "Is it true that it rains all the time in England?" "Can it be true that if one of our men tries to marry one of your women he will be stoned?" "Is it true that all Christians hate Moslems? Why is that?" "What do you know of our religion?" We were both amazed and saddened at the image these kind friendly people had of our home. I was learning how powerful propaganda is as we tried to give a fair and honest picture. Their answers to our questions indicated again that misinformation was alive and well. "The war in the south is a minor skirmish." "No we don't hate the black people, but they want to take over our land." "The Aid agencies from the west are full of CIA spies." I wondered about how much of what we read and are told in our own country is the complete truth.

Not long after arriving in Sudan we'd begun to notice how white people's teeth were, particularly in comparison to the Egyptians. We suspected that this was due to the price of tobacco in the Sudan. A lot of smuggling goes on over the border but not it seemed enough to stain most of the population's teeth. You could tell a rich man by the colour of his teeth; all of our dinner companions for example were obviously poor.

The oldest of our companions had grey hair, which he incongruously kept covered with a fur-lined hat. The earflaps on the hat made him look like Biggles, the hero pilot from my schoolboy novels. He also had the dirtiest feet of anyone I'd seen anywhere. They were cracked and split like the landscape and his soles were covered in thick waxy layers of skin. I'd been impressed with the thought of him walking on the sand in the heat of the midday. That same heat had been really uncomfortable even through the thick soles of my bike boots.

I was desperate to take photographs – the train roof, the way stations, prayer time and the crowded corridor. The face-painted honeymoon party next door that kept awake until the early hours each night, singing their songs and laughing, would have all made great shots. Even the faded, fly blown colonial mirror above the waterless hand basin in our compartment told a story all of its own. The desert was stunning too, and I really wanted a picture of the train as it curled around a big bend in the track for apparently no reason at all, but I didn't dare. This country was at war and the signs said, in English, 'No photos without permits from Khartoum.' I snapped a couple out of frustration and received warning looks and stares from our fellow travellers, so put my camera away again. It would have been sad to spoil the cramped, but easy atmosphere and breaking the rule felt like a total lack of respect.

The countryside changed. Scrubby farms appeared with windmill water pumps, and donkeys. Then we started to see overloaded trucks, gravel roads and houses with paint on them. The market at the first town of consequence straddled the railway track, and the train considerately stopped in the middle of it. Some of the women I saw in the market that morning were absolutely beautiful. Their rich tanned skin combined perfectly with soft Arabic features and broad perfectly shaped mouths. But the most fascinating thing about them was their eyes. They seemed to be pure white and were centred with honey brown irises that glinted and gleamed when they smiled, and they smiled a lot. When they saw Mike, Jeroun and I, they'd look coyly at us, smile, giggle and turn away as if teasing us – the perfect flirt.

That night we pulled into the town of Atbara. We were due a long stop here, so Mike and Sally decided to take a stretch and to try to find us some water. We'd drunk thirty litres between us and even that hadn't been enough. They came back with water, Pepsi and ice cream. Sally looked exhausted and they had to force their way back in past five newcomers who insisted that they had reserved seats. It was a mad situation in which tempers were more than a little frayed. The corridor was so crowded now that she couldn't get to the toilet that way at all. Tears finally fell as she sat wedged in a heap of total misery. I could see that Mike was also close to the edge. Not with sickness, but with the frustration of not being able to do anything to help her. Eventually she got to the loo by climbing down the outside of the jolting train on a thin metal bar that ran along at floor level. Even when there, she still had to push her way back into the carriage and then persuade the inhabitants of the now stinking, stifling box to get out. She had to do that several times before we finally got to Khartoum.

By this time there were sixteen of us in the compartment and with a little grin, I longed for the relative comfort of the previous night. The only way to sleep was to take it in turns to hang half in, half out of the window. White dust swirled in and covered everything and everyone. There was still room for the journey to get worse, so of course it did. The train driver had brakes that were obviously either off, or on! Every couple of hours the train would jolt massively to a halt, and then just sit there for no apparent reason. No prayers, no food stop, no male urinal stop and no sand on the tracks. We'd just sit there until the engine thundered with the effort of heaving the now dangerously overloaded train. With another wild jolt, we'd be off and once more facing the task of trying to sleep. Not one of us was comfortable, and in joint misery the frustrated anger of Atbara disappeared. The sixteen of us waited patiently and during the night the Immodium seemed finally to work for Sally; she was feeling a little better. I'll always be impressed with the way she handled herself on this grim but wonderfully bizarre train ride.

Khartoum was now close and we felt that a new, more comfortable adventure was surely about to begin. My dreams were of a hotel and a shower, of ice-cold cokes, and a large meal, mail and photography permits. Then we'd be ready for nice touristy things and Ethiopian visas for Mike and Sally.

Finally we arrived. When we got to the cargo carriage, good news, the bikes were still where we'd left them. It may sound silly but I had worried that during one of the stops along the way, they might have been quietly off loaded. The bad news was that they had fallen over with the constant stop start journey, but thankfully no real damage had been done. Mike rode down from the train on a four by two plank but I chickened out and eased mine down with the help of three passers by. I felt terrible. Not from being a chicken, but three days and nights without going to the toilet had left me bunged like a cork in a barrel. I was constipated, in pain and sweating as a result. Sally and I laughed at how we'd managed to be at the opposite ends of the scale. Each bump that Khartoum's streets could put in my way, hurt. How many tourists have had to resort to laxatives in Khartoum before?

Leaving the two sufferers to wait with some of the kit, Mike and Jeroun set off to find a hotel. They were gone a long time but it was worth it. They found a hotel that was cheap, had a lock up garage for the bikes, clean rooms, showers that worked, friendly staff, and was conveniently placed in the city. The big bonus was a refrigerated coke machine at the end of every floor. The overhead fans in the rooms worked, and at the end of the street was a small supermarket that stocked all sorts of goodies. Mike, Jeroun and I pigged out on yoghurt, cheese spread sandwiches, tomatoes and ice cream. We felt pretty darned good afterwards, but poor Sally still couldn't bear to watch. Bed that night was a wonderful horizontal event, though it did feel rather lonely without fifteen fellow travellers to share it with.

We decided to be pure tourists on our first day and set off early while it was still cool. The city, set in three distinct parts at the confluence of the Blue Nile from Ethiopia and the White Nile from Uganda, is an odd mixture of Arab, British colonial, modern and village. The main city streets were grandly laid out by General Kitchener in the form of the Union Jack. Patriotic maybe, but he'd had other thoughts in his mind at the same time. The angles of the streets allowed near perfect lines of fire for his machine guns. In our time though, the odd layout seemed to play havoc with traffic flow.

The cars were mostly new and often sported hastily painted out Aid agency signs – there had to be a scam there somewhere. Big Western hotels stood in streets whose pavements hadn't been finished. Donkeys jostled with trucks and taxis, and on almost every street corner was a stall selling chilled soft drinks. By ten thirty, we knew why there were so many of them. By twelve it was over forty-five degrees Celsius in the shade, and there wasn't much of that. Sometimes the soles of our boots actually felt as if they were sticking to the paving stones as we walked. Deciding that only mad dogs should be out and about, we retreated to our rooms for a siesta. Sally was feeling miserable again.

The British embassy in Egypt had asked us to check in with the Embassy in Khartoum on arrival. By late afternoon it was cool enough to head out again and besides checking in, we thought that the embassy would be a good place to find the address of a doctor for Sally. With luck they'd tell us who their staff used. She was really ill and seemed to be getting worse. Cairo's embassy had been a grand affair – Khartoum's was perfect for a country at war. The tall walls were topped with razor wire, had steel gates and armed guards. Inside these walls, plate glass separated us from the very helpful and friendly officials.

In the 45-degree heat the bikes were an absolute bonus. The few backpackers who had made it to Khartoum trudged miserably from one side of the city to the other on their hunt for the amazing list of permits that the government required for tourists to move anywhere. Some took budget-wrecking taxis; we cruised. A permit was needed to go to the next town, a permit to get a permit to get petrol, a permit for going to the Ethiopian border, and so it went on. Some required a series of signatures from offices on opposite sides of the city and the official we needed never seemed to be there. I expected to be told at any moment that a toilet permit would be needed! I still didn't have a problem with that, but Sally did. The Doc said she'd picked up both Bacillic and Amoebic dysentery. While she was recovering the days eased on by, rush, slow, siesta, rush slowly, siesta.

On the way back one day, I stopped at our local bakers for fresh bread. At this baker you got to queue in the shade and he baked twenty-four hours a day. The permanent row of people waiting was a perfect opportunity to 'people watch'. Women were allowed to go straight to the front but rich people, (men, women and children) also queue jumped, much to everybody's frustration. Small boys hawked brown paper bags that were made out of old cement sacks. They wandered the line calling "Kiss, Kiss", which raised an eyebrow until it clicked that 'Kiss' in Arabic is the word for bag. The police and army were also 'allowed' to push in, which elicited muttered under the breath curses from the rest of us. The best of the situation though was that although I was very obviously a foreigner there was a sort of bond between everyone in the queue, and I was included.

I discovered a lorry park one afternoon. Beat up, mainly round-nosed Bedford trucks of indeterminate age collected there, their owners touting for loads. The trucks alternated their colour schemes between dull bare metal, and pale blue. Surprisingly, British barge painting style flowers, patterns and murals decorated the blue backgrounds. The trucks were the newer version of the age-old camel. Their owners treated them with equal pride, but heavily overloaded them. Periodically, a rumbling truck would waddle its way out of the park causing a flurry of activity. Youths would leap up from wherever they had been waiting patiently, and they'd run behind the truck with the ambition of pinching a free ride. The drivers must have known that this was what was happening, but like the youths who ran pretending that they'd not been seen, the drivers pretended that they hadn't seen either.

Armed with our new photographic permits and with Sally feeling much better, we got back to work, and to being tourists. We travelled across to the old city of Omdurman to watch the famous 'Whirling Dervishes' whirl their amazing dance. The dancers are the descendants of the reputedly ferocious men who banded together under the leadership of the Mahdi, a religious leader supposedly descended from Mohammed himself. They had been so committed and cleverly aggressive that they had actually defeated and killed General Gordon. The current Government has virtually outlawed them and their dance is just about the only right for public display that they have left.

Finding the dancers wasn't an easy task though. With the end of day cool, the wind builds and blows in off the desert. The stronger gusts make your face feel like it's being sand blasted and the streets look as if they are fog bound. We were lost and about to give up when a voice from behind asked, "Are you looking for the dancers?" The young man had been on a bus and had recognised our bewildered expressions. He'd hopped off his bus just to show us where to go. Hospitality and care towards strangers was a Moslem trait I was beginning to rather like, and this guy was living his faith.

The Dervish costumes were of bright greens and reds. They were led by an elder who was dressed in a raggedy cloak that looked like Joseph's technicoloured dream coat might have done after it had been through a combine harvester. On his head sat what looked suspiciously like a rope floor mop. The main theme of the dance seemed to be to twirl either on the spot, or to twist with one foot never leaving the ground. They spun for ages, but never looked as if they were about to drop. While we watched, Abdul disappeared, to return with tea and doughnuts that he refused to let us pay for. The Dervishes danced until the sun went down behind the dome-roofed mosque and palm trees, in a red tinged dust haze.

Abdul invited us back to see his rooms, but we didn't take him up on the offer. His landlady had been a political dissident and had only recently been released from jail where she'd been badly tortured. We knew she would be afraid that our presence would bring the police down on her again. Once more our journey had caused us to step into a different world.

The twenty-year war had been going on in Sudan in an ever more vicious manner. The fighting was, put simply, between the Arabic peoples and the dark skinned Nubians. On the surface it seemed to be a religious war between the Moslems of the north and the south's Christians and Animists, but I'd heard tell that there was a large dollop of greed thrown in too. The fertile south, it had recently been rumoured, was oil rich.

The markets in 'Omdurman', (which translates as 'The Elephant's Trunk' after its position on the Nile) were a medieval maze of fascination. Copper pots, camel skin bags, fruits, vegetables and wooden farming tools were on show next to a medicine man's herbs and potions. Sally was glad she was feeling better when she saw the latter. The pride of the souk seemed to be something called a Phoenix. These black beauties were bicycles made in China but assembled in the souk itself. Row after row of these gleaming bikes stood awaiting their proud new owners. For many, their price was equivalent to a year's wages.

The street in front of our hotel was by day a boring concrete hotel front on a boring concrete street. By late afternoon it came alive. Tables and chairs appeared, loud-speakers were hung on the wall and screechy music drowned out the streets background noises. White robed, hook nosed, turbaned men came to sit, hookah pipes were lit and soon the smell of strawberry flavoured tobacco wafted on the cool breeze. At dusk a pickup truck would ease past with a giant fan and large steel bottles loaded behind it. The fan whirled and the bottles were opened one at a time. This mega bug killer was the reason that there were no flies in the city, no birds either. I felt depressed and sat down at one of the tables; Sally's convalescence and the paper chase had eaten too much time. My visa for Ethiopia had expired, but in a way luck was still with us. We all had new visas but the trouble was, they were stamped 'For Entry by Air Only.' Was the chance for riding through Ethiopia really gone? I didn't want to fly. I wanted to ride. My neighbour took a puff on his pipe and passed its long stemmed mouthpiece across to me. "You look as if you need this, my friend." I decided to chance that there wasn't anything dodgy in the mix and took a long puff. The water in the bottle bubbled furiously; strawberry tobacco. I relaxed with a little head rush; I'd given up smoking two years before. My new friend turned out to be a camel driver. "I buy camels on the eastern side of Sudan and take them loaded with goods across the desert to the west. I sell the goods and the camels as I go, and

then return to buy new," he said. I liked his obvious intelligence, his sharp wits and very dry sense of humour.

We talked round my problem. "There's always a way in this part of the world", he said. Bribes? But who? Was it worth the risk? By morning I'd had a brain wave. Young lads who were refugees from the war in Ethiopia tended to each floor of the hotel. I'm sure that their existence was a pretty miserable one as they probably worked for room and board only, but our lad was a cheerful, honest faced fourteen or fifteen year old. I'd been buying him cokes and always had a quick chat when passing. He'd been teaching me phrases in Amharic, the main language of Ethiopia, but this time he translated a new phrase for me. I checked it with another of the lads, and before I could change my mind, wrote it across the top of my visa. Fortunately, my only pen was exactly the same colour and width of ink as that of the visa-issuing officer. 'Permission to enter and ride overland by motorcycle'. That should do it. One way or the other!

I was by now taking my camera with me wherever we went. Permit in pocket it was still wise to be careful not to take shots of police, soldiers, government buildings and railway stations, or in fact anything that looked even remotely official. In Khartoum, that covered a lot of ground.

On the way to the British embassy, two children playing in the street caught my eye, great shot. I checked the background for things governmental and even asked the kids permission. That spoiled the shot but I'd asked, so I took it anyway. Within seconds, police and soldiers surrounded us. Rifles and pistols were cocked and pointing in our direction. They wanted my camera. I was really ticked and there was no way I was going to let them have it; I knew I'd never get it back.

The Sergeant grabbed the camera; I hung on to the strap and pulled back gently. The situation could get out of hand very quickly, but I was on a roll. Talking in my best authoritative but 'Mr Innocent' voice, we carried on in the direction of the Embassy. A fine tug of wills followed for four blocks - me versus the Sergeant, the troops and the ever-increasing crowd of curious. Mike and Sally wisely eased to the edge of the mob and at the embassy there was consternation. The guard called for help and soon the security officer came to the gates. The man was dressed in a Harris Tweed suit and wore a walrus moustache. "You seem to have a touch of bother old boy, are you British by any chance?" He listened to my story. "OK, just a moment and I'll come and sort these chaps out!" Sort them out he did. The situation calmed as he arranged to develop the film, and to give them the offending photo and negative the following day. "Do you realise what the problem was?" he asked. "You took photos of the two children belonging to the General in charge of security for the whole of Sudan!" He apparently wanted them to grow up normally so playing in the street was OK so long as the 'trees' were full of soldiers.

While the permit chase had been going on, the British embassy in Khartoum had been faxing their counterparts in Ethiopia's capital Addis Abeba. Was it safe for us to come? We'd been hearing all sorts of scare stories but at last there was a reply from Addis. Roughly translated, it said that the journey south would be dodgy, but it wasn't a flat 'no'. Great news and to fit in with our mood, by chance, a party had been planned at the Embassy. We were invited to join the staff, their families and guests.

"We don't get folks like you through; come on in for a drink and a chat." Behind the walls and the wire lay green shrubs, a pool and a 'cold drinks' bar. The party was like a little oasis —quite wonderful and a fine ending to Khartoum for us.

With perfect timing, Sally was well, and we finally had all of the rubber stamps and signatures we needed. The route was planned and now we had the green light from the Embassy. But, with one thing and another we were running late and that could be critical. The dry season was coming to an end. If the rains started before we covered the next section, we'd be in trouble – very muddy trouble.

Chapter Five

"The Brigadier's Parade"

By seven-thirty in the morning, we were on the road out of Khartoum heading east. We reached the outskirts before it started to get hot, and fuelled the bikes before following perfect asphalt across the sun-baked countryside. The permits for fuel worked as they should, and our permits for travel got us through the first checkpoint. For as far as I could see, the land was beige and the sky a clear blue. Suddenly we were very glad to be free of the city; we had open road at last. The calm night air and heavy desert dew had settled the dust and the ground had yet to get so hot that the sky would be distorted by shimmering waves of heat. But the black surface of the road was a different story and heat pounded up at us from it. The dry slipstream sucked moisture away from any bits of exposed skin and by ten thirty it was forty-five degrees in the shade again. Our weeks in Sudan had made it obvious why the desert tribes covered themselves up so completely. Stopping for regular slurps of tepid water, the ice-cold cokes of Khartoum became just a tantalising memory. Checkpoint after checkpoint treated us with grudging respect, and the day slid by.

Eventually, at the town of Gedaref the road split in two, east to the Red Sea and south to Ethiopia. Gedaref was also the last chance to fill fuel and water tanks. From here on it would be bush, a dirt road and small villages. And we'd been warned that the further away from the main road we were, the more likely there was to be trouble with armed bandits. The warning hadn't really sunk in though; it had felt decidedly unreal.

Trouble of a different sort started as soon as we hit the outskirts of town. The petrol station manager said our permits weren't valid. Arguing wasn't working and neither was gentle persuasion, but we had a stroke of luck. By chance a senior official was at the police checkpoint on the road. He authorised the permits with a wonderful flourishing signature, and we filled up.

In the days of trip preparation, I'd been warned that it was really dangerous to over-fill a fuel tank, as petrol expands with heat. I mentally tossed a coin as I dripped petrol in past the safety line. The end of the day cool was getting closer and as we had no idea where the next fuel stop would be, each extra drop could be vital. With the war only just finishing in Ethiopia we could reasonably expect a lack of supplies of anything, let alone fuel. With that thought, I chanced a little more.

I'd said that coming to the Sudan had felt like stepping out into the unknown but going to Ethiopia felt like stepping out into nothing. I'd no experience of a devastated, war torn, drought stricken country and that was how the stories made Ethiopia sound. Perhaps we should never have been heading that way, but instead of thinking 'what if?' the best plan seemed to be to get on with it – to cope with each situation as it arose, or hit us.

The mid afternoon heat was exhausting and we'd been using our supplies of water fast. I'd begun to feel naive and unprepared as the only hotel we could find with off street parking and a vacant room, had just a thin dribble of water from the taps. We'd gone out in search of a better supply only to find that a bureaucratic cock up somewhere along the line had cut off the entire town; no one had any. Gedaref was to us a noisy thirsty hole. Filth lined the streets and lethargy lined the people's faces; I knew that I'd be happy to leave in the morning. There was a dangerous and rather volatile, shifty air to the place but at least we could ride out of this trouble; I suddenly felt very fortunate. The place also made me ponder a statistic I'd read. With each flush of the loo at home, I would use more water than the average third world dweller would use in a whole day, for all of their requirements. Just thinking about that then made me even thirstier.

In the morning before setting out across the scrubland we had to report to the police again. Three valuable riding hours were wasted when a bout of aggression and chaos started as we'd finished our breakfast of bread and bananas. 'Officers' came to the hotel before we could get to the police station. They were in plain clothes and had no identification papers. Their faces mirrored the mood of the town and Mike took an immediate disliking to them. All three were thin, sallow skinned and unkempt. The leader had a skinny face that, underneath a hooknose, held a set of blackened and broken teeth. His breath smelt of rot and he talked in a demanding, weasel like manner. His belligerent and surly second in command had a face that was moon shaped and badly pock marked. This one was the 'heavy', though he struggled with the role. The sycophantic runt of the litter hovered behind, hopping from one foot to the other.

For all we knew, the three of them could have been in league with the bandits down the road. So, we demanded to see ID before allowing them to inspect our papers or gear. The men disappeared to return with identity cards whose mug shots didn't match theirs. They got really angry with us when we told them that we would go to the police station to do the paperwork. Meanwhile, a sullen entertainment-seeking crowd had gathered outside the hotel. Eventually we made it to the station to find that the officers had got there before us. They were indignantly complaining to the desk Sergeant, and Mike was pushed around by one sunglass-wearing policeman who obviously thought that the pride of the Sudanese police force had been dented. But we knew we had done the right thing and finally with papers correct, we escaped. A long day was on the move.

At the edge of town there were three tracks out into the sand but no signposts. The police wanted to have nothing to do with giving us directions and the town's people didn't seem to understand what we wanted. All we could do was take a compass bearing and head off down the track that seemed to be the best bet. We were feeling pretty stubborn by this time and were determined that the morning's efforts weren't going to be wasted. It was time to leave Gedaref behind us and strangely, it was the perfect mood to hit the trail with.

The beige soil and sparse growth changed to black earth and scrubby bush. Most of Sudan is a flat featureless plain that covers great latitude – it's the size of France and a good chunk of Spain put together. For much of the year the country would be dry and could only produce crops with considerable effort. I'd read that for all its miles of desert, vast acres in fact were fertile enough to produce tremendous quantities of food. The missing element was water in regular supply. We'd seen the results of aid agencies attempts to help in the form of derelict and rusting farm machinery dumped along the roadside in decaying heaps. Vital parts had been stripped and the carcasses left to rot. Each country in the world has its priorities but Sudan's I struggled with. The seemingly endless war sapped the funds and brainpower that could so easily have improved so many people's basic quality of life. This was one side of the Moslem religion that I didn't understand. In fact, I find any religious war hard to make sense of. Perhaps in the end, wars like these come down to personal ambition rather than anything else. It was a good point to ponder on the easier sections of the trail.

After a while, the track started to twist and turn for no apparent reason. The soil in the corners had been pounded into a fine deep dust by the heavily overloaded trucks that kept the villages supplied, and acted as the local bus service. The battle for us was with a combination of deep ruts still left from the last rains, and with the soft thick pockets of dust that would instantly suck power. They were rather like riding into baths full of talcum powder. Mike's motocross experience paid off, but we both fell. The track was so soft that on one occasion, the only way to get the bike upright again had been to scoop holes under the wheels and then push it into them. The struggle was then to get the now upright bike out of the holes. A stop-go rocking motion and a shove seemed to be the best way to do that. Another notch on the learning belt but I was glad that the imminent rains hadn't started; this section would have been a black quagmire.

So far, at each unmarked junction the compass had kept us heading in the right direction. Then in front were five tracks, three of which could have been right. We needed a three-sided coin. Half an hour later we realised that the track that had been the best bet, had turned west and it didn't look as if it was going to twist back again. We needed southeast and nothing else would do.

Time was marching on desperately fast. The road conditions were making the bikes drink fuel much quicker than I'd thought possible, and the lack of shade in the intense heat was making sweat pour off us. We stopped to drink another litre of warm, decidedly odd-tasting water. Going back and hoping to find the right turning was out of the question – it would eat too much time. The only choice was to ride through the chest high scrubby bush and hope that we would cut across the right track, and miss picking up any thorns. We were already feeling tired and weren't even half way through the planned day's ride.

The chase across the bush was a brain tease. Common sense kept saying, slow down, take it easy. A broken leg or indeed a broken bike at this stage would have been a disaster. But it was another 'don't think about it' moment. Don't dwell – just go. Knobbly tyres and a lot less weight would have helped, but the BMW's power compensated for my fear and lack of experience. By the time we humped across a new track, my trousers were ripped around the knees and my legs were scratched bloody from the low-lying thorn bushes. But, I'd learned some more and the well-used track continued in the right direction.

The halfway point to the border was a large village that was surrounded by fields full of withered maize and a few bony cattle. Doka was packed with excited people and I realised that we'd crossed an

invisible line. The local skin colours had changed from the light tans of the Arab world to the dark honey tans and Nubian jet of the south. Scrawny goats wandered around eating discarded orange peel, mango pips and even bits of old newspaper. The twenty or so huts were straw roofed and walled with branches that had come from goodness knows where. I could only see three trees and hadn't seen anything even remotely resembling a forest since arriving in Africa. The gaps between the wall sticks would make the huts cool and would be enough of a deterrent to keep any animals out. But mosquito's and 'Peeping Toms' would have had a field day.

Conversations stopped dead as we rode across the bare uneven compacted dirt of the village centre. The Gedaref police sergeant had told us to report in to the local cop shop which, when we found it, was of course another straw roofed hut. The policeman was dressed in a djelalaba which did nothing to hide his girth. He had a young lad shifting the air around the inside of the station with a palm frond mat that was suspended from the roof beams. The policeman didn't seem especially surprised to see us. In the corner sat a large army type radio so we guessed that he'd been warned that three crazies were heading in his direction. His manner was rather benevolent and of complete authority. Around him sat a collection of men who had the manner of courtiers attending the king. To our delight there wasn't a trace of the aggression we'd found in Gedaref. The Police chief advised us in a rich baritone, that suited his bulk perfectly, "You will have to travel to the border in a truck convoy. Bandits for you are now, to my very great regret, a serious problem." The trouble was the convoys were few and far between, and several days wait in the village was not something we were looking forward to. All of the delays in Khartoum hadn't left enough time on our Sudanese visas and the big worry was still the imminent rainy season. It could hit at any moment.

The chief of police asked a series of questions most of which we seemed to give the right answers to. Then the subject of convoys came up. Our luck was in – the excitement in the village was for a very good reason. The local tribal chief's oldest son and a princess from a neighbouring region were getting married that same day. People had walked or travelled by truck for days to show their respect and a wedding convoy would be leaving at some time later that day. The bad news, when we thought about it, was that according to 'Africa time', 'sometime later that day' could well turn into 'much later that day'. Riding in the dark on these roads didn't seem to be a good idea. I could just imagine thick dust in my headlights making it even harder still to see where the next hole or rock was. The police chief was obviously on the ball though and read the worry on our faces. He listened to our concerns, and decided to let us go the final seventy kilometres on our own. Absolutely delighted, we scooted out of the village without even filling our water bottles from the murky waters of the village pond. Later, we realised that there was another reason why he'd thought we would be safe.

After just ten minutes we took the wrong track again. Both options had looked as well travelled as the other and of course both headed in roughly the right direction. The sun was beginning to fall and once again we were faced with the same set of problems: fuel, water and time – not to mention the bandits. This time our luck was really in; there on the horizon was a man herding goats. He stood leaning on his long black staff. At first it looked as if he only had one leg, but on drawing closer, I realised that he had his right foot tucked behind his left knee. It's a typical pose for this part of Africa. The man stood absolutely still with an unperturbed expression on his face. Whilst approaching, it seemed almost as if he was totally used to seeing two dirty, large and overloaded motorbikes thumping across his world.

Now we only had to make him understand what we wanted. The next village down the road that we should have been on was called Maliha. Perhaps if we pronounced this in as many ways as we could manage, then at least one of them would be close to the mark. Well, the man stood one legged and still with his unperturbed expression until we had finally run out of variations and were beginning to feel a bit desperate.

"I do speak perfectly good English you know", he suddenly told us in an excellent Oxford English accent. "If you ride for half a mile in that direction you will come to the road, go left on it." Feeling decidedly silly, we asked how he spoke such good English. It turned out that he was the son of a wealthy Chief. His father and older brother had been killed in a truck accident, which had left him head of the family. Now, to get back in touch with his 'old world', he'd decided to herd goats for a couple of weeks. We chatted on for a few more moments and then, thanking him, set off again. Perfect directions and minutes later we were turning left and on to Maliha.

The landscape was changing from scrubby flat desert to rolling hills. In the distance were the blues and greens of mountains - Ethiopia. As the sun dropped further towards the horizon I noticed the silhouettes of armed soldiers standing on the hilltops. In one way they were a comfort but also they were a sharp reminder that we really were in a dodgy part of the world. If everything hadn't been happening so quickly, I think I would have been scared. Surviving the moment was more important. The road surface was firmer but now great boulders started to appear and I wondered how the trucks managed to manoeuvre over some of the drops between them. It was difficult enough with the bikes and on one of the drops a rock put a split in my stainless steel water canister. Ten litres leaked away uselessly before I realised.

Catching a whiff of wood smoke was the first hint that we were approaching a small village. Lining the road was the bizarre sight of a crowd of people, men, women and children, dressed head to toe in pure white robes and white turbans. Black Arabic lettering decorated the long white banners that they were waving on poles and when the people saw us, the women started to ululate. Their high-pitched wailing, that seemed to rise and fall in an odd sort of harmony, was clearly audible even over the noise of the bike and through my helmet. The crowd parted as we rode closer and then the people swarmed around us. With obvious pride, a tray of purple coloured drinks was proffered. It was one of those situations where refusal might well have offended. The juice was diluted pomegranate, and delicious, but after seeing the last village's water supply I wondered how long it would be before I fell ill. We thanked them as best we could and rode on, leaving a strangely confused crowd behind us.

The road continued to get rockier and the hills higher. At the next village we were greeted in much the same fashion but this time a bellowing cow was dragged out in front of us. To our horror its throat was cut with a large curved sword. Blood spurted out across the road and we kept on going, it was a little bit too bizarre for us to linger. Meanwhile the soldiers still stood watching from on high.

The last thirty kilometres to Gallabat, the border town, went by in a weary haze. By now I was tired, thirsty and was looking forward to whatever hotel the border might be able to offer. I didn't really care how bad it might be. We would try to cross the border in the morning.

Once again white robed people greeted us at the edge of the village but this time there were lots of soldiers around, many of them officers. As we eased dustily through the crowd, they directed us up an immaculate section of gravel to an obviously new concrete building. Perhaps this was the hotel, but something didn't feel quite right. Of course four overloaded motorcycle tyres leave a bit of a mess in thick, freshly raked gravel but we could only do as we were told. The crowd excitedly swirled around us, a child touched my hot exhaust and got a nasty surprise; other children were tussling with each other to get into the best position to stare at the dials on the bike's instrument panel.

Suddenly the atmosphere changed. An army convoy had pulled into the village, and in the second jeep sat a brigadier wearing dress uniform and an angry face. An officer hurried up our tyre tracks. "You leave now", he ordered. We didn't need telling twice and eased as quickly as possible through the confusion. The only place to go was the local hotel down a rough back road. There weren't any rooms, just an enclosed space with rough wooden beds arranged around the edges. It would do, we'd been up and battling with the day for almost eleven hours.

We were still puzzled as to what the problem with the soldiers had been, but had a more pressing need – water. I was so thirsty I couldn't even work up enough saliva to spit. Mike and Sally were on the edge of thirst exhaustion too. A wash, several cups of tea and a feed were needed. As we relaxed we congratulated ourselves on making it through the day without any serious mishaps, and started to wonder what the next day would bring.

Suddenly the rough wooden gate swung open and in rushed a group of soldiers who made it quite obvious that we were no longer welcome. They kept pointing towards the south and to begin with the only understandable word was 'Ethiopia'. I was finding out what the results of 'raining on someone's parade' was all about. It was the brigadier's parade we'd ruined, and he was mightily pissed. He'd apparently travelled from Khartoum to open the new concrete hospital. By distracting and confusing the roadside welcoming committees, we'd stolen his thunder all the way for hours. But the brigadier's journey was no doubt why the policeman in Doka had been reasonably happy for us to travel the last section to the border on our own, and why there had been so many soldiers on the hilltops.

There was no point in making a fuss as we realised that the brigadier wasn't giving us any choice, but to leave. We rode from the 'civilised' newly white washed walls of the Sudanese border post onto the Ethiopian side, and into a crowd of teenagers in disintegrating camouflage uniforms.

The air of aggression followed us across the rubbish-filled gully that formed the border. Rifles and AK47's were pointing in our direction; the words of Amharic I'd learned in Khartoum deserted me, and the noise was overwhelming. An English speaker would have been very nice to have around at that moment and someone was reading my mind. There in front of us was a friendly face: "Do you need some help?" His English was broken but understandable.

As soon as we were talking, the tension of the crowd relaxed. Our new friend explained to the soldiers that we were tourists and had come to their country on holiday. I got the feeling that not only was he having to explain what tourists were, but was also struggling to explain what a holiday was. Twenty years of war had officially ended just a few weeks before; so most of these kids had never seen people like us. A Martian landing on Earth for the first time would probably get the same reaction – holiday trip or not.

Guns were still pointing at us as our translator led the way through the crowd and along the dirt track that doubled as the border town's main street. The huts along the edges were in a ramshackle state, and the village animals, goats and dogs, looked as if they were not long for this world. The track itself was rutted and full of rubbish. The troops' post wasn't in any better condition. They told us that the commanding officer wasn't on the base at the moment and that we should wait inside the compound. That was fine, except that the sun had dropped still further and more importantly, there was no way to get the bikes in. Sally bravely volunteered, "Go on, you go inside with Sam, I'll be ok out here with the bikes." The situation was far from ideal but with once again, no other choice, Mike and I moved inside.

The yard was strewn with soldiers still sleeping in whatever shade they had been able to find. Around them were women who looked as if they had been working most of the previous night and in the centre of the yard was a hut, falling to bits like most of the others. The soldiers pushed us towards it and indicated that we were to wait inside. Ducking our heads, we did as we were told. With eyes slowly becoming used to the musty gloom, we realised that the strange half-light shapes were more sleeping soldiers, and that the tremendous buzzing noise was from all the flies that our arrival had disturbed. We were brought chairs, and settled down to wait.

Moments later there was gunfire, shouting and screaming out in the street. We rushed towards the gate as the soldiers scrambled for their guns which had been stacked surprisingly neatly in little wig-wam shaped groups around the yard. No one wanted to let us out but there was nothing to stop Mike. "My wife's out there!" He was shouting, in English of course but they got the gist. We made it to Sally as an odd bullet or two was still sporadically whistling through the air. When the shooting had started she had been pulled to the ground and leapt on top of by the soldiers. "Very scary", she said. "But not quite as scary when I realised that they were only trying to protect me." When it was over, the raggedy young soldiers went back to playing catch with their grenades and we were hustled back into the compound. The up side of the shooting was that it had woken up the Captain; he'd been there all the time. This guy, in total contrast to his troops, was a very snappy dresser and to our relief he spoke a little English. This was good news since the boy soldiers hadn't let our interpreter into the compound with us. On his head sat a clean red beret whose badge was a shiny skull. His uniform was well pressed pale green and even his belt and boots held a high gloss. I knew that I looked as filthy as I felt, and the bike was still dropping oil over my right boot. I'd never managed to find the cause of the Greek leak.

The gist of the captain's questions was, "What on earth were we doing at this border?" "Didn't we know that it wasn't safe and didn't we know that tourists were only allowed in by air?" Time for some fast-talking, Sudan wasn't going to take us back that was for sure. Talking hard, we heaped on the praise. "How wonderful it is to finally be allowed to visit your beautiful country." "How pleased you must be to have the war finished so that life can get back to normal, and we tourists are the first signs of this happening." "Do you know if there was a 'good' hotel in town and is there anywhere to get petrol from, oh and a little oil would also be useful."

With one ear on what was still rumbling outside and the other on our friendly jabber, he inspected our passports –upside-down. Eventually, in mine, he came to the visa from the London Embassy and my forgery. Well, this was the moment of truth, jail or freedom. I knew at that moment that I'd taken a stupid risk – Mike rolled his eyes. The captain couldn't read a word of English but he could read 'permission to enter and ride overland by motorcycle' in Amharic. Once again we brought out every piece of official looking paperwork we had; the newspaper articles, the fax from Addis and typed letters. I could see him mentally tossing a coin, so kept on talking pleasantly as if we had every right to be there.

"All right, all right, you can go", he said. Fantastic! Outside there was an hour of daylight left, did he know of a place where we could stay? "No, you don't stay here", he said. "You go now!" The border tension made it seem a wise thing to do. Sally meantime had been practising her Amharic with the prostitutes. We climbed aboard the bikes and rode out of the village before he could change his mind. We'd now been on the go for twelve and a half hours.

I don't actually remember much about the next hour; I must have been on some sort of physical and mental overdrive. But I do remember the wildly coloured birds that kept darting across the road, which was in far better condition than it had been on the Sudanese side. We swooped on, swirling dust behind us as we passed burnt out army trucks and tanks. Fords over deep dry riverbeds told the tale of the road in the rainy season and we knew that the decision to press on from the half way village of Doka had been both mad, and very wise.

Around us, the low forest grew ever denser and finally we reached a village. The sun was about ten minutes away from dropping below the hillsides. Slowing up, we eased on down the only road trying to get the lie of the land. With darkness only moments away, it had become critical to find somewhere to stay, and fast. This, being the main road to and from the border, made us sure that there must be a hotel of some sort somewhere. At the end of a day like this we didn't feel like trying to find somewhere to camp. Once again we were a conversation stopper. In fact, many of the people ran away to hide behind the huts. Having doubled back, in the centre of the village, the only thing to do was sit and wait for the people to come. The first was a child and it was he who clicked the fastest to our sign language game and badly accented Anglo Amharic version of 'where is the hotel?' Wherever we'd been so far, children had always seemed to understand us first.

The lad ran off in front of the bikes leading us down a dirt track into the inevitable stick enclosure. Inside the kraal was a collection of wood, thatch, mud and hide buildings that seemed to have been stitched together with bits of old string and wire. The people looked baffled, scared and bewildered – two motorcycles had just driven into their living room! But when Sally got off their bike and one of the women recognised that, underneath all the dusty bike gear was a woman, the ice started to break. Sally had a smile that had already melted a lot of ice on this journey. Yes, this was the village hotel; our young guide was the hotel owner's nephew. At that moment, the sun finally disappeared.

Our wattle and daub cells had bug filled straw roofs and corrugated iron doors. Old rickety iron beds that had definitely seen better days were each covered with a straw, and probably bug filled, mattresses. Air circulation was not an issue in the windowless rooms but we didn't care. It was slowly sinking in; we had made it, not only through the bandit-ridden bush lands of eastern Sudan but over the border, and through a shooting. It also dawned on us that with the chaos at the border there hadn't been a chance to organise any Ethiopian money to pay for the hotel. Honesty works so we owned up and told them that we still had Sudanese money, which of course there hadn't been a chance to change at the border either. At rip-off rates they accepted what we had. Perfect.

All that any of us wanted to do then was fall into bed and sleep, but we were too wired, too tired and knew that we badly needed to drink - lots. I'd already drunk countless litres but was so thirsty that I was feeling light-headed and rather sick. The little voice in the back of my mind reminded me about the brigadier's pomegranate drink. Delicious, but potentially loaded with samples of every bacteria that Africa could offer. Out came our water filter pumps and with buckets of water from the village pond we set about entertaining the hotel family and clients alike. As fast as we pumped and drank, the liquid sweated out again with the effort. The filters constantly clogged and then the work of pumping increased. The murky pond was an absolutely multi purpose water source. Drinking water, cooking water, body-washing water, clothes were washed in it and animals came down to it to drink; I'd even seen a child pee in the pond. But by this time I'd discovered the leaking water tank on the bike, so pumping fresh supplies was even more important.

Knowing that we should eat and that in this environment, we should cook food ourselves, out came a tomato soup mix and a bag of Egyptian pasta spirals. In the flickering light that was gently cast out by our hosts' paraffin lamps, our little petrol stoves drew a crowd and we ended up with the difficult sign language task of explaining how they worked. Not easy and I'm still not sure to this day if they did ever understand or if they just politely gave up. Periodically, groups of people would linger by the entrance of the kraal. Quiet voices were obviously discussing these odd strangers that were suddenly in their midst. I wished even more that I could talk to them but my twenty-odd words of Amharic were just not enough. Smiles had to say it all.

At that moment the hotelier presented us with an Ethiopian border village's version of champagne. A cobweb covered wooden soft drink crate containing three rusty-topped Pepsi bottles was handed to us with great ceremony. The tops flipped easily and the warm but still fizzy contents eased wonderfully down sore throats. There was still enough Sudanese money to pay for them too.

Securely locking the bikes, and with assurances of their safety, we bid good night to our new friends. The day had been a very long sixteen hours. Too tired to check the bike for any loosened nuts and bolts or to clean the air filter, as I knew I should, I fell into bed as totally exhausted as I'd ever been. Sucking my still swollen tongue, I fell asleep listening to the sounds of donkeys braying in the enclosure, a radio playing distinctive Ethiopian music, cocks crowing (on Africa time) and the noises of an animal scrabbling about on the roof. My dreams were of bugs crawling over me, saucer sized spiders, of scorpions in my boots and cows wandering around with slashed throats. Even after all those litres of liquid I suspect that it was dehydration that caused me to hallucinate the night away.

A cockerel woke us all the next morning, with rather too much enthusiasm as far as I was concerned. My body ached from head to toe, my throat was sore and tongue still swollen. Then I remembered where I was and nothing else mattered; we were in, we'd made it!

Chapter Six

"Living the Dream"

'An ounce of luck is better than a pound of wisdom'

Ancient proverb

The three of us emerged from our cells to find breakfast fires floating smoke across the rays of sunlight that had worked their way through the surrounding Eucalyptus trees. The radio was playing a catchy tune, and the hotel family greeted us with smiles and an invitation to join them for a cup of the locally grown coffee. The smell was totally tantalising and the friendly atmosphere was the perfect start to the new day. They'd made a big effort for us and had brought out what had to be their best china. The thin porcelain was totally unexpected in this world of sticks, mud and string.

Soon after breakfast had been eaten, when the bikes had been checked and loaded, I had a feeling that the coming days were going to be something quite special. Of course we'd no idea what surprises were in store but we did know that we'd be heading up into the mountains. The thought of cool air and cold water was a strong pull. The night before, I'd thrown my leather jacket on the floor in the corner of the cell. There hadn't been any hanging space for it, or for that matter, anything else. When I picked it up in the morning, at first it looked as if it was covered in dust, but the large white marks were salt stains from all the sweating I'd been doing the day before. The salt made the jacket incredibly stiff to pull on but happily it still smelt quite clean. We hadn't been able to wash ourselves for several days but strangely, we also still smelt OK. It made sense that, as in the desert, all the sweating and water drinking had purged our bodies of whatever it is that gives armpits a 'hum'.

The road meandered through the hills, little by little gaining height as it went. Every so often we thumped through a river ford, some of which were surprisingly deep, and again we were thankful that we were making the trip in the dry season. The few trucks we scooted past tooted their horns in greeting as they ground along in

91

low gear. We passed monkeys, cattle, cattle and more cattle. This was no surprise though - my research had told me that Ethiopia has the largest cattle population in Africa. They were sway backed, bony-hipped, hook-horned and their colours varied from dusty red to dusty brown. The dry yellowed grasses of the roadsides had been cropped close by their feeding.

With increasing altitude the road turned to almost pure gravel. There were very few pot holes but those that there were had to be treated with caution. Though the holes were large and often over two feet deep they weren't a problem unless we got too close. The big hassle was keeping momentum on the loose gravel, particularly the deeper ridges of stones on the tight corners. The bike would pull sideways, back wheel spinning hard. It made me feel like I was a 'motocross' rider on a drunken camel who had no sense of direction at all. I could see that Mike was having fun though, in spite of being two up.

We passed a group of vultures that looked at us indignantly as we disturbed their meal of an anteater that some truck had sprawled across the road. Our Michelin map showed us to be at five thousand five hundred feet, the highest I'd been with the bike. I was proud of it. The thinner air was supposed to affect its performance but it didn't seem any different.

Rounding one corner, we found a band of heavily armed militia waiting expectantly. They'd obviously heard us coming from quite a way off, so were fully alert. Even though the sounds of the bikes must have been quite unfamiliar to them, they hadn't shot first and asked questions after – during the war that had apparently been the norm. We stopped as soon as we saw them and immediately turned the engines off. Taking our helmets and gloves off as a sign of innocent respect, we carefully climbed away from the bikes to wait for them to come to us. This time we remembered our Amharic and were quick to greet them. Handshakes, suspicious at first, soon became friendly as they realised that there wasn't a threat from these 'Ferenji's' on motorbikes. Their weapons were a rag tag collection of rifles and machine guns. The only ones I could recognise were the inevitable AK47's and also a rather ancient Lee Enfield rifle. The militia's ages were not a surprise. Most were boys in their very early teens and nearly all the rest were grey old men. We'd heard that in this part of the country, almost a whole generation of men had been killed off by the war.

By the time we reached the city of Gonder our fuel situation had become critical. As we rode into the ancient capital of Abyssinia, we passed a long queue which ended at a petrol station. "Yes", the man at the rusting pump said. "We have some petrol." But would he sell it to us? "No." We didn't have the right permits of course. We shouldn't have been there and it seemed that we were about to pay the price. We tried to pay any price for the fuel, but with no luck.

To cheer ourselves up we booked into an expensive hotel. At five pounds a night for the three of us, the hotel offered off-street parking for the bikes, clean but basic rooms, a cold shower and a balcony overlooking the street. The real bonus though was that it had a bar. Locking the bikes and dumping our gear in the rooms, we took our grubby rather despondent selves for an Ethiopian beer. Perhaps a brew or two would loosen the grey cells I thought. There had to be a way to get petrol from somewhere, even for we 'illegals'.

Our luck was in. With just the first beer slipping down it seemed that we had made friends with a bike fan. He'd seen us ride into the city and had followed to try to get a chance to meet us. Daniel, a student, spoke very good English so the beer and conversation flowed well.

"How are you enjoying my country, are you having any problems?" "Fantastic", we said. "But we can't get any petrol." He gave us a sideways look and told us that his brother worked for the government motor pool and that the next day we could go with him to see his brother. "The new government would want to help you", he said. We weren't so sure but kept quiet. "Though first", he added. "You must try the Travel office for the correct permit; I'll show you where it is."

Fresh in the morning it was time to be proper tourists. Daniel took us up to Gonder castle. In the sixth century, when the city had been the capital, the ruler of the day had built the first castle in a giant, fortified hilltop compound. The following 'Lion' Emperors had each built their own home within the compound, leaving the older castle every time to the remaining family of the deceased ruler. I rather liked the sound of this system. It was certainly a lot more people-friendly than the descendants of the ruler would get in many cultures. But the thing that impressed me most was the grandness of the architecture; it had been built at the time the Saxons had been invading England. This was not at all what I was expecting to find in Africa.

The city itself had outside influences from more modern times. Though Ethiopia was the only country in Africa not to have been colonised in the nineteenth century, Italy had occupied a part of it just prior to and in the early days of the Second World War. You could easily see this by what they had built, and by the local taste for pasta!

Ethiopia's altitude had made it strong enough to resist invaders for a very long time. It all came down to manpower verses animal power. The vast majority of sub Saharan countries had been forced to rely on manpower to cultivate the land. The deadly tsetse fly, carrier of sleeping sickness and inhabitant of the lowlands, had meant that draught animals had not survived there to plough the land. Manpower had only been enough to produce sufficient food to survive. The Ethiopians had been able to plough their fertile fields and had produced enough surplus food to be able to trade, as well as simply survive. They'd traded as far as China and their wealth had enabled them to buy modern weapons when they needed them – when they could get more advanced countries to supply them that is. In fact at the time of the Italian invasion, the British and French had misguidedly placed an arms embargo on Ethiopia which basically favoured the Italians. It was the time of appeasement in Europe, and estimates from that time say that the Ethiopians had a similar amount of weaponry to the amount the Italians expended in just one battle. The Italians still had a hard time but won as a result of the black shirts amazingly brutal behaviour, sheer numbers and the use of mustard gas. This was the first time that gas had been used indiscriminately upon civilians and literally thousands were either horrendously maimed or killed. Complaints were made to the League of Nations, but nothing was done.

The British eventually helped to kick the Italians out and had therefore been the next nation to influence the country. Besides help to free the country and set up some infrastructure, it seems that they had mainly built bridges, and we'd already ridden across a few. They did teach the locals the value of a good brolly as well and today no sensible person who can afford one is without. The umbrellas go up in the midday sun as well as in the teeming rain that hits the country in season, when there is no drought. Though the Ethiopians had the advantages of altitude, they historically have a cyclical drought problem. They can go for years of prosperity and then be hit by countrywide drought that decimates the nation. As a result, Ethiopia never took a permanent place amongst the worlds powerful.

As we strolled with Daniel, the local kids ran after us calling what sounded like "You, you, you!" They loved Sally and before long she had a dozen of them all trying to walk with her holding her hand. It was a pretty sight to see as we wandered down the sunny, dusty pathways to the church of Debre Birhan Selasie. The children darted around her like butterflies.

Daniel said that we were some of the first tourists to come to Gonder since the war ended and as far as he had heard, we were the first to come overland by motorcycle from Sudan for twenty years. He said that people knew all about us and that Sally was rather a celebrity. People couldn't remember a woman having done this trip on a motorcycle before at all.

The church itself had a dark interior that was decorated with mural scenes from the Bible and also from St. George and the Dragon. Though ancient, they were in excellent condition, which I put down to the lack of light inside. Ethiopia is a Christian country in the main, though there are Jews called 'Falashas' whose history seems to go back to the year dot. You can find many Moslems and Animists there as well.

The only downer on our wanderings came from the ragged children in some of the back streets. These kids not only shouted 'You, you, you' but someone had taught them to call "Give me pen!" in a very demanding way too. Daniel steamed when this happened. "The children of Gonder should never become beggars", he said.

I felt dizzy, light headed and generally rather dodgy as one afternoon of exploring came to an end. We'd walked quite a lot, with me telling myself not to be a wimp and just to get on with it. But when Sally took my temperature, it sat at 102 – time for bed and a couple of paracetamol. Putting feeling so grim down to the altitude and lack of sleep, I dropped off quite quickly. Ethiopia's highest point is at Ras Dasha where the land peaks at 4,620 metres. Gonder was nearly as high – maybe the thin air was getting to me.

The paracetamol did its stuff and I slept the best I had for days, but woke at five fifteen in the morning with a shock. Whilst asleep I'd developed diarrhoea and it was a nasty wet feeling that had woken me up. I'd well and truly messed myself, and the bed. Oh gloom, but no time to think about that, my guts were rumbling again! As fast as my aches would let me, I dragged myself out of bed and ran naked and filthy down the corridor to the toilet. I made it just in time and squatted over the hole in the floor toilet in misery. I was shivering, aching, exhausted, filthy, stinking and I still had to make it back down the corridor to the basin in my room without anyone seeing me. At least I'd had the sense to flip the door latch on the way out so it wouldn't have locked on me. Ahh yes, life on the road.

Later that morning, we hit the trail again. Our fuel tanks were full, courtesy of the correct permit that had been surprisingly easy to get, and I was suitably bunged up with Immodium. The price of filling up had knocked our budgets but not as much as it must the local peoples. At a non-black market rate of exchange, petrol was a steep, US $1 a litre. Ethiopia has no oil of its own and the struggling economy was making hard work of it. The average yearly income was a little less than a $100, which put things into perspective for we 'rich' tourists. There were obviously very few cars on the road but trucks were the blood in Ethiopia's veins. We saw them everywhere and the drivers were a really friendly bunch. They always had a smile and a wave for us as their ageing Fiats ground along making great clouds of dust. When they did see us, they would always courteously pull over to let us on past. The dust was so thick though that unless I rode with full beam headlights on, Mike and Sally up in front would lose sight of me. I knew from the way I was battling with the road that I wouldn't have been happy if I'd had to search the dust behind to see where a travelling companion was.

I tried to kill myself on this road, though not on purpose. Suddenly, out of the dust, there was Mike's tail light just four feet in front of me. The only way to go was off the road. I'd no idea what was there, the dust was absolutely opaque, so hitting the ditch was a surprise and so was making it through without falling off! On the other side was a soft grassy verge, a large rock to swerve around, a deep gully too wide to be called a ditch (but still three feet deep), a soft sandy patch, another ditch, a bush and finally, a deep ridge of gravel that shouldn't have been there unless it was a corner, and yes, it was a corner. Thank goodness for Immodium...

The next days of riding through the mountains saw us standing at the Blue Nile Falls. The waterfalls are supposed to be thunderous in the wet season, but now were just a healthy rumble that hadn't even a trace of blue in them; just muddy brown. The real reward for dealing with the road was our first sight of the Rift Valley. We'd just made it through an army checkpoint where the soldiers had fingered triggers nervously, but not stopped us. Every time we'd had a confrontation like this it was as if the soldiers were so surprised to see us they didn't know what to do. We could almost see the cogs going round in their heads... 'Well, if the previous check point has let them through, then it must be OK for us to do so too', and off we'd go. We were riding with fingers crossed that there'd never be a soldier who was having a bad day.

Up over just another rise in the road, there it was - the stunning and magnificent Rift Valley. Looking down into the faded greens and tans of its hazy depths, we could see little clusters of round straw roofed huts that were clinging to slopes that seemed to fall forever. The road could be seen winding its way down, following the contours as it went. Along the valley bottom, a silver thread like river meandered its way along the sleeping fault line. The deepest point in Ethiopia is in the valley at 100 feet below sea level and dropping down into it from the high plateau was an incredible temperature shock. The air below was stifling, and so incredibly humid that it felt like we'd just ridden into a rice steamer.

On the steep road out, we had our first puncture. Squatting by the roadside to change the inner tube gave us the chance to watch the world go by. Elegant women carried unbelievably large bundles of wood on their heads. Some of the bundles were larger than the women themselves. Tyre off, we found a foot long split in the inner tube. How it had got there was a total mystery, as there didn't seem to be anything sticking into the tyre.

A group of boys herding goats straggled past us. They were entranced by our mirrors and they acted as if they had never seen themselves before. We guessed that if they had, it was probably only in the still waters of the village pond. They stood in an orderly line, everyone waiting their turn to stare at themselves. Each boy was a delight as he poked and stroked his face, the others in fits of giggles.

With the wheel almost back on, a car screeched to a halt just down the road. It was the first car we'd seen outside a large town in Ethiopia. The driver leapt out and ran back up to us. "Can I take your picture?" he yelled. After all the pictures we'd been taking of the locals, it seemed only fair.

The higher the road took us the more the land was cultivated, but in a very neglected sort of way. Along the roadside, wrecked trucks, tanks and army personnel carriers were collecting rust and dust. In one we could see a heavy machine gun with the ammunition belt still hanging from it and the only thing that seemed wrong was that the APC's giant tyres had been slashed. Passing each village, we noticed that the land close to them was well and intensively cultivated. The story was that the 'shoot first' policy of wartime had meant farmers had stopped working anywhere other than in clear sight of their own villages. These farmers could produce enough food for themselves and for trade locally, but not enough to feed the desert and city folks if something were to go wrong. The recent drought was causing a lot of problems.

The road levelled out into a green rolling land that sat under a clear blue sky. The riding temperature was perfect and before long we started to see horsemen. These riders wore black costumes and hats that made them look like they had just stepped off the No 5 gondola from Venice. The horses were superbly trained and high stepping along the roadside. Their hides shone with health and their bridles were decorated with fist sized woollen pompoms in pinks, reds and white. One of the horsemen saw us and spurred his horse across – a race was on. I could hear the horse snorting and its hoofs thundering on the ground as we sped down the road. The horseman was flashing a white against dark tan grin at me. These few minutes brought home to me what an amazing country we were in, and suddenly, the risks seemed worthwhile.

In the next town, we had to refuel. There were pumps, (the first we'd seen since Gonder) but no fuel. There wasn't a drop at any of the five stations. While waiting at one pump for an answer I noticed a face that stood out clearly from the rest of the inevitable crowd. This face beamed a cheeky grin at me and then disappeared only to return a few moments later. The young lad, face still beaming, proudly opened out a centre page spread from a motorcycle magazine. It was a bright red Ducati. He seemed to be saying to me 'Look, I'm a biker too'. I still wonder where he got the pages.

Out of the town, we hit the deepest gravel we'd been on and in spite of the cool air at this altitude, sweat was pouring off us again. Trucks had left dangerous ruts in the walnut sized stones that pushed and pulled two wheels in whichever direction the ruts chose to go. It was scary because speed was the only way to make it through the drag effect of the gravel. After two hours of this, I'd almost had enough. My bike was clearly still overloaded, but what could I dump? There was already a trail of my belongings across northern Africa and I'd even gone as far as cutting my bar of soap in half. Now there were only two pairs of socks left, one for wearing, and one for washing. Losing my umbrella would help, and in this country it'd go to a good home that was for sure. But really, it was the heavy spare parts that needed to be cut down on. Most of them had been expensive so just the thought of getting rid of them hurt. I was beginning to think of them in terms of 'this cost fifteen beers' or 'that one cost a weeks stay in this nice place'. But mostly, the problem was that I'd no idea what was really likely to be needed, if anything at all. Sod's Law says that whatever was dumped would be needed just down the road. I kept it all.

The closer we got to Adis Ababa the more modern life we saw. New cars and four-wheel drives crunched towards us on the gravel, each driver's face a picture as they realised that they were looking at tourists on motorbikes coming out of the back of beyond. I hoped we wouldn't come across a government official who would know that we shouldn't have been there.

Addis, third highest capital city in the world, was a touch of bedlam after the relative peace of the countryside; people, noise and traffic everywhere. Adis Ababa actually means New Flower and it's located in the cool clean air of 9,000 feet. Emperor Menilk II's wife, Empress Taitu, actually founded the city because she found it far too cold up in the heights of her husband's preferred location on Mount Entoto, which you can see from Addis. I thought the temperature she'd chosen was just perfect.

Our out of date guide book only told of places to stay that were well out of our budget so when one of the street lads volunteered to show us a cheap hotel, we decided to risk that he wouldn't lead us down some dangerous dark alleyway. As my top box covered the passenger seat on the bike, he had to sit on top of that. Potholes in the streets, rubbish and mangy dogs were everywhere. The buildings were ramshackle concrete structures with rusting corrugated roofs, and all were in desperate need of paint. The people were excited, friendly, and much more open than the country folks. The children ran alongside the bikes yelling "You, You, You!" This, we'd decided was the local version of, "Hi, hello, how are you." But I still worried; riding as the centre of attention could well attract unfriendly officialdom.

Finally, we made it to the Bel-Air hotel – very nice indeed and not a dark alleyway in sight. It had bougainvillaea on the walls, asphalt on the car park, and a bar/restaurant tucked away inside. The rooms were still a bit pricey, but to us well worth the money. After a night of cars coming and going and strange noises from the rooms around us, we realised it was an upmarket version of a brothel. But, at least the sheets were clean and the bikes were safe under the watchman's eyes.

In fact it was so pleasant we decided to hang around for a few days. This was our first chance to get a few things done, and top of the list was check in with the British Embassy. The past days had underlined to us the importance of registering with them. If we did go missing then at least someone would have a starting point in the attempt to find us.

We also desperately needed money and young Theodorus offered to be our guide – he would help us change money on the black market. Teddy had an open friendly face that seemed without guile and his smile always seemed to start with a tentative twitch that rapidly split into a happy beam. I liked him and trusted him. Changing money on the black market in any country is always a risk. When you do it you dip into the underworld and when you are in an unfamiliar land you are vulnerable. There must be a million and one travellers tales about being ripped off in an under the table money change deal, but having a local guide you can trust goes a long way to both keeping safe, and keeping your money.

The Adis Ababa market was supposed to be the largest in Africa but I wondered if the war would have shrunken it. When we got there though, life teemed. The market was also famous for its diversity and I think that we probably passed a version of just about everything that Africa had to offer for sale. In fact, you were supposed to be able to get hold of anything there. Just out of interest, and because, to my western mind, it was a nice bizarre request, I asked Teddy if there was a tank for sale. "Of course", he replied. "You want to look, there's a Russian T52." I wondered who would buy it. Not me, I was happy with the bike.

Teddy led the way through the alleys to a corner of the market. This was the money changing area. We'd walked through the vegetable, hardware, clothing and scrap areas to get there; each item for sale having a section of its own. We'd even walked past the toilet area. Nothing discreet here, if you needed to relieve yourself, you just dropped your trousers or pulled up your robes, did your business and then carried on with life. The smell stayed in my nostrils for hours afterwards.

In the dimly lit rear of a curio shop were a couple of men, very obviously dealing in large quantities of money. In fact it looked rather like another set from a bad Hollywood movie. The lead character was wearing his shirtsleeves in garters and had a cardsharps visor on his head. His customer seemed to have fallen into the act as well. Between them and us were the 'heavies'. Teddy explained our story and we were told to wait in the corner. Around us in the darkness was an amazing collection of historical 'artefacts'. Everything from round leather shields and feather trimmed spears, to pith helmets that had presumably started life in the Italian Colonial services.

Then it was our turn and well worth the wait. 8 Birr as against the banks' official rate of 3.5 Birr to the dollar. We'd already asked around about the black market rate, so knew that we weren't being ripped off. What a difference this rate would make to just about every aspect of the trip through the rest of the country. Teddy turned out to be a gem and he earned a large tip for his services. We wondered how far up the ladder a lad like him could find his way. He hadn't a lot besides enthusiasm, determination and trustworthiness to help him. In Ethiopia's developing situation, I hoped that they'd be enough, and that he didn't have to change too much to survive.

That last night in Addis, Dagnachew the manager of the hotel came over and asked to join us. I liked this guy. He had a typical Ethiopian skin colour, like a tanned Asian. His hair was also typical. The locals jet black hair curled in a way that was half way between Negro and wavy Caucasian. Dagnachew's eyes glowed honey brown and like so many Ethiopians, he had perfectly shaped, stark white teeth. His love of life shone through a dazzling smile. But, like everybody in this part of the world, he had a story to tell. "I inherited the hotel from my father but I actually trained to be a textile expert", he said. While doing that, he'd travelled in Europe. Back in Ethiopia he'd become head of one of the trade unions for which the previous government had arrested him and thrown him into jail. "Jail in wartime Ethiopia was not a pleasant experience", he said with a deadpan expression. His upward twist to the story was that the unions had called a countrywide general strike and the government had had no choice but to let him go. I could imagine that he had a lot of friends. He seemed positive about the new government but worried about how things were going to turn out. "The problem is", he said. "The long war has killed so many educated people and has exhausted the country's resources."

It was time to move and if we moved fast we could make it to the border with Kenya in just a couple of days. The road south was supposed to be fair to good asphalt all the way, though the Embassy warned us that this part of Ethiopia had big security problems. It was bad enough that we had even debated flying to Nairobi, but in our naïve enthusiasm we opted to risk the ride. A long but easy morning sped us past towns and villages that seemed to be going about the business of daily life and nothing else. There didn't even seem to be much of an army presence.

In the middle of the afternoon we rode straight into the middle of a hailstorm! Over just a few miles, the sky turned to a heavy purple black that should have warned us that a change was literally in the air. But, being in Africa we'd just not expected that within moments, golf ball sized chunks of ice would be ripping the surrounding banana trees to shreds and pounding on our helmets with a deafening noise and neck jarring impact. After just minutes, the roadside ditches were full to overflowing and we were counting our blessings. At least the road was asphalt and not the now greasy red mud of the roadsides. As the hail stopped children rushed out from under bushes and straw roofs to play, shrieking with laughter in the icy waters of the ditches.

Life changed as we rode into the half way town of Dila. Here, the people seemed scared and they moved furtively. The usual crowd of children still collected, but these kids just prodded and poked at everything without any respect at all. Men with guns sat on doorsteps but the hotel seemed a secure bet as high walls surrounded it. None of the guests parked out in the street and the walls had broken glass and barbed wire strung along the top. A bonus was that some of the staff spoke a few words of English, but we were treated with considerable suspicion by both the staff and other hotel guests alike. The only likeable person I met there was a lad who was smart enough to realise there was some money to be earned out of us by fetching soft drinks and fresh bread. We were happy not to have to go out into the surly crowds more than was absolutely necessary so he did some good business that day.

Late in the day whilst sitting on the veranda to cook dinner, a man who said that he was the local schoolteacher, told us that from here on south, it was too unsafe for us to travel. "Even locals are thinking twice about the journey", he said. He also warned, "There is an Army checkpoint and these soldiers are dangerous men, they will rob you if they have the chance."

The border looked so close on our maps, just five hundred and forty seven kilometres, and we had made it this far, we reasoned when he'd gone. Going back could be just as dangerous as going forward. Out in the street, truck after truck, and bus after bus were heading down the road. We'd no idea how far they were going, but at least none seemed to be coming back. Good news, or bad? We decided to sleep on it but even then I think we all knew that we were going to risk it.

The buses still seemed to be running south in the morning so we decided to carry on. We'd ride much faster than normal as if in some sort of way this would make it safer. The bikes would guzzle more fuel but it felt important to be doing something that might help.

In the villages we rode through, the locals had spread coffee beans across the tarmac to be dried and winnowed by passing vehicles. It was much the same sensation as riding over loose gravel and was a real surprise the first time it happened. I knew that coffee was traditionally one of the country's major exports but we'd seen no signs of giant plantations, even though the roads we'd been riding along were supposed to be across good land for the plant. These coffee beans had to be destined for local tables I assumed. We actually get our name for coffee from the Ethiopian 'Kaffee' and some say that Ethiopia is the original source of the plant. The village people seemed much happier out here and we sped on past kids selling bananas and pineapples by the

roadside. They walked with great bundles suspended on either end of a pole rather like a Dutch milkmaid of old would carry her buckets. The children laughed and waved when they saw us, and the scary world of Dila seemed like a bad dream.

As we moved out of the mountains the scenery changed quite dramatically. Now there were rolling hills and plains again, but this time the soil was a rich orangey colour. The trees were mostly all much scrubbier and many seemed to be thorny. The heat was back with us again but far less intense than the weeks before. Then, from the top of one of the hills, we spotted the roadblock the teacher had warned us about. Easing our bikes back from the crest of the hill we stopped in the gentle heat to watch for a while. In the valley far below, the temperature was obviously much greater. A large barrier had been dragged across the crossroad and was moved only when the soldiers had checked a vehicle. No one passed us, but traffic in the other directions seemed to be getting a thorough going over. This did not look good, but the soldiers didn't always pull the pole back across the road and that might help.

We decided to zip through as if we had every right to be there, but to wait until the barrier wasn't in the way. Going back was never considered. The moment came and to begin with I coasted down towards the checkpoint. I couldn't hear Mike and Sally's bike so assumed that they were doing the same. A hundred yards before the still-open checkpoint we gunned our engines, and with open throttles and a friendly wave we sped on past the surprised faces. We kept going as fast as possible whilst trying not to look totally suspicious. There wasn't any reaction at all from the soldiers until the roadblock was disappearing in our mirrors, then loud bangs. We never did know if they had fired upon us but in our ignorance we seemed to have got away with it. If they were shooting at us, they'd missed.

The day cruised on and the road remained one of the best since Europe. We hardly saw a soul, either walking or in vehicles. The only wild life we'd come across crawled along the roadside in the form of a tortoise or belted out from the bush as a tiny antelope called a Dik-dik. It ran straight into the side of Mike's front wheel; there was no damage to the bike at all, but the antelope was definitely dead. Sally was stunned and a little shocked by the violent impact, but Mike was stoically calm.

In Ethiopia we'd been learning that danger always seems to hide around a corner. Around the next corner was a small burnt out bus with a thin trail of smoke still whisping up from inside it. Sad remains of personal belongings were scattered by the roadside and several dark stains spread across the asphalt. We opened our throttles again. It wasn't clear what had happened, but it didn't seem a good place to hang around.

Slowly, signs of cultivation started to appear and we knew that it couldn't be too far to the border. The best sight of the day for me came next. The soil was still a rich orange colour and the landscape had levelled out. The trees were mostly thorny and the few single palm trees stood out like nature's skyscrapers placed amidst villages of low scrubby bush. The orange soil was freshly tilled, forming a perfect colour contrast with the bright green of new growth on the thorn bushes. Then there they were in the middle of a field lit by the golden glow of a sun that was well down its afternoon slide.

An old man dressed in a long white curve bottomed shirt and a loincloth, was followed by a small boy dressed as a miniature carbon copy. The man was ploughing and the boy was scattering seed as they went. The boy's hands dug deep into a sacking bag that was slung around his neck and for each fling of an arm, his legs would stretch out to scoop soil over the seeds. He seemed to be scattering and scooping in perfect rhythm, as if he was listening to a beat that no one else could hear. The old man, plodding along in front of him, leaned onto the wooden plough that he'd harnessed to two fully-grown camels. They seemed to be working the field as if this was in fact what camels had been born to do. The furrows in the rich soil were perfectly straight, prize-winning work.

Not long after passing through fields full of tall sentinel-like chalky white termite hills, we found ourselves on the outskirts of the border town of Moyale. Trundling quietly into town still made people stop and stare as we went but this time the usual curiosity was tinged with looks of, you got through? It was an odd combination of exhilaration to have made it, and quiet relief; we were sure we'd been lucky.

Most towns in Ethiopia had reasonable streets even if it were only that the potholes were under control and the dust kept down. Moyale, just a few hundred yards from the border with Kenya, was the complete opposite. The main road wasn't too bad but the roads and tracks between the unkempt houses, shops, hotels and restaurants were grim. Deep dried out rain gullies veined the orangey-red coloured dirt tracks whilst huge potholes chequered the tired, raggedy-edged asphalt sections.

The petrol station, a ramshackle affair with rusting fuel stained pumps, didn't look like the best place to get clean fuel from, but at least it had fuel. Between the pumps the broken concrete had that matt black patina that comes as a result of decades of diesel and oil spillage. A crowd of men, women and children hung around the office, as was quite normal when a station had fuel. In fact petrol stations seemed to be the hub of information as well as being the best place to grab a lift. But some of these folks looked as if they had been waiting a long time.

We hadn't seen any buses in the far south at all, and when there weren't any buses, trucks would do the job. The trucks we'd seen around the country had always been well overloaded. So much so that their manufacturers would probably have either cringed, or been proud. On top of the loads, a mass of people and their belongings would collect. The driver's mate would not only be chief gopher, he'd be chief loader and fare collector as well. We'd seen these guys climb through the window of a moving truck, onto the running board and then up to the literally leaping and jolting cargo to collect money from the passengers, or to strap a section of goods back into place. These men appeared to have suction feet and a perfect sense of timing. They were also raucous and always seemed good-humoured.

Other than those in the cab, the prized and most expensive seats on the truck were on the cab roof. Some trucks had rough and ready seats built there but most didn't and on those we reckoned that the ride would always be white knuckled. But up there at least, you'd get a journey mostly out of the swirling dust which the front wheels would whip up to blanket everyone else. The trucks seemed to transport anything and everything, so the ride you had was potluck. You might be lucky and get a load of rice sacks to travel on. But at other times you'd be stuck for hour after hour, clinging to thin steel railings across the horned heads of a load of nervous cattle. If you fell in you'd be in big trouble, but people still seemed to think that the risk of a few hours was preferable to a three or four day walk. Never again would I complain if the bus back home was a few minutes late.

The opportunists at the petrol station were quick to sum up what the two dust covered bikes that had rolled in across the waxy concrete actually meant. Money! The price of petrol (for us) immediately inflated. However, by this time the three of us were considerably more streetwise than we'd been seven weeks before. To begin with, today we knew enough to fill up with petrol before looking for a hotel because at least today the station had petrol. The next day it might have run out and anyway, in this area anything could happen overnight. We also knew what a fair price for fuel should be. Having said that, I'd long before decided that I should never expect to pay 'local' price for anything in a third world country. I knew that to the locals I looked like wealth on wheels and though always grubby, in effect I was. An expensive motorcycle and foreign number plates opened the door to price hikes wherever we went, but these guys were a bit too optimistic. Our scornful reaction made the price drop rapidly from completely ridiculous, to just a bit higher than it should have been. And bearing in mind the conditions through which it had to travel to get to Moyale at all, face was saved on both sides.

That night, we left the bikes parked on the street for the first time. The few hotels down near the border looked like they held ratings of minus five stars and I'd had the feeling that our bikes would have been stripped of anything shiny or even remotely useable within ten minutes of our going to bed. Back up the street near the petrol station was a guesthouse that looked safer and cleaner, but it didn't have a courtyard. In the end the view out over the valleys into Kenya sold it to us.

My first set of tyres was pretty much worn out. By now they'd had a hard life and had done well. Our map said that we should expect some extremely rough roads over the next days so I decided to put my spares on while Mike and Sally went to explore. The end-of-day-cool was the perfect time to do the job so I got stuck in, but an hour and a quarter later I was still struggling to get the rubber to break away from the alloy rims. My inexperience showed as I trapped a finger, peeled a sliver of alloy off the rear wheel, hit my thumb and pulled a lot of curses out of mental cobwebs. I could now swear in English, French, Italian, Greek and Arabic - satisfyingly colourful but in reality, no help at all.

Meantime I had an audience but at least this time it was only one man. White haired, he sat on one of the guesthouse steps next to his bundle of firewood. He calmly watched with his head cocked slightly to one side and an expression of curiosity on his deeply lined face. Other than greeting me in Amharic he'd said not a word, which was rather unnerving. I was getting more embarrassed and more frustrated, but I wasn't going to let it beat me. I was determined to get the job done before Mike got back. I felt that I'd asked for his help with the bike more than enough already. No one could learn for me; there had to be a way to do this and I was going to find it. What I didn't know then was that even experienced bikers would have been struggling. The weeks of intense heat had welded the rubber to the BMW enduro wheel rims and no one was going to find the job easy.

Except the man with the firewood that is. Suddenly, he greeted me in Italian. Now I was embarrassed about my language. I hoped that he hadn't understood, though suspected that it was those very curses that had prompted him to talk in a form that perhaps we might both understand. Coming closer, he indicated that he wanted to try. He moved me gently and respectfully to one side, like a parent might move a child in need of encouragement. Then he placed a foot on the rubber and with a hefty thump struck the tyre between his foot and the wheel rim with the blunt edge of his axe. The tyre was off in minutes and he never hit his foot or the rim. I wasn't so sure that I could have managed that feat, though I was absolutely positive that the tyre had come off so quickly because I'd done so much to loosen it in the first place... Yeah well, pride you know.

Mike and Sally's shopping expedition had been successful in true Ethiopian style. They'd found potatoes, onions, oranges and bread. The menu was thick onion soup with oranges for dessert, unpretentious, but a feast.

There's something really fine about three good friends cooking simple food over camp stoves in a setting like this one. We'd had special weeks full of amazing sights that had been made extraordinary by our having sped through the most dangerous part of the world that any of us had ever been to. We'd made it safely and this time, following our instincts had well and truly paid off. We ate, bowls on knees, sitting on the steps with the rolling valleys of Kenya spread before us. A gecko was chirping under the eaves, the cicadas were singing their evening song and that same distinctive Ethiopian tune was being played on someone's radio somewhere near by. It was one of those moments where you need to pinch yourself to make sure that it's not a dream. Yes, this was us, alive and glowing with tired, end of day happiness. We were living the dream!

Chapter Seven

"Swahili Chanting"

"The difference between stumbling blocks and stepping stones is how you use them.'

Anon

We were sitting there on the steps, warm breeze floating around us and happily turning over a mental page on Ethiopia when Safu Baba arrived. I immediately suspected that Safu would never just turn up somewhere, he would always arrive! He radiated personality from a very ordinary looking face above an equally ordinary looking body. His features were not Ethiopian at all but Asian. It was his piercing eyes that dominated, and they did so in such a way that it was impossible to take offence. It would be far easier to just let yourself get swept along with this man's overflowing spirit of adventure. "Come and drink beer with us", he insisted, his eyes shining with enthusiasm for the idea.

Safu drove a shiny black vintage Cadillac which he proudly told us he'd bought from Haile Sellassie's estate when the old Emperor had died. A row of bullet holes decorated its side. Apparently he'd collected these on his last attempt to make it up the road that we'd just ridden down! He'd been stuck at the border for days and he said, leaning down towards us with a pleasantly theatrical manner, "A bus this very day was stopped and robbed. Its occupants were raped, mutilated and then killed." His voice swelled with drama. "Local people are on the rampage, it's difficult to stop them, the new government is out of control in the south so the people are getting rich and married." This left me none the wiser. But Safu Baba explained; one of the major local tribes had a bloodthirsty marriage rite. To earn the right to get married, a young man must present proof of his manhood. Traditionally, this was done by killing a man from a neighbouring tribe and then presenting his victim's genitals to the potential bride. "With the loss of control in the south there are a lot of marriages going on", he said. "And they don't care what colour the marriage gift is either." With this comment he pointedly grinned at Mike and me.

Safu introduced us to his friends. Malesa, a tall skinny guy, had just run away from his French boss at the aid agency he'd been working for. They'd had a blazing row and Malesa had stormed off in the agency's 4x4. He didn't know what to do next. His other friend Dejemi was a smuggler of goods from Kenya. We suspected that Safu, as a general merchant and dealer in semi-precious stones, probably got a lot of stock from the rather dandified Dejemi. The odd thing was that in spite of these guys' unusual stories it seemed the most natural thing in the world for us to be with them.

The enormous vintage car floated on its soft springs down the dirt tracks that meandered their way behind the slightly more orderly main street. Many of the grass huts on the outskirts of town had blue plastic sheets strapped to their round straw roofs. Safu told us that at the end of the dry season there was nothing left to repair the roofs with. The long grass had all been used by the people or eaten by the cattle. "Normally the huts would not need big repairs", he said. "But Moyale is regularly attacked by bandits and the bandits damage everything they can." The plastic sheets were from European aid agencies.

The guys were hungry and wanted us to go and eat with them. "Local food", they said. I was still feeling quite full but they'd spoken magic words to us. In the weeks we'd been in Ethiopia we'd nearly always cooked for ourselves.

We came to a halt outside a café whose frontage was a butchers. Two young lads stood out on the track carving strips of meat from carcasses that hung from the porch roof beams. We'd seen butchers like this before. If the meat wasn't attended to constantly it would hang dark with crawling flies. This time, if there were any flies, the dusk made it too hard to see them.

We were led across a small, beaten earth courtyard, past stacks of coke and beer bottle crates, then into a brightly lit room where a huge, very black lady stood with a wide smile. Safu had arrived, and was obviously well known. Other diners shuffled round to make space at the plastic covered tables as he collected nods from all present. Above us the paraffin lamps hissed and hairy moths danced mesmerised in the brilliant glow.

The main items on the menu were Injura and Wat. Wat is a sort of heavily spiced stew which can contain any kind of meat and sometimes is even vegetarian. Chilli is a main ingredient. It's served with the Injura, which looked very much like a pancake of grey coloured stomach lining turned inside out. In fact, it's bread-based and is slightly sour.

Our hosts taught us that the meal is eaten communally, right hand only for sanitary reasons. One breaks off a large chunk of Injura with which you mop or scoop up a dollop of stew. It smelt delicious and my mouth had been watering like crazy. In Ethiopia, the ultimate compliment you can pay a dinner guest is to feed them with your own hand. It could have been a repulsive experience but from Safu, who'd thoroughly washed his hands before sitting down, it wasn't – just intimate and an honour. A juice-laden torpedo headed in my direction and instantly, my mouth zinged alive with hot spice and tender chicken. It was perfectly complimented by the sour yoghurt flavour of the Injura. Absolutely delicious, and all of it washed down with Tetcha, the local honey-flavoured beer.

After the meal and subsequent burps (a very important sign of appreciation) an enamel bowl was brought to us to wash our hands. Then coffee cups, so thin I could see my fingers through them, were laid on the table.

"You must see the coffee ceremony 'Boonah bir Kibbi' before you leave our country", Safu said. And the next hour passed gently. With reverence and concentration, coffee beans were roasted with a pale green incense that sent tantalising smells floating through the air. Then the beans were ground carefully with a carved pestle and mortar. A brazier full of red-hot coals heated water in a tall, narrow necked, almost Arabian looking brass coffee pot. The freshly ground coffee was then carefully measured into the water and left to steep. The final touch was to float, foul smelling rancid butter across the coffee before it was poured.

"The ceremony is traditionally carried out by a virgin," our host told us. A pretty, honey skinned girl with a shy smile and a touch of coyness to her manner poured the thick black coffee into the beautiful cups. She offered them up with gentle elegance and as she did so, I decided that it's better not to know the answer to some questions. Surprisingly, the rancid butter complemented the rich flavour of the coffee perfectly, but it didn't improve the smell.

During the evening we persuaded Malesa to go back to the aid company to sort out his troubles. He told us that he'd go, but not before trying Kenyan beer at least once in his life. After the coffee we left them to it, no doubt they'd be trying many; it was a good night for a party.

I eased into sleep that night, happy and proud that I'd made it across this beautiful country. Also sad that it'd had to be such a rush, but we all accepted that a longer journey could well have ended up in a totally opposite way, so we didn't complain. We'd been very fortunate. My last thoughts were that the next day would see us trying to explain to the border guards how we had got into the country with our bikes. My fingers were going to be crossed that the visa forgery would not be picked up. During the night, the drought broke.

In the morning the rain had stopped but over Kenya lurked heavy clouds tinged with a suspicious shade of purple grey. Bikes loaded, we headed for the border. It was minimalist, just a length of string with an old yellow rag hanging from it stretched across the road. A solitary guard sat in an old-fashioned single sentry hut. To our delight, the guard on duty only gave a quick glance at our passports before dropping the string into the mud for us to ride over. It felt too good to be true. The guard went back to his seat and we rode away leaving him looking as if he were sitting in an open-fronted out-house! I couldn't resist a grin once we were safely over the line; the forgery no longer mattered, it had done its job.

The Kenyan side of the border was a different world. Neatly painted concrete buildings lay behind a smart red and white striped pole that sat efficiently across the road. The pole was raised with a salute from the uniformed guard, allowing us to ease on up to the clearly sign-posted offices. By now rain was falling furiously. Unlike the Ethiopian officials, these customs officers knew what our bike temporary importation carnet was, and what to do with it. The immigration officials were just as efficient, and our being British seemed to make the procedures very straightforward. A throw back to colonial days perhaps? I wasn't so sure but for once, the red tape was easy. In fact the whole business was so easy after the past months I felt that there was something seriously wrong. I kept expecting some disastrous discovery to be made about our paperwork that would mean that we had no choice but to go back to Ethiopia. But it didn't happen, and soon the paperwork was all over. The loud drumming noise on the tin roof told us that it was raining outside with monsoon-like enthusiasm. We pulled on our layers of rain gear again and stepped out into what was my first tropical downpour since childhood. My parents had worked in the Congo and being in this hammering rain brought memories rushing back. For a moment I was a child again and gazing out over the sodden jungle. The dank earthy smell of a wet Africa is unforgettable.

The rainy season in the Congo, or Zaire as it became for a while, was a time when life was hard for many. But it was also the time when new life began. Long summers without rain would toast the land to a crisp. Wells and rivers would dry up, and dust coated everything - little would grow. Finally, after days of darkening, heavily oppressive air, the rains would come with a cooling vengeance. For week after week, tons of water would fall until the land was saturated and trickles became raging torrents. Rivers would burst their banks and force new routes across the land, dragging trees and dead animals with amazingly violent strength.

In my parents' day, a bridge had often been no more than a couple of trees felled from one bank to the other. When the water was up, the tree trunk bridge could be hidden by the muddy rushing flow. My mother would wade out into the swirling, debris-filled waters to show my father where at least one of the tree trunks was. That way he'd have an idea where to put the Land Rover's wheels. Sections of roads would get so badly holed and waterlogged, it was said that whole vehicles could disappear into what looked like just another long puddle.

As the rains calmed, new life would be literally bursting out from just about everywhere. Seeds would sprout, flowers would bloom and a new generation of life would be born; many animals choose this time to give birth. Mud huts could be rebuilt and new roofs would be growing fast. Crops could go in, and now in the intensely humid air, the land would rapidly transform from yellows, faded browns and beiges to one hundred and one shades of green.

In Kenyan Moyale, I stood wondering if these heavy rains would last as long and what their effect would be on the dirt road we had to use next. Outside the customs offices the parking area sloped quite steeply, and when we'd stopped there I'd made the big mistake of parking the bike leaning almost at the point of no return; pure stupidity. I climbed aboard and heaved at the handlebars. I'd just got it upright and was feeling pleased that I hadn't dropped it or even had to ask for help, when I stood on a banana skin. It couldn't have been scripted better. The world went into slow motion and bike and I went down in a soggy heap. It took a moment or two before the spectators realised that I wasn't strong enough to pick it up, and then there was plenty of help from my laughing audience. Welcome to Kenya! I'd broken the other indicator now as well.

It wasn't even mid morning and we were free to start our hotel hunt, or move on in the rain. Though the town on the Kenyan side of the border was also called Moyale, the similarities ended there. We'd thought that the Ethiopian Moyale had been a shambles, but this one was full-on outback Africa border town. No money had been wasted on anything that couldn't be lost or left behind if necessary. The only hotel that didn't look as if it was flea-ridden was neither friendly nor welcoming. But it did have a yard, which with a bit of effort we could just get the bikes into. We'd learned after this many weeks on the road that it wasn't worth starting a ride this late in the day, and the police had said that shifta (bandit) activity was still strong on this side of the border. All vehicles had to travel in an armed convoy and we'd just missed the day's convoy as customs had finished with us.

With the end of the war in Ethiopia there were suddenly a lot of unemployed guns floating around this traditionally volatile area. They were in the hands of a generation who had grown up with the gun being an 'easy' means to an end, as well as being a way to survive. This time we decided that it would be prudent to follow official advice. Besides that, our map said that the next two hundred and fifty kilometres were over really rough dirt and that meant slow going again. The convoy seemed unavoidable. Meanwhile, nature was laughing at us and the torrential rain continued to fall. Little rivers swirled like tomato soup through the streets.

Our first floor room had a covered balcony, the perfect place to watch life go by. Below us, the town's inhabitants were getting used to the rain and were venturing out in it to do whatever had to be done that day. Those without umbrellas ran from one porch to another, pausing at each to look skyward to see if there was a chance that the rain would stop before their next dash. Or they hopped from one firm-looking patch of road to another with sheets of old plastic covering their heads and shoulders. Everyone's clothes took on a red stain that started from the bottom and headed on up the legs. Children splashed, oblivious to the fact that one obviously wasn't supposed to get wet, and mangy-looking dogs slunk bedraggled from one dripping overhang to the next.

Hours passed and still the rain fell. For the local farmers it should have been good news. A Somali vet told us that thousands of cattle had been dying due to lack of water in Ethiopia and Somalia. But, I wondered how much damage was being done to the over-dry countryside by the quantity of water that was doing the drought breaking. With the vegetation having been cropped so hard by all the hungry cattle, there was bound to be severe soil erosion. I felt sorry for the people; it was just one thing after another, war, drought and now this. However, I knew that a lot of the damage would be down to culture-led mismanagement. For many tribes in Africa, wealth is still measured by how many cattle a man owns. Their health or milk production doesn't seem to matter as much as their numbers. To them it was just too much of an immediate loss of wealth, prestige, power and security, to cull in order to keep the strongest and best alive. With the world's climate changing faster than these age-old cultures, I wondered just how desperate things were due to become - sober thoughts for a wet day.

Down in the café on the other side of the street, some of the local men seemed to be using the rain as a good excuse for not doing very much. Cigarettes were smoked, coffee and beer drunk, and long stems of some sort of leafy green plant were being lazily, and lengthily chewed before being spat out as a spinach-coloured sludge into the street. This was our first encounter with 'Mirra' or 'Chat'. Many people in East Africa chew it for its mildly narcotic effect. We were told that it also suppressed hunger. For sure we never saw a 'chewer' eat anything other than, more chat.

The rain fell on through the night and in the morning we knew that we just had to ride the sodden road, like it or not. At the start of the way south, a collection of trucks, jeeps, people, soldiers and dogs milled around two ridiculously overloaded motorbikes and three worried bikers. The first hundred metres of road looked a nice firm red, then the ruts started and puddles were forming little lakes down the tyre tracks. Mike and I had talked long about where we should try to ride in the convoy and had decided that the best place was right at the front. There we would avoid freshly made ruts and with luck we wouldn't be left behind if something went wrong with one of the bikes. In the back of my mind was the thought that if the convoy was attacked then we could just keep on riding out of the danger. It was another of my naive little ideas.

Whilst the truck drivers for some reason were telling us to do the exact opposite to what we'd decided, I realised that the liquid dripping down my fairing wasn't just rain. Somehow the reservoir for the front brake fluid had come loose and the level was down below the safety mark. My spare fluid was sensibly packed in the most inaccessible place on the bike. Sod's law. The trucks by now were revving up and passengers were climbing aboard. A crowd had gathered noisily around us as it began to dawn on me that I'd have to miss the convoy; there was no way to get the fluid unpacked in time. Then a hand thrust through the crowd to wave a bright yellow bottle at me. One of the truck drivers that I'd been talking to had seen what was going on and had dug out his spare supply. He'd also been urging me to put my bike on the back of his truck. The fee was quite reasonable, but I wanted to ride.

Finally, once the soldiers were on top of the trucks, we were on the move. The rain continued to fall enthusiastically as Mike and I wobbled out along the road. Inside my rain gear, sweat was already running. Mike and Sally splashed cautiously through the first puddle with their rear wheel skipping rapidly from one side of the rut to the other. Their enduro tyres had instantly choked with mud and had become smooth and slippery. When Mike sped up I realised that at a certain speed the collecting mud flicked out of the treads. I tried to go faster too, but wondered how long it would be possible to hold on at that speed. Behind us there was a rattle of gunfire as the soldiers let the shiftas know that their weapons were in perfect working order.

Out in front of the trucks, I wasn't having any fun at all. I was absolutely not in control of my three hundred and fifty kilos of bike, gear, food, fuel and water. The style of riding was probably best described as 'Crisis Management'. The slushy ruts were roller coasting me from one puddle to the next and every now and then, the cooling fins on my engine would leave skid marks on the sides of a gully. Every puddle was a guessing game. There was no way to tell if a stretch of water was a couple of inches, or a lot of inches deep. You just had to open the throttle as wide as you dared, and go for it. With each slippery rush the bike threw red spray over the roadside bush. My goggles misted over in the humid air so I had to pull them down, which meant trying to see through rain and mud streaked glasses. Just to make life a little more interesting, the front brake seemed to want to be either on, or off. I needed all the gentle control I could get, and I'd lost half of it.

My first fall was in a three-foot by ten-foot strip of power-sucking red gunge. One minute I was hanging on at a scary thirty kilometres an hour and the next, the bike had abruptly stopped, tipping me into a layer of red, porridge like filth. Mike skidded to a halt and the two of them slipped their way back to help me, bless 'em. The trucks were moving up on us fast and as I pulled free, our lead on the trucks had been halved. By the third fall, they were on my tail and I could hear the passengers taking bets on how long it would be before the next one. Side bets were also being taken on what it would be that actually got me, a hole or a sideways slip down the camber into the thorns. Up ahead, Mike and Sally were taking their fair share of abrupt tumbles as well but in fact, in spite of being two up, they were doing better than I was. Mike's experience and skill were again showing through.

In the rare moments that there was time to look in my mirrors, I could see that the trucks were now so close that with the next fall, I'd be lucky if one didn't drive over me. The pressure increased and I admit it, fear made me go faster. I later wondered how I would have coped with this road without the pressure of having to keep up with the convoy. For sure I'd had to ride much faster than I wanted to. There was no time to look ahead and plan which way to deal with each obstacle in the sea of mud. It had been more a case of, point the bike, open the throttle, and hang on.

A slightly better stretch of road gained a bit of falling-off space. Then of course, I fell off again. This time, Mike and Sally couldn't leave their bike to help me and it was impossible to get free on my own. I felt pretty pathetic as I wallowed in the mire, feet and bike slipping in all directions except the one I needed to go in. Then, four sets of hands were suddenly there, the bike was out of the hole and it was being held up for me to get onto. Amazing! The guys were the same passengers who had been taking bets on me. They'd rolled up their trousers and slopped down into the muck to help me out – getting somewhere seemed to be becoming more important than entertainment. It had taken us three hours to drive thirty kilometres. With three more falls over the next hours, I finally found that I no longer had the strength to pick the bike up on my own. Amazingly, the same guys enthusiastically leapt down to help every time. At one point the ruts had given me no choice but to ride into a hole so filled with mud that it threatened to ease in through the air intakes above the engine. If more than two of the guys climbed into the sludge with me, the level rose dangerously high. Only three of us could work at getting the bike to the edge of the hole and whilst doing so, I sensed impatience behind us.

The bike eventually came free with the customary sucking noise. It felt like it had taken hours to get out and I'd started to feel really embarrassed as well as tired. I was reaching my limits. The whole convoy was being held up in the potentially dangerous area and behind me the trucks had slid to a halt with the guards nervously pointing their guns out into the bush.

But there wasn't any time to think, the convoy was on the move again and by now Mike and Sally were out of sight. Quite a few trucks had eased past me and I was now riding in their freshly carved ruts. Amazingly the going was easier there. The trucks had pushed the sloppy, loose mud to the sides and my tyres were gripping the firmer mud underneath. We should have listened to the drivers. Of course they'd have known.

Every so often a driver would lose control too and his truck would slide almost sideways into the thorny bushes. Then it was the time consuming task of the truck to the front and the one to the rear to pull it back into line. If that didn't work, the out of line truck would power along, engine bellowing, front two wheels up on the track, rear wheels pushing and struggling on the cambered verge. In time they'd find something firm enough to grip on so that all the wheels would end up back on the track. Sometimes it would take them several roaring, bucking kilometres to get back up. The verges were inevitably in as much a mess as the road itself. It was like watching a truck rodeo.

My last fall of the day was a big one and the bike ended up almost upside down in the 'tourist trap' in the road. Enough was enough; I was so tired I could hardly stand up let alone hold the bike upright. There'd been no time to drink anything so I was badly dehydrated, and as I stood punch-drunk in the middle of the road almost unable to move, my friend the driver beckoned to me. This time I didn't need telling twice, but worried about how to get the bike into the truck; the load bed was a good five feet up. I shouldn't have been concerned though, this was Africa, a land where everything and anything is possible.

My mud covered friends leapt down one more time onto the road. Chanting a Swahili sing-song version of 'heave, ho', they picked up the bike and all the luggage in one swoop that made the three hundred and fifty kilos look as if they were just thirty-five.

I used the last of my strength to flop up into the truck and we were off. As the truck crashed through the next big hole we were all airborne and the bike crashed down sideways onto the truck bed. It wouldn't take many of those to wreck it. The guys helped me strap it upright to the side railings and finally I could relax enough to take a proper look at the scenery. Beyond the mud sprayed bushes, the rain had brought out a profusion of new growth. Bright young green shoots on the thorny scrub combined with hundreds of brilliant yellow, pom-pom shaped clusters of flowers to make an almost unnatural contrast with the red mud.

My fellow passengers were filthy: some from helping me, but most from the condition in the rear of the truck. Apparently, the load beds were always empty on the way back from the border; there was nothing to carry except passengers. Without weight on the trucks, the journey was a series of leaping jolts that had been slamming the men (there were no women on this particular truck) against the remnants of everything dirty that the truck had ever carried. A mess they may have been, but they were full of good humour. There were ten of us, all soaked from the rain and from standing in six inches of muddy water that was sloshing back and forth as we hit one hole after another. Mini waterfalls jetted out from the sides of the truck as we went. The men's bags had filled with water and some of them bobbed around along with scraps of paper, bits of rope, a plastic shoe and some old bottles.

Through stilted conversation held in a delightful mixture of Swahili, English and sign language, I learned that my helpers were two students, a soldier on leave, a farmer and a businessman. The latter, whose black trousers and white shirt were black and white no more, seemed absolutely delighted to have been able to make his regular journey more interesting. All ten of us bounced along in an unspoken sense of camaraderie. I had to grin because the bike had given me another great experience and because, if Kenyans were like these guys, then this country was going to be a special place to visit.

Up in front, Mike and Sally had also made the inevitable decision when a deep mini lake had flooded their electrics. Sally waved at me from her five feet off the ground perch.

The convoy made much better time and by late afternoon it was pulling through a refugee camp a few kilometres before our destination, the town of Marsabit. The camp was full of anyone in need of safety. Most had come from the border areas of Kenya, Ethiopia and Somalia. They sat in wet misery beneath too small, agency plastic covers that were slung over rough frame-works of branches. Better than nothing, but it brought home that in spite of my hard day there were plenty of people having an even harder time. The convoy drivers seemed to make a point of stopping to drink tea from the makeshift stalls that straggled along the roadside. It was as if they were doing their bit of 'aid' work by helping the camp's obviously struggling economy.

It was getting late as the convoy pulled into Marsabit. The last kilometres had been an even wilder ride with the trucks jostling furiously for lead position. But we made it and before I knew it the bike and I were standing by the roadside wondering what to do next. The businessman had told me that there was a northbound convoy and that our drivers were dashing to book the hotel rooms while there were still any left. With no sign of Mike and Sally, I decided that I'd better do the same and once again our luck was in; the last rooms were ours. Then it was just a case of waiting out by the road for them to arrive. Their bike still wouldn't start when they did, so we pushed it to the hotel only to find that the manager had let out one of our two rooms. I was furious and must have looked quite silly as I raved away some of the day's frustrations. He took pity on us though, and for a small fee I could have an empty room that had no bed in it. Suddenly it was dark and the mosquitos were swarming more thickly than we'd ever seen them before. In the pond outside the hotel a chorus of bullfrogs sang with the cicadas up in the trees, and we realised that it had stopped raining. It had taken eleven hours to travel the two hundred and fifty kilometres.

In the morning the sun was shining. We could see by daylight that our attempts to wash the night before had been quite pathetic – we all looked as if we'd been sleeping in the mud! Down in the courtyard, the bikes were covered in terracotta from tyres to handlebars. The bad news was that the hot engines had baked the mud into a pottery casing. Seeing the mess made us decide that a day's holiday was in order. It would take a while to clean the bikes and check them over for damage but also, Marsabit is in the centre of a National Game reserve so we wanted to explore a bit. We had to chisel the pottery off the bikes but most of it came away in chunks, particularly where my old oil leak had smeared itself as a non-stick coating over the engine. One of my panniers had broken and everything, including my spare paper air filters, had been soaked, but the brake fluid leak seemed to be just a loose connection. Nothing else appeared to be damaged, and Mike's bike started easily once the ignition system had dried out.

Chapter Eight
"An African Pearl"

'Experience is what enables you to recognise a mistake when you do it again.'

Sam Manicom

Marsabit was our first taste of a sub Saharan old English colonial town. The buildings were either concrete or wood. The wooden houses had verandas and flower gardens, the concrete looked more official with parking spaces and an occasional flag. The poorer locals lived in a collection of shanties on the edge of town, or in run-down, paint-peeling houses none of which, for some reason, seemed to stand up straight. In the cheerful bustling market we found all sorts of greens, roots and fruits. Beside them hung hunks of meat, rolls of barbed wire, and tools with bright 'Made in China' stickers on them. Beat-up trucks, Land Rovers and 'sit up and beg' black bicycles worked their way patiently through the brightly coloured throng. Squawking chickens, bleating goats and the loud calls of vendors competed with scents of cattle dung, diesel fumes and stagnant drainage ditches to assault our senses.

The three of us were so much into the swing of relaxing after our day off that we made a silly mistake. Whilst exploring Marsabit we'd asked as many truck drivers as we could find about the state of the road up ahead; quite sensible as we were about to cross the Kasuit desert.

This time we'd woken to a perfect biking day. It was dry, cool and there were blue skies. In front of us lay two hundred and seventy seven kilometres of what everyone had assured was 'a bit rough but easy, it will only take you six hours.' We shouldn't have listened. Relaxed and reassured, we didn't set off until ten - after all, surely it wasn't going to be wet. We rode out from under Marsabit's trees and started into the desert with eager anticipation. Going into these conditions felt nice and familiar and I was buzzing – sunshine does that to me. Being alive and kicking after the series of hard days added to the buzz, and I was feeling safe in Kenya. I felt far more at one with what I was doing, and with the bike. We'd come a long way, and I'd learned a great deal. I was actually quite proud to have made it this far, but my mood was probably tinged with a touch of overconfidence.

The shady trees disappeared behind us, with the distinctive flat-topped acacias and the softer outlines of scrubby thorn bushes replacing them. In the distance, the horizon almost disappeared as a pale beige against pale blue line on one side, and softened into the misty sages and violets of a mountain range on the other. The road surface was mostly firm earth with just an occasional section of washboard, and that made the ride nice and easy; it looked as if our advisors had been right. I relaxed a little more and sat back to enjoy the scenery.

A few doubts began to creep into my mind as the washboard sections grew longer. These corrugations were a chore to ride. Strong winds combined with erratic rainfall (either not enough or too much), had made runs of little ditches that lay directly across the road in front of us. They were often no more than an inch deep, but could be several inches wide. They weren't evenly spaced either and the tops of the ridges were hard. The front wheel and the back wheel soon began to feel as if they belonged to different bikes. The books I'd read about desert riding offered two pieces of advice for dealing with washboard. One, go very slowly and just accept that it will be a long, uncomfortable, ball battering, teeth chattering ride. Two, open the throttle until you reach a speed where you skip across the top of the ridges. The latter option the books said would be smoother, faster and cause less damage to the bike, as the vibrations would be smaller. Put like that I had no choice and opened the throttle wider. Yet again, I wasn't completely in control of my three hundred and fifty kilos.

Every instinct said that this was totally mad, but I hung on and kept the throttle open. The bike seemed to go where it wanted to, meandering me erratically from one side of the road to the other; I began to feel that I was just some sort of biking accessory. Thankfully the road was pretty straight and so far we hadn't seen any other traffic.

After about an hour and a half of this, I thought I saw a little mirage. It wasn't though. Running along the roadside was a half-kilometre or so of smooth, pale ground and I eased across to it as best I could. The pale colour was soft sand and my seventy kilometres per hour disappeared in a blink. I was completely unprepared and the bike landed on my foot with my boot digging its own gully in the gravel. There was a moment of silence. Then, through the still swirling dust I heard the worrying hissing sound of fuel dropping onto a hot engine. I started to feel the first touch of panic as I realised that one of the fuel taps was out of reach. My foot was firmly stuck under the engine but at least the bike had stalled. The heat from the exhaust pipe began to work its way through the thick leather of my motorcycle boots as I lay helplessly, trying to be calm and to think what to do next. The petrol was still dripping and hissing.

Riding up in front, Mike and Sally had realised that their dusty shadow was missing. Their first move was to pull the bike off me and with that there'd been an instant rush of relief as we'd realised that there weren't any broken bones to deal with. My boot sole was almost completely ripped off though, and I wondered what state my foot would have been in if the boots had been anything less rugged. Duct tape made for a good temporary repair. Amazingly the bike looked pretty good, but the engine was dead. On starting the trip I'd accepted that if the bike were to break down and my ignorance were to get the better of me, then a truck would have to be hired to take us to someone who could help. I'd felt that this would be possible because there would always be a truck along sometime, and the BMW was relatively simple.

However, when I'd had these thoughts, I'd also accepted that I'd be riding the trip with mental fingers crossed.

Fortunately Mike was far more knowledgeable than I. While Sally sensibly tucked herself away in the meagre shade of a thorn bush, he gave me my first lesson in 'on the road' problem solving. Two hours later only one truck had passed us and he was beginning to scratch the back of his head. The midday sun was high above us and the surrounding land was bouncing heat up into the sky in shimmering waves. We were working under the bike when I had the strange feeling that we were being watched. I turned round to see a Rendille tribesman patiently watching our efforts. He stood tall and motionless, except to acknowledge our greetings with a nod. His head was a mass of tight, red stained braids. Around his neck and arms were a series of multi-coloured beaded necklaces and bands. He was dressed in skins with a bright red cloak thrown over his left shoulder. We carried on working and when we looked up again, without a sound, he had gone.

On a whim Mike split open the ignition switch, which looked quite undamaged. Inside, somehow, a tiny sliver of contact metal had bent enough to break the electrical circuit. Problem solved and we went back to skipping the bikes across the corrugations. This time I ignored the smooth bits!

At the Laisamis road junction, where the desert began to peter out, another hour of the riding day was lost. We had to stop for a police roadblock where thankfully the whole business was speedy and polite.

"It is our duty to check the papers of everyone coming from and going to the border areas", the neatly clad policemen told us.

Their checkpoint was an old trestle table that had stood empty in the sun but was rapidly manned when they'd seen us. They'd sensibly been waiting in the shade of a gnarly old tree. By this time we too automatically headed straight for any shade.

Back at the bikes and ready to go, Mike's wouldn't start. The constant vibrations had worked the negative lead to the battery loose and the battery itself was flat. The policemen lived with no transport of their own at the roadblock and there weren't any cars around so we had to strip the racks off my bike to get at its battery. Out came jump leads that I'd nearly dumped in Ethiopia, and the engine fired up nicely. Fifteen minutes later the racks were back on, and as the last straps were fixed into place, Mike's engine died again. The whole process had to be repeated as a bit more of the day slipped past. Now it'd be a close thing to make the town of Isiolo before dark, but it was still possible. Between Isiolo and us were a couple of small villages and another wildlife reserve.

We hit the road again and thankfully, this time it was in better condition – just rough with the occasional washboard. We picked up speed hoping to make up some time, but also to give Mike's battery a chance to charge up a little.

There in front of us in the deep blue mid afternoon sky hung five spectacular sights. Five oval shaped clouds floated on top of individual dark grey curtains of rain. They looked like a fleet of space ships cruising over the bush.

We sped towards them. Two were dropping their watery loads right across the road, but being able to see through them we kept the throttles open. Time now mattered! Mike and Sally hit the rain curtain and a series of ruts at the same time, and over they went with a bang. Sally lay gasping helplessly for breath, completely winded, while Mike shakily picked himself up. He and I heaved their bike upright and tried to help Sally, but she was still struggling to get a breath. We both feared the worst - such a hard fall must surely have broken something. When at last she got her first breath, shock began to take effect. As miserable, stunned tears fell down her cheeks, Mike and I faced the fact that she probably shouldn't get back on the bike. She really needed a doctor. Meanwhile, Mike's bike had stalled of course. The buzz of the early morning was long gone.

Before we could make a decision about what to do next, a newish Land Rover stopped. Eight immaculate Kenyan businessmen piled out to see if they could help. They too thought that a doctor was a good idea and told us that they were on the way to Isiolo. There was a hospital there and they offered to take Sally with them.

She looked instantly relieved. This day had been a touch of hell for her. Hanging on over corrugations must have been really hard work, and as pillion passenger she had virtually no control. Her trust in Mike was absolute, but part of her shocked state I think was the forced realisation that with bikes, the cow dung can still hit the fan, however good you are.

Sending her with the Land Rover felt exactly the right thing to do, so without really thinking about the potential dangers of packing her off with eight strangers, we carefully lifted her onto a seat. Instinct had taken over again. We jump-started Mike's bike from the Land Rover before it left and with no doubt that we'd see her soon, we waved goodbye to a still shocked and white-faced Sally.

For us the race was on again. It was past the point of making it to safety before dark but now the ride had to be done anyway, to find

Sally. We took off riding as fast as we could go. Mike's arm was dripping blood from what he later showed me to be a two-inch gash below his elbow. Skirting the trees of the Shaba National Reserve, the road got better but the daylight had almost gone. When a truck came towards us through the half-light, its headlights on full beam, Mike decided that he should put his lights on and his bike instantly died again. The battery was a wreck, it wasn't even holding enough charge to run the headlight and keep the bike going at the same time. As the truck thumped slowly past us, Mike dived for the bushes frantically undoing his trousers. I hadn't realised until that moment that he had a dose of the runs and had been riding on will power for some time. He must have been shocked too but he wasn't one to make a fuss. A pale but relieved Mike returned to contemplate the thought that once again we were going to have to strip the luggage off my bike to get at the battery. Another lost hour would take us, without doubt, into complete darkness. The day at this moment was getting so bad that it was almost laughable. In fact it had been incredibly tempting at that moment to just sit down and laugh until tears came.

Instead, we started trying to work out how to ride in the dark with only one headlight between us on a track that now had two definite tyre-sized ditches to ride in. At that moment three trucks came our way and the lead one stopped. An Asian Kenyan leaned out of the cab to see what the problem was. He was out in a flash telling us that he had two twelve-volt batteries in tandem and that we could jump start off his truck.

We tried riding with me behind Mike as usual, but gave that up as a bad job when he said that he was looking into his own silhouette shadow. The next attempt was with me in front which seemed to work reasonably until I got a funny feeling that he wasn't there anymore. I stopped, turned the lights off and waited for my eyes to get used to the dark. No sign of him at all, and from the bush came the sound of a lion coughing and grumbling. Mike had come off; a long patch of soft sand had slowed the bike until it had stalled. The lion grumbled again, but in the calm night air it didn't sound very close. We had just resigned ourselves to another hour of dismantling, when a pick up truck stopped and gave us a jump-start. Now I rode beside Mike in the middle of the road. The right hand tyre track aimed my light too far to the right of Mike's left hand track. That meant I had to bump over the rocks, holes and tussocks of grass in the middle.

Finally, in our headlight there was the police roadblock. At last we'd made it to Isiolo. It had taken us ten hours. That taught us not to be so slack in the morning - another of our 'hard way' lessons. The day had also taught me another valuable lesson. This was our second rush to beat the falling sun and this time it was a pressure that hadn't needed to be there. It had been a dangerous day, but only because we had made it so.

The officer on roadblock duty knew all about us and gave directions straight to the hospital. A tired, still rather stunned looking Sally sat in a room that had two tones of green paint on the walls, and smelt as hospitals always seem to do. A doctor hadn't seen her; they were all busy, but apart from being sore and in some pain she didn't think that anything was broken. The Land Rover ride had been rough, but she knew that the back of the bike would have been ten times worse. We rode into the town to find a hotel, leaving her in the waiting room that was still full of people, waiting.

131

Mike and I agreed that a good hotel was in order so we blew the budget. A maroon jacketed, brass buttoned porter showed us to a room with space for three and a shower that was strong enough to blast the dirt off with a jet of hot steaming water. This was what Sally needed, a hot water massage. When Mike went back to the hospital, Sally still hadn't been seen so they decided not to wait. Room service fed and beer'd us before we all eased battered bodies into our beds. Another long day; I wondered how many more there were going to be like this.

Isiolo is the frontier town for north-eastern Kenya. It had a detectable air of lawlessness about it, which combined with a sudden availability of most material things. The town and its people were living on the edge, and the streets were filled with characters. There were conmen, hunters, tribesmen in full regalia, truck drivers who seemed to have the same mentality as those in 'Wild West' wagon train movies, farmers and traders, all rubbing shoulders with those who just lived there. The town itself was still visibly 'Old British colonial', but tired, very tired. Poor Sally was still in pain and breathing seemed to have become really hard for her, so we decided to stay in the town for a few more days.

One evening in the hotel we bumped into Babu. He was the truck driver who'd helped us with his battery on the road near where the lions had been complaining about whatever it is that lions complain about in the dark. He seemed to be a thoroughly nice guy, but was totally fed up with the state of affairs in Kenya. We listened to his story.

For every load he carried, a palm would have been greased to get it. Then at each police roadblock, another bribe would have to be paid. That could mean a lot of money on a long journey. He said that the system of corruption went as high as the cabinet officials and top army officers. The little people were being well and truly bled.

Babu, his face tense with frustration, told us that the odd feeling in the air of this town was there because tribal warfare and banditry were on the increase in the north and northeast.

"The people say that President Moi is the one that is orchestrating these problems. He's under pressure from outside to hold multi-party elections and he knows that he will lose if that happens." Apparently the plan was to prove to these 'outside influences' (and I knew that Britain was probably one of them) that Kenya was far too unstable to successfully hold completely democratic elections.

I wasn't sure what to make of it all, but Babu's comments had the earnest ring of truth to them. I'd read enough about African politics to know that it's as oddball a convoluted game, as any politics could be. And that it was also full of twists and turns that outsiders would find hard to accept. African priorities in so many things were either totally different, or simply had to be looked at from an unexpected angle.

Mike had hunted out a private hospital - thank goodness for travel insurance. They gave Sally a thorough checking over and confirmed that she didn't have any broken bones; they were 'just' badly bruised. But she did have a lung infection that had developed because the damaged ribs had made it too painful to breathe properly. Unpleasant, but both could be dealt with.

Livingston, Carlo and Sammy proudly introduced themselves to us as Bantus. The Bantu are a race really, the core of a massive gene pool that spreads across much of Africa. Carlo had said the word to us almost as a challenge, but Livingston seemed more laid back. "Would you like to go to an African disco with us?" But when the guys turned up that evening, it was obvious that Carlo had been drinking all afternoon. He was very pissed and decidedly obnoxious. Sammy and Livingston still had their act together though so we went with them with fingers crossed that Carlo wouldn't get out of hand.

The disco was in the dingiest part of town. The guys took us down dirt roads and past battered houses of concrete, wood and corrugated iron. Skeletons of cars sat forlornly in the shadows whilst groups of people sitting on their doorsteps grew quiet as we were guided past. My senses tingled big time. When Livingston beckoned us down a gloomy cluttered alleyway, I began to feel really happy that I'd brought only beer money and a photocopy of my passport with me.

Our little group trailed through an unmarked wooden doorway that was set into one of the damp smelling concrete walls. Inside were dimly lit corridors and the distant sound of music. We squeezed past small groups of people who were propping up the walls. Though some of the girls were obviously wearing perfume, most of the people had a dusky, to my mind, rather exotic scent. The air floated with the odours of African cigarettes, beer and stale vomit (not so exotic). At the end of the second corridor stood a cage-like construction into which you paid your entrance money to a large, round faced perspiring man who I certainly wouldn't have liked to upset.

At nine forty-five it was still pretty much deserted inside, but the music was fantastic. We took a seat at one of the rough wooden benches and settled down to watch. We couldn't fail to listen! An ever changing collection of African and extremely up to date European music pounded out of speakers that looked like they had been on tour with a rock band for a couple of decades. The lighting was simple but effective, with shadowy corners and a dance floor that was alive with flashing colours.

By ten fifteen the beat was hotting up and the floor was full of people dancing in a style that was totally different to the slightly reserved gyrations of dancing back home. This was uninhibited wild rhythm and complete animal grace. I'd never seen arms, elbows, knees, bums and heads flung about with such fluidity before. And it was all in perfect time with the music. My feet had been hopping up and down under the table for ages. I wasn't able to resist it.

Livingston told me that he could arrange a girl for me if I wanted.

"But she will probably have Aids; half the girls in the club are prostitutes and nearly all have Aids", he yelled at me over a new and even louder track. Of course I'd been looking at the girls and fancied that a few had been looking at me. To see so many women with such a lack of inhibition was exciting and fresh. But by this time the scent in the disco wasn't fresh at all, and my solitary bed beckoned.

For us, one thing above all others marked Isiolo out as a wonderful place - the start of the tarmac road all the way to Nairobi. With the city just a few hundred kilometres away, Mike's battery problem was a pain rather than the dangerous nuisance it had been. We were now around enough traffic to make jump-starting a relatively easy task and we were pretty sure that he'd be able to get a suitable replacement in the city.

Much of the route we'd been riding was the same as Ted Simon had done on his Triumph way back in the mid 70s, when riding a bike through Africa was a decidedly brave thing to do. Every so often we recognised sections of his journey - some things don't really change much in this part of the world. This next section of road through the lush farmland around the base of Mount Kenya made me feel that I was almost riding the pages of his book 'Jupiter's Travels'.

Just south of a town with the wonderful name of Nanyuki, the Equator slices across the main road to the capital. We stopped amidst the ramshackle market stalls to savour the crossing moment and take photos in front of the mustard yellow Equator sign. Above us loomed the clouded heights of Mount Kenya. Legend has it that the gods of the Universe made Mount Kenya as a sign of their power, and as a resting place for them when they visited Earth. The local name for it is 'Kere Nyaga' which means, 'The Mountain of Brightness'. The local people still pray and offer sacrifices to this awesome mountain and there are many legends about it. The one I liked the most was the one about the tribes and the land.

The gods had three sons and they wanted to give the sons the gift of all the land that could be seen from the mountain. The gods knew that they had made a paradise and they wanted their sons to be happy in it. The sons were all strong men who were wise, but also young with much to learn, so the gods decided on a plan. The sons came to be the fathers of the Kikuyu, the Kamba and the Masai tribes – the digging stick, the bow and the spear. The father of the Kikuyu took domain over the fields, the Kamba the forests and the Masai the herds on the plains. In this way, all could live in peace alongside each other.

In fact it's still pretty much that way today. One side tale to this story is that the father of the Kikuyu had nine daughters. These daughters and their descendants became the traditional trustees of the nation and it is said that even today, when you scrape the surface of much that happens in Kenya, you'll always find one of their fingers in the pie somewhere.

Over the generations though, East Africa (and Kenya in particular), has become the melting pot of both Africa's races, and its outside influences. Swahili, the language of the eastern lands, is the classic example. The word itself comes from the Arab word for coast, 'Sahil'. The language adopts a little bit from almost every culture it has come into contact with for any length of time - Bantu, Arabic, Persian, Indian, English, Portuguese and German. For a hybrid language it's well organised and has a simple, logical structure.

Just as English is the default language in many parts of the world, so Swahili is in Eastern Africa. It's the form of communication that most, regardless of their own specific tribal language, will understand. It sounds great too. "Jambo, habari?" – 'Hello, how are you?' "Me me nataka…." – 'I would like…' "Kwaheri." – 'Goodbye.' I'd read that 'Klingon', the language of 'Star Treks' chief aliens, was actually worked out to be a language that can function. It's based on Swahili.

With the road no longer demanding that its every metre be watched, there was plenty of time to relax and take in the passing scenery. Mud villages, concrete towns, rolling farms, forested hillsides and fast flowing rivers kept us entertained as we meandered through the cool air. Young boys actively fish these rivers and every so often we'd come across a cluster of them with their catch for sale. The metre long fish would be held high with two fingers stuck up into the pink slits of the gills, and hopefully offered to us as we rode by. Tempting, but the thought of the lingering smell of fish on my luggage was not.

The bikes were behaving perfectly and even the inevitable mangy dogs seemed to be looking both ways before crossing the road, but the closer we got to Nairobi the more traffic there was. There were plenty of the usual trucks and four by fours, but now there were cars as well, some of which should never see a rough road. And, there were crazily driven mini buses called Matatus. Most of these drive regular routes as the local bus service. Their drivers work long, hard, fast days. The buses inevitably belong to a 'Boss' and the drivers rent them on a daily basis. The rent is so high that to make any money a driver has to make as many trips as possible, picking up as many people as possible for as many hours as possible. Twelve-seater vans would squeeze in twenty people, with cheerful bantering enthusiasm from the drivers' mates and resignation from the passengers. It must be a hard life and many of the drivers only manage it by being stoned in one way or another. On the road, we treated them with complete respect.

From a distance, the view of the city is quite spectacular. With its giant modern tower blocks thrusting out of the plains, it looked to me like a vast spaceship, so out of keeping with its surroundings as it is. The outskirts are low and the traffic moves steadily along wide roads. Seeing it this way made it odd to think that its cemetery was the city's first permanent structure back in the days when it was a squatter's town spawned by the new railway from the coast. This was the 'Lunatic line', so called because of the considered madness of the attempt to build it. Nairobi was built on the last section of flat land before the hills and the Great Rift Valley started. Now, cars and trucks jostled for position while lean men pulled wooden carts loaded almost to toppling point with goods for one or the other of the markets. The men glistened with sweat and breathed in the dense fumes, but their families would get fed and clothed via their efforts. Day after day we were being taught how hard life is when you live on the edge.

I'd heard of the area to the south of the city, which in effect is more than just an area, it's a full on suburb that no one in power wishes to admit exists – even though President Moi's own home had a grand view out over it. The area is called Kibera and it's home to an estimated one million people, but no one really knows. When I was told about it, my first thought was, 'some home!' It's a mish-mash of narrow earthen alleyways, with open flowing sewers lining these walkways. The shacks are cobbled together with whatever can be scavenged and one of these shacks can be home to a whole family of 6 or 7 plus. This doesn't sound too bad until you realise that they are often no bigger than a small bedroom in an English home. Families come and live there for generations, each enduring the conditions because there is at least a chance that they might pull their family above the poverty line. The attraction is the chance of work, but the emphasis is on chance. Days later I met a man in a market and we got talking. James told me he was from Kibera, and when I asked him if it was OK for me to visit him there, he looked shocked that I would want to go at all.

"Why?" he asked. "You don't need to see it and besides, you won't be safe there, even if you are with me. Life is difficult." I decided to listen to the advice. His quiet, considered way of dealing with my question made more of a point than a dramatic reaction would have done.

Our destination within Nairobi was a legend. For twenty-odd years Mama Roche had been running an overlanders' oasis there. There were many stories swirling around as to how she started the business of running her hostel. The stories were filled with great treks, murder and banditry with dollops of bribery and corruption thrown into a mix that also contained portions of bravery and determination. Each one is as far fetched as the other but as you get to know Mama, an immigrant from Poland at the end of the Second World War, you realise that each is quite possible. Mama's gardens were the temporary crossroads home for travellers coming from all parts of Africa. Land Rovers, jeeps, a truck or two, motorcycles and a lot of backpacks get parked in the ramshackle flower gardens; initially for a couple of days 'R&R' from the strain of being on the road in Africa. The dorms were always full with an ever-rotating stream of travellers, and the lawns were covered with tents from all over the world. On any one day you would hear conversations in at least ten different accents, about at least ten different parts of Africa. The traveller's information grape vine was flourishing amongst the mango trees, the washing lines and the shrubs. The couple of days' R&R would inevitably turn into several days as the total convenience of the place took over and battered bodies began to relax and feel safe. For many, Mama's was the first place for weeks where they were able to do normal everyday things without an audience. How nice it was.

I hunted out the few folk who had been in Uganda. This was yet another country that had recently been at war so there wasn't much up to date information available. And of course we'd been pretty much out of touch with the outside world for a couple of months. The folks with the best information were those who had just made it through West Africa. They'd been the lucky ones as they had made it across the Algeria-Niger border before it had closed. I heard the story of one poor couple on bikes. They had made it across the Sahara to arrive at the border very late in the day. Tired, they had decided to cross it when they were fresh after a good night's sleep – a good plan except that the border closed during the night. This was a total disaster, they were travelling on a very tight budget and the lost time and miles meant that their dream had to be put away for another day, they hoped.

The longer we stayed at Mama's the more we began to realise that we were, as Daniel had said, probably the first to make it north to south across Egypt, Sudan and Ethiopia for a long time. There'd been an Israeli in Aswan who had made it going north with a Swedish passport in his pocket and a monkey as his companion; an English guy, Jonny Bealby, was in Adis Ababa trying to get north on his Yamaha, but there was no news of anyone else. Our brains were picked mercilessly by travellers who were realising that a travel 'window' was opening up a new route to replace the still closed western trail. None of us liked to predict how long the window would stay open and we carefully explained the risks of this road, but dwelt on the fun bits.

The Uganda news was good. Things were decidedly unstable in the north, but calm in the centre and south of the country - two out of three seemed pretty good. Mike, Sally and I parted ways now. They'd managed to find work and a place to stay with one of the Aid agencies. After all our time together it felt quite strange to be setting out on my own again. We'd become a family in a comfy sort of way. We'd grown to trust and rely upon each other. We'd laughed and cried together, and had survived, together. A lifetime friendship had been set and our final parting was in a way, rather odd. It was almost as if a page in a book had turned. New adventures were beginning and we were eager to see what would happen next. Yes the parting was sad, but the sadness didn't outweigh the dreams and fears of the coming day. For the first time since Greece, any mistakes would be my own and I'd be reliant on my own resources. But it also meant being able to make 'spur of the moment' changes in plan. I was ready to roll with the thought that one day Mike, Sally and I would have a reunion that would also be a memory worth having.

The road west along the Rift Valley took me past the wonders of the Masai Mara and Nakuru National Parks. I'd still seen hardly any wildlife on the trip so far, but as the weather was right for a dash to Uganda it made sense to do my sight-seeing on the way back. Some of the game came to me though. Sections of the main road overlook the Rift Valley's salt lakes, which are home to literally thousands of pink flamingos. It's a dramatic sight, the lakes seem to shimmer with the birds' beautiful colours. When something creates a scare, the sky fills with swirling lines of panicking, screeching pink.

Half way to the border, when contentedly enjoying the temperature and the mustard colours of the land, a herd of Zebra charged across the road right in front of me. It was as if I'd suddenly ridden my bike through a TV screen and into a wildlife programme.

The town of Eldoret was as far as it felt comfortable to go that day so I started my hotel hunt in plenty of time. This time there would be no one to stand with the bike when I went into a hotel to ask about parking, the price, and of course whether there was any space. The jaded old colonial New Lincoln Inn was the only place with parking. Even so, it was only just within my budget. To my delight, I was warmly greeted by more staff in neat burgundy uniforms. The bath in the room I was shown was a mini swimming pool and yes, the tap ran hot. Too lazy to explore the streets on a food hunt, the hotel restaurant seemed like a good bet and a nice treat. Faded fly-blown pictures decorated three of the walls and on the fourth hung a large, very serious photo of Kenya's president, Mr Daniel Arap Moi. He looked rather uncomfortable amongst the ageing memorabilia of colonial days gone by. A couple of Tusker beers helped the tough-as-old-boots chicken slip down and I headed for a long wallow in the tub; the perfect end to a good day on the road.

The next day I eased out of Kenya without a hiccup and slipped into Uganda with the same efficient smoothness. Everyone was helpful and polite. When I smiled at someone, there was always a smile back. When I said thank you, I was always given a version of, 'you are welcome'. Customs knew what they were doing and immigration gave me the same respect that I gave them. When they asked how long the entry permit should be, I doubled the month I'd planned, just to cover the unexpected, and was told, "No problem."The rubber stamp hit the inkpad, then my passport and I was dismissed with a "Have a great stay."

The border marked a very obvious change in the vegetation. On the Kenyan side it had been mainly mustard and sage, bush or farmland. In Uganda the difference was dramatic. Everything was suddenly green; green grass, green bushes, green trees. After trundling on through the tidy lines of banana and tea plantations, I had to twist my neck to look up at the first trees I'd seen of any real size in Africa. The shade was so dense in some sections that it actually felt cold, and I could smell as well as feel the temperature changes. The road took me swooping and curving through the land and deposited me in a butterfly valley. Literally thousands of butterflies filled the air and the road seemed to be almost carpeted by these stunning, multi-coloured creatures. I could only get through by riding at a snail's pace and wondered how many were killed each day in their search for whatever they were looking for in this particular valley. Then a truck blasted past me killing more in a few seconds than I could have done in ten minutes of wanton slaughter. I moved on.

It was a delight to see the local women walking along the roadsides with bundles piled high on their heads. Their dresses were always an eclectic clash of bright colours. These were wrapped around them in such a way that their basket on head posture made them look more elegant, to my mind, than the highest of Paris fashions would have done. The fruit stalls that lined the roadsides were loaded with the colours of mangoes, pineapples, oranges and

bananas. These vivid splashes of colour rivalled the dresses for vibrancy.

The road surface was absolutely fantastic and for once I was able to hear the drumming noise from the tread on my enduro tyres. I was tickled by the road signs too. 'Driving on the hard shoulder is prohibited' was a good one – until now everyone had driven wherever they'd thought the smoothest bit would be. 'Spilling of petroleum-based liquids on the road is prohibited' - some hope. Drivers often did their oil changes by the roadside, the old oil just emptied into the sand. But, in true African style, there were no signposts for Kampala.

Because the border had been so quick, it was quite possible to make it to Uganda's capital city, Kampala, before it got dark. I had somewhere to stay as well. I'd known Heather for years, and now she was working for the Christian airline 'Mission Aviation Fellowship'. Their job was to take medical and food aid to troubled areas, to fly doctors and nurses to where they were needed, to take sick people to hospital, and aid workers and missionaries to their far-flung posts. As Christians they taught the gospel wherever it felt right. They would also fly businessmen and government ministers around the country, though these definitely had to pay their way. The airline worked from donations and from what fare paying passengers they could find. It was good to see where some of my sponsor money would be going. The chance to go up in a spare seat on a flight brought back another memory from childhood for me. Sometimes the only contact we had with the 'outside' was by the tiny Cessnas whose pilots seemed to be able to go just about anywhere.

Over the next weeks I would learn that there is no better way to find out what really goes on in a country than to spend time with someone who eats, sleeps and breathes the place. Heather was great company and a never-ending source of information and contacts.

The city itself was a dodgy place to be living and bullet holes decorated many of the walls. Crime was a major problem and once again,

HOW NOT TO LOAD A TRANS-AFRICA BIKE

FISH RIVER CANYON - THE LARGEST IN AFRICA

MEALS ON WHEELS — MATOKE BANANAS

SMILES — AFRICAN MAGIC

CAPTAIN JOSEPH'S DAUGHTER CHECKING THINGS OUT

THIS IS ONE
LOADING
TECHNIQUE I
DIDN'T TRY!

CURIOSITY - KIDS IN CENTRAL AFRICA ALWAYS WANTED TO KNOW...

MY FAVOURITE ANIMALS

LUNCHTIME AT THE VILLAGE

LAKESIDE VILLAGE - MALAWI

THE LAKE BUNYONYI PROJECT

ZAMBEZI RUSH HOUR

CAN'T SEE THE BOTTOM? — CHECK IT!

THE 'DRY' END OF THE MOYALE ROAD

THE BUSHMAN'S QUIVER TREE FOREST

A LUCKY SHOT

THE LOCAL BUS SERVICE

ETHIOPIAN ROADSIDE

THERE IS A STORY BEHIND CATCHING A CHICKEN FOR LUNCH

IT'S HARD WORK GETTING TO THE TOP — BUT WORTH IT!

MIKE AND BIKES — THE ROAD TO GEDAREF

TAKING IT EASY ON ONE OF THE BETTER DIRT ROADS

DESERT PEACE

UNMARKED ROADS ARE WORTH EXPLORING

AND I THOUGHT I WAS OVERLOADED!

at the end of a war, there were too many guns floating around. The houses of Muzungus (white folks) were sealed inside compounds, barbed wire on the walls and guard dogs patrolling the yards. Everyone kept in touch by CB radio and unknown locals were treated with caution. The situation in the city had been very bad indeed and there were still occasional flare-ups. "In the main", said Heather, "you get used to it."

To me, Uganda's recent history seemed completely mad. In the 1960s, shortly after independence, Milton Obote came to power with a reign of corruption, mass detentions and armed reprisals. The country fell to pieces. Then things took a turn for the worse. In 1971 Idi Amin Dada took over in a coup, which started with a massacre of hundreds of troops and police. The 'new broom' was sweeping with a vicious vengeance. It carried on sweeping and in 1972 Amin expelled the thousands of non-citizen Asians. These people had held many of the supervisory, management and small business jobs. Without them, a small number of people became very wealthy and at the same time, the structure of the country began to disintegrate.

Amin's reign of absolute terror continued, with no one strong enough to oppose him until 1979 when the Tanzanian army invaded alongside the Ugandan UNLA. During Uganda's past twenty years an estimated 800,000 Ugandans have died. Successive coups over the following years failed but a military commander named Museveni, who had helped lead the Liberation Army, ended up as head of the disciplined National Revolution Army. As Museveni climbed to power, the country began to breathe a hopeful sigh. Hardly a family had been untouched and the country was an almost bankrupt shambles of distrust and open sores.

By the time I arrived, Museveni was the President and making all the right noises. This hopeful air was a good time to arrive in the country. People were making an obvious effort to get life back on an even keel. There was still considerable unrest up in the north, but in Kampala paint was appearing on walls, the shambolic telephone system was being repaired, roads were being rebuilt and the people were being quietly positive.

I was starting to like the Ugandans. The ones I'd met were quiet talking, beautifully mannered people. They placed great importance on a good solid handshake that seemed to say 'Hello, it's great to meet you; I'm glad that we are having the opportunity and I suspect that we could become friends'. I always got the feeling that these greetings were important and quite a contrast to the often cursory European version.

Changing money in the bank was an event. For just ten pounds sterling I'd be given a fifteen centimetre high stack of paper, and that was the high denomination notes! Inflation was a problem. The first time this happened, I left the bank feeling that my bulging pockets were a beacon for muggers. The next time I took a large bag.

The police in Kampala caught my eye. They all looked incredibly smart in their beige and black uniforms but they seemed pretty ineffectual. They had very little equipment and no cars. The crime rate actually appeared to be controlled by the people themselves and if someone was caught stealing or was a murderer, then vigilante rough justice would be quickly meted out. Most caught were severely beaten, even to death. However, house burglary was treated as an unfortunate fact of life and one of Heather's friends told me that there was a 'thieves' market'.

"If you are robbed", he said, "go down to the market the next morning and you can almost always buy your things back!" At first glance it was a sort of Robin Hood style of sharing the wealth. It was probably cheaper than paying out for insurance too, if you'd been able to afford any in the first place that is. As for stolen western goods, it was far easier to buy them back than it was to arrange for replacements to be imported into the country, and cheaper.

Over those first days in Kampala, the driver from Heather's company was kind enough to take me out with him on his errands and deliveries. As many Ugandans do, he spoke good English and that allowed me to be introduced to another side of the city. This was the 'behind the scenes' world of the shops and offices, and Joel knew many of the people. With him as my chaperone, people behaved in a relaxed, matter of fact manner. Joel in fact was rather an odd person to look at.

He made me think of a human version of a Gnu. This beast of the plains, so legend has it, was put together by God out of all the pieces that were left over from the task of creation.

One day, when the jeep had gone to be serviced, I gave Joel a lift home on the bike. I think that he got a kick out of being on the back, particularly in full view of his neighbours. I enjoyed his happiness and the thought that it was a nice way to pay him back for all the time he'd spent with me. His home was up a steep dirt road that would be a slippery chore to get up and down in the rainy season. The house stood on the side of the hill where it was sheltered by a clump of trees. He'd built the four-bedroom building himself and it was quite large, though it wasn't anything like big enough for all the relations who'd moved in with him and his family. In this part of Africa, family looks after family but that can take in the extended 'clan' as well as immediate relations. The house was packed with aunts, an uncle, cousins and nieces and nephews. To the rear of the house Joel had a plot of land on which he grew bananas, potatoes, the versatile root manioc, calabash, tomatoes and beans – all the things that the average Ugandan had to grow to supplement any wages that might be earned. Half a dozen rust, black and emerald coloured chickens scrabbled around the plot, scratching and pecking at goodies that I for one couldn't see. They were skinny, so perhaps they were just being hopeful.

Joel introduced me to what was his Ugandan version of the 'apple in the eye'. Pineapple of his eye didn't have the same ring to it! His youngest daughter was called Victoria. Not out of any royal connection but because her birth had been so hard that it was, Joel said, "A victory that she is alive."

Heather had known that I'd be turning up sooner or later so she'd arranged some holiday time and to hire one of the agency jeeps.

"I want to show you the south", she said. Over the next week we did a big loop down through the lush patchwork quilt terraces in the hilly southeast. We went almost to the border with Rwanda and then back up on the western side to Kampala. We took in the once famous Queen Elizabeth National Park on the way. Heather had warned me that most of the game had gone, either killed for food by the soldiers or sold in 'bits' as souvenirs. She was right, but we did see hippo from a distance and buffalo from far too close. The drive through the park took us up over a volcanic escarpment where small round lakes along the trail had attracted a pretty good selection of Uganda's bird life.

The weaverbirds impressed me a lot. They are called weaverbirds because they literally weave their nests. As you ride or drive, you see trees festooned with these straw teardrops that are anything from six inches to a good foot and a half in length. They hang from the tips of the branches with the bird's front door on the underside, all this to try and keep unwelcome visitors away. The weaving is so strong that a freshly made nest is hard to rip apart, even for human hands. These cheerful birds reminded me of the resilience and character of London's sparrows.

I'd also been amused by another of Uganda's feathered characters, the Marabou stork. My first encounter with these rather gruesome birds was very appropriately at a restaurant. These storks had none of the elegance and grace that I'd always associated with birds of that family. They stand with long, knock-kneed legs and their black feathers never seem to sit quite as flat as they should. We were drinking coffee when one fixed me with a single-eyed glare. He stood there motionless, like a cross between a Walt Disney cartoon waiter and an undertaker. Red faced with wobbling jowls, his bald head, hunched shoulders and long beak all turned in my direction. He watched me with his baleful, fish-eyed stare, whilst hopping from one foot to the other as if he was afraid that we were going to escape before giving him his tip.

The view from the top of the escarpment was absolutely panoramic and the feeling of wide open space quite magnificent. Below us for as far as we could see was nothing but a gently rolling green and gold plain that seemed to be sleeping in the sultry warmth.

There was a rustle and a snort behind us; we had company. A herd of buffalo had moved into the scrub nearby. They stood stiff legged and frowning, like a group of grumpy old men who have just discovered that their favourite seat in the park is already taken. They actually made me feel quite uncomfortable with their indignant stares and when they began pawing the dust, we made a quick exit.

Winston Churchill called Uganda 'The Pearl of Africa' because it's so lush and fertile. For a large part of the country, the soil quality, the altitude and the year round availability of water make the agricultural possibilities endless. But the constant wars and corruption had pretty much snuffed out the greater possibilities. Years of tribal sniping, the problems of colonial borders, tradition, greed and outside interference kept the brakes on development. But, the new President really seemed to be a glimmer of light on the skyline – he appeared to have the ability to turn ideas into reality. As we travelled we could see that the country was in the main getting on with life, one tentative step forward at a time. Fingers were firmly crossed and when the chance came up to help a little, I decided to stay for my extra 'unexpected' month.

I found myself back down in the south on a lake that was close enough to the Rwanda border to hear gunfire at night. No one could tell me if it was rebel action or bandits. The sounds were so normal that locals treated the noise as a western city dweller would treat the sounds of heavy traffic. I didn't have time to be worried though, I had a job to do. For my extra month I would be work co-ordinator for an aid project out on an island in the middle of Lake Bunyonyi.

Once, there had been a large cottage and staff quarters on the island. These were now semi-derelict, thanks to neglect and theft over the war years. Our job was to get the buildings habitable again and build a camping site on one of the beaches. The island would then be used by the various agencies at work in Kenya and Uganda for staff holidays, training and conferences. The public could use it too. Once running, the project would generate its own funds and hopefully enough to renovate the hospital and school on the neighbouring islands. It would also provide employment for some of the people living in the villages around the lakeshore. My job for the month was to make sure that the local guys got on with the work, that supplies were ordered on time and that they didn't mysteriously go missing. All well and good, except that I didn't speak a word of the local lingo.

"Wine with no Label"

'A man who knows he is a fool is not a great fool.'

Chuang Tse.

The weather was idyllic, the work hard and the local guys were just your average bunch of guys. One was a hard worker, one was the joker, one was incredibly lazy; one was a villain who seemed to be checking what was stuck down and what was not, and one was strong but classically, a bit simple. M'Agandi, the hard worker, was a talented man. He was a skilled roofer, general builder, and could whistle the calls of local birds. I could never tell the difference between him and the real thing and as he worked he would string the various calls together as a sort of song. He could whistle seemingly without effort for hours. With his straw pork-pie hat shoved to the back of his head he'd given us a lesson in recycling; each nail he pulled out of a roof would be straightened and used again. Every piece of wood and every broken tile that could possibly be reused was stacked neatly on one side.

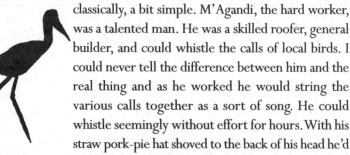

Lake Bunyonyi had a mystical quality. In the evenings at the end of an inevitably hard day it was difficult to believe that these islands had seen so much cruelty. As if to remind Jeroun, Paul (fellow Aid workers) and me of that, a faint crackling of rifles would sometimes float over from Rwanda on the warm breeze. The mist that settled on the lake at nighttime would take on a wavering glow from the campfire and the only things that broke our peace would be the popping of the fire and the occasional rustle of eucalyptus branches up above. It seemed like our island fire was the centre of the world and that whatever it didn't light up, didn't exist. All three of us felt this, and some evenings while the hours slipped by we hardly spoke a word. None were needed.

Morning always brought reality with the lakeshore villages coming alive as a rising sun burnt off the mist. Thin tendrils of smoke would wisp up from cooking fires and if there wasn't a breeze the lake's calm waters would carry across the sounds of people talking. Sometimes we could hear whole conversations, the humour and the scolding – though we didn't understand a word. Fleets of dug-out canoes would then set out to ferry people to their jobs and children to school.

Our supplies were delivered by John the boatman in his dugout. Part of his charm was that he would bend the rules, but always with a grin. We had to watch him but he was good to have around. John had the major advantage of speaking English so would often act as interpreter if we got stuck. One day he asked me if we'd like to go to his village to eat dinner with his family. It was a nice surprise as when he'd been shuffling from one foot to the other I'd been wondering what was coming next. Once or twice before I'd asked where he lived and he'd just given me the answer 'in the village'. This time he pointed to a small settlement no more than a mile away on the side of the lake.

The next evening John brought us 91 crayfish. There were so many, I had to count them; in Europe they'd have cost a bomb. The lake teemed with crayfish but amazingly the locals didn't eat them. When I asked John why, he said, "We don't know how to cook these things!" I was a bit stunned that here was a major food source they couldn't eat – time for a cookery lesson. Tradition (or perhaps pride) said no wives were allowed, but the men turned up and watched avidly.

Take a big pot, boil water, chop tomatoes, onions, garlic and sweet potatoes, add to water. Bring to boil and simmer. All easy to do on a wood fire and the smoke added a rather pleasant flavour which I'd love to replicate now. Finally, in with the 91 crayfish and five minutes later, with a wonderful scent floating through the trees, tuck in to a rich red stew. The three of us loved it, but the locals were not impressed at all. Most of them took just one mouthful and one even spat it straight out, unaware that I'd seen of course. The crayfish would be safe in their haven for a little longer.

The day of the dinner party came round and Jeroun, Paul and I took our end of 'shift' bathe in the lake before donning our cleanest travellers' clothes. John eased his canoe up onto the sand. He'd lined it with dry reeds in our honour and we settled down cross-legged to help paddle. With four of us working at it we sped across the deep water, leaving a little wake behind us. The shores of the lake were quite steep, and John's village was set up high on the slope out of the way of floods. His house stood out from the others as it was the only one that wasn't made of mud, wood and straw. It was square, the others were round; his walls were breezeblock, the others were mud brick; his roof was corrugated iron, not straw. I looked at him with new eyes - John was obviously a man of consequence. With an unusually small family for Africa, he'd been able to spend his savings on building his home.

We ducked our heads under the rough wooden door beams and were shown with great pride into the living room. The rough plastered walls were decorated with bead jewellery, some wooden carvings and a small collection of photographs. These were arranged according to age. On the left, a sepia shot of John's grandfather wearing a Victorian bowler hat above his best tribal robes. The next was a black and white shot of John's father. He stood proudly in shorts with a solar helmet on his head. His face was seriously stern, and unusually for the region, his chin was covered with a grey beard. The next was of John himself wearing his city outfit. He was clean-shaven but had an equally serious expression on his face. If you looked hard enough though, you could see the usual twinkle in his eye.

John left us to ourselves for a moment saying that he was going to get his wife. We gradually became aware that a full-blown argument was going on. When he came back into the room his head was down. His wife had prepared nothing for our dinner. "When I told her I was bringing three Wazungu (plural for foreigners) for dinner, she thought I was drunk", he explained. He told us that the best plan was to go to the shop to buy beer while his wife organised the food. He warned us that it would be nothing special because there wasn't time. My stomach rumbled - there hadn't been a chance to eat since breakfast.

It was raining outside and John's 'not far' to the shop turned out to be a two-kilometre red mud slide up and down the valleys around the village. Three round straw huts stood surrounded by banana trees out on a point over the lake, not a shop at all, but the village pub. We slipped our way down to the last which John said was the one he drank in.

"The landlady is my sister" he said. With the dark clouds overhead stealing the last of the day's light, the hut interior was pitch black. John pushed us inside. The only sounds were rain falling on the straw roof and a chicken clucking quietly from somewhere in the gloom. Nine pairs of eyes, seemingly suspended half way up the walls, watched us with hardly a blink. I felt like an invader.

The room stayed silent. Then John eased his way between us and told our tale. Our eyes accustomed themselves to the dark and now we could see nine sets of white teeth to go with the eyes. When John told the story that his wife had thought he'd been drunk, everybody laughed and the mood was set. Extra chairs were brought in and the drinkers shuffled round to make space for us to sit, but we were one chair short. Jeroun and I mimed that each other should have the seat. The eyes watched our visual discussion back and forth until we both sat down on the chair at the same time, and promptly fell off it. With that the silence was broken for good.

Our bodies, elbow to elbow, papered the wall, and in the middle of the room stood two wooden bench tables. John asked if we'd tried maize millet beer. None of us had, particularly Paul who happened to be a teetotaller. He was in for a rough night. The beer came in one and a half litre, handle-less plastic mugs - small buckets really. Inside my red bucket swirled what appeared to be watery mushroom soup. Small black lumps floated on the surface; to my eyes they looked suspiciously like drowned flies. No one spoke a word as they waited to see what we would do. Jeroun and I picked the mugs up and tried to look enthusiastic as we took our first tentative gulps. The first mouthful told me that this was not a drink for me. I could feel the lumps floating over my tongue, and both the consistency and sour taste were unpleasantly alien. My stomach rumbled a complaint this time.

Over the next half hour what was left of the light outside disappeared faster than the beer. The atmosphere had eased and little conversations were flowing around the edge of the hut. I began to think about John's wife sweating over a hot cooking fire on our behalf, and started to feel awkward about being in the pub still when we were supposed to have just popped down to the shop. I did wonder if she was well aware of the results of John's visits to the 'shop' so in fact was at home with her feet up. I chugged down the last of my beer and nudged the guys, should we go. It couldn't have been too soon for Paul but Jeroun pointed out that he still had a long way to go with his beer. Within seconds, another beer arrived in front of me, and it looked even worse in blue plastic. "You like it, eh", said John. "But, what about your wife?" I asked He told us that she would still be quite a while and that we should relax and enjoy. So, feeling that there was no choice, I started on my blue beer. Whenever Jeroun or I spoke, everyone else stopped to listen. It felt very odd, most of the guys didn't even understand what was being said and I certainly wasn't saying anything earth shattering. Paul suffered in silence.

The lumps were slipping down easier now and my stomach was beginning to feel quite full. John told me that many of the local men would drink beer for lunch for just that reason. I thought about pub lunches at home and my tongue tingled at the thought of a pint of good real ale. The blue mug was empty now, but this time I was quick enough to stop another one ending up in front of me. I was feeling very relaxed.

"Well, if you don't want any more beer then you must try the other of our drinks, it's called Banana wine", said John. Banana wine didn't sound as if it could possibly be any worse than the beer so to be sociable I agreed. Jeroun too was ready for a change, but Paul was still staring miserably at his almost untouched beer.

The wine arrived in a bottle that had no label. If I'd been smarter I'd have realised what we were about to receive. This time proper glass glasses were produced. We all raised our drinks, the whole hut joining in as they realised that we were paying. Pure banana moonshine packs a punch. It slides easily down into the stomach where it hits with a thump. Dinner was forgotten as words around the room began to slur. Laughter rolled out into the night and tall tales were translated to and fro. The last thing I remember was standing to make a speech.

Jeroun and I were woken up by an over enthusiastic cock crowing in the morning. My senses told me first that I was lying on some sort of coarse material that smelt strangely musty. I pulled myself up to realise that we were laying head to toe with two other of the night's drinkers, with John and the landlady; we were all in her bed. There was no sign of Paul. The cock crowed again, waking John this time and the three of us said sore headed, weak stomached goodbyes to our companions of the night. Jeroun told me that as hardly anyone could speak English, my speech had actually been quite good!

Back on the island Paul waited, trying hard not to be shocked at us and with no sympathy for our delicate state. We declared the day, for us at least, to be a holiday. Not such a good example, but we hadn't had a day off since we'd arrived. The two of us perched under the biggest tree and as the day's heat increased we sat watching life float by on the lake. When John arrived we apologised for our behaviour and asked him to pass them on to his wife.

"That will be difficult", he said. "She isn't talking to me, but she will get over it!" I hoped so. I was also concerned that we might have embarrassed him in front of his friends. "No, no", he said. "You are the first white people to come to our village, most of them were scared of the Wazungu - they aren't now, they realise that you white people are just like us really!" From down by the waters edge came the call, "Hey, Mr Sam, Mr Sam!" Down in a dugout sat a man from one of the nearby villages. "Hey, Mr Sam! Hey, hey, hey!" he yelled at me with a grin as his right arm made an unmistakable motion. The word it seemed had travelled the lake already. We had a lot of arm flexing visitors that day.

Working towards the end of the third week on the island, my thoughts turned to getting on the road again. I washed clothes, packed gear and checked over my paperwork to make sure that nothing had gone astray.

Page eleven of my passport told an awful tale. For the past week I'd been an illegal alien in Uganda. My entry permit had been stamped at that 'oh-so-easy' border for just six weeks instead of the two months that had been agreed. It was the classic traveller's mistake of not checking at the time. The whole business had been so straightforward that I'd been lulled into a foolish sense of security. It began to sink in that my situation was potentially quite dire. Quite simply, I was a stranger who had been hanging around a border conflict area for several weeks and now didn't even have valid paperwork. The army had at least five checkpoints for me to face before reaching Kampala, where I hoped I could plead stupidity and get away with it. It was one of those moments in my life when panic threatened to make all clear thought impossible. The sensible side of me said that panic was a big mistake and the coward in me said to find a big hole to hide in with the hope that it was happening to someone else. Optimism joined in with the comment that if I believed that I could make it, then it would happen.

Feeling that I didn't have a lot to lose I decided to carry on and work the full four weeks. It was really just postponing the inevitable with the vague hope that 'something' might happen. When my time on the island was up nothing had and I didn't even make it past the checkpoint on the outskirts of the town.

Heather had braved the long journey down to the lake by matatu just for the hell of the ride back up with me on the bike. I think she'd soon begun to wish that she'd stayed at home. We were stopped at the first checkpoint and the almost inevitable hand came out with the sods law question "Can I have your passport please?" Trying to bluff my way out with a dumb tourist act didn't work, and with a stupid lie I fell into a hole that was going to be an even bigger problem to climb out of. An armed guard escorted us back into the town to the police station where one of the senior officers told me that I was being detained for having invalid paperwork in the border area, and that my bike could well be confiscated.

Unbeknown to me, at that very moment a pair of legs were pounding away on a bicycle to the next town where the local Bishop of the Church of Uganda was working. The islands belonged to the church and I'd met the Bishop just a week or so before. It was with his blessing that the project was going ahead. The man on the bicycle was one of his workers and he just happened to see us being led away by the soldier. Hours later, after hurried phone calls, Gary and Karen, the aid project leaders, got the word that everything was sorted out. Their idiot ex-worker and his friend were free, but not until I'd received a severe telling off from the senior policeman who said, "We aren't idiots you know, if you'd only been honest and come to me in the first place, it would all have been OK." He also gave me a pass to show all the other checkpoints on the way back north. I felt nearly as stupid as the dumb tourist I'd tried to pass myself off as.

Another lesson learned the hard way, but ironically not one of the other checkpoints even glanced at my papers. In Kampala's immigration offices the formalities were completed with ease and once again I felt safe. Heather graciously said she'd enjoyed the ride, despite the side adventure.

I spent a few more days with her and then, with a big hug for all the good times, heeded the call of the road. This time the border crossing was even easier and I rode back into Kenya thinking that it had been too easy. Someone somewhere must have forgotten to do something. I stopped a short way out of the border town and checked all my paperwork again; it all seemed fine.

The room with the en-suite 'swimming pool' at the New Lincoln Inn was available and suddenly I was delighted about that. I felt the need for something familiar, for safe ground. The receptionist was the same, the manager was the same, the waiter was the same and the same sorts of flowers were blooming in the garden. Even the noises from the street felt familiar and I could park the bike in her old safe spot. An hour in the bath, a long read of an awful paperback novel (that I won't embarrass myself by writing down the title of), a cup of tea made in the room on my cooker, and half an hour of washing my socks and shorts was enough to make me want to do some exploring again. The book, by the way, was a classic swap. English language books are hard to find in shops and are expensive when one does. I'd worked out that a book would have cost the equivalent of sixteen beers or five days food. From then on, whenever I met another traveller I'd try to swap a book. Some of the swaps were grim and I always wondered, with those, if the traveller breathed a sigh of relief when he or she got rid of a poor read.

But, swapping got me into reading a lot of books that I'd never have picked up at home. I read my first ever science fiction book in Kenya, and had re-read 'A Tale of Two Cities' in Egypt.

The New Lincoln's manager recommended a barber's and it was a colonial museum piece. Outside hung a superb example of the traditional red and white striped pole, and the glass half window held faded black and white photographs of 1930s 'western' haircuts. The walls inside were hung with gilt edged, rather fly-blown wall-to-wall mirrors, but the chairs were the real feature. I'd only ever seen white enamel swivel-based chairs like these in a movie. The red leather covers were a little ragged and very faded but they were highly polished and the white-jacketed barber snapped his scissors as if to say 'The edges may be worn but the heart still beats strong'. Well, he did a really good job using an enormous comb that no doubt had last been used to tease out the knots from crinklier hair than mine, and a shiny pair of hand clippers. With memories of my mother's determined short back and sides with similar clippers, I sat with fingers crossed. As a bush town, mission station, nine-year-old I knew nothing of fashion, but never liked having my haircut. This time all went well until he said "Beard?" to which I nodded without thinking. I walked out of that dash of history with a very white chin that glared visibly through the stubble the barber had been kind enough to leave.

That evening after dinner, some of the local men and their girlfriends invited me to join them for a few rounds in the bar. The debate swirled over such important matters as, which has the more strength, White Cap or Tusker beer? Which girls from which bar were the prettiest, and they wanted to know if I was completely mad to be riding a 'piki piki' through Africa? (Swahili for bike - presumably because of the noise that the small local bikes make!) 'Didn't I know that it was dangerous and how often had I had to pay a bribe so far?' That was an awkward one. The truth of the matter was none, but by that time I knew of course that these men lived in a world where not a lot got done without a fair spreading of palm grease. It felt right to change the subject without answering, so I bought another round instead.

Breakfast was a good old-fashioned English spread that was served in the cool flower gardens by the maroon jacketed waiter who called me 'Sir'. Sitting there already togged out in my dusty oily bike gear, I almost had to check that it was me he was talking to. He brought me porridge, bacon and eggs, toast and marmalade and for a splash of local colour, some very good papaya that was decorated with a slice of lemon and a bright red hibiscus flower. This all made for a superb start to a blue-sky day.

I'd learned pretty quickly to hit the road in the early hours of the day. It's a lot more fun to ride a piki piki in the cool. By midday, the asphalt is almost at melting point and the heat hammers up at you off the black surface. You can imagine what happens to your tyre wear at these temperatures, and something else I'd learned by now was that my concentration wasn't at its best when I was slowly cooking in my leather jacket. My six a.m. breakfast in the garden got me on the road for seven, which would give me at least three hours of cooler temperatures to ride in. The low, softer morning light was better for taking pictures and there was a much greater chance of seeing wildlife that also takes advantage of the cool to feed and move.

At the checkpoint a few kilometres down the road, a long line of traffic waited. Two matatus overloaded as usual, with their drivers' fingers tapping at the delay, formed the tail of the queue. Matatu drivers are a traditional target for palm grease so I suspected that the finger tapping might have a tinge of frustration to it. The policemen indicated to the first driver to pull over, and an argument started. Suddenly, one of the officers walked round to the back of the mini bus and using his rifle butt he smashed the taillights on one side. Back at the cab, money changed hands - the driver was now 'legal' in this policeman's eyes and free to go. At least that is, until the next checkpoint where the broken taillights would cause more problems.

Then it was my turn. Another policeman directed me out of the line of traffic. I stopped the bike, pulled off my gloves and helmet and sat waiting. The extremely smart officer strode arrogantly over and stared at me from above the razor-edged creases in his trousers. He had a semi-automatic rifle slung over his shoulder and he didn't say a word, just watched me from below the patent rim of his hat. Not being able to see his eyes in the rim's shadow made him feel really menacing. He strutted around the bike.

After moments that felt like ages, he demanded abruptly "Where are you coming from?" "Eldoret", I told him, wanting to keep things simple. "No, before that!" he snapped. I began to wonder if there was some sort of sting about to occur, was my paperwork from the border in order or not? I'd no choice but to tell him, "Uganda." "I know", he stated in reply, but by then he was stroking the bike with what I thought looked like boyish admiration. He then looked up and said, "What is this?" "Um, a BMW motorcycle", I replied not quite knowing what else to say. "No", he said. "This is a car on two wheels!" and burst out laughing. "Ha, ha, fooled you didn't I?" He'd just stopped me for a chat!

It turned out that he had been on the checkpoint between the border and Eldoret the day before and had seen me ride through. Normally in Kenya I'd been just waved on through the checks, so hadn't thought twice about it. As I breathed a sigh of relief my new 'friend' started walking round the bike muttering such things as "What a machine", "A super bike", and "Oh yes, indeed, a car on two wheels". He then chortled again with laughter and pushed his rather forbidding hat back from his eyes, which shone. Here was a uniformed bike enthusiast. "Would you like a ride?" I asked. "Me, on this?" "Sure", I said, and within seconds his hat and rifle were in the surprised hands of one of his mates, and he was on the bike. We set off down the road with him yelling "Faster!" So I did. One hundred and thirty ks an hour was quick enough on that road though, so after a few kilometres I turned around to deposit him swaggering with glee back at the roadblock. Was that a bribe? No, too much fun to be a bribe.

I'd decided to return to Nairobi but this time to take the back roads through the Cherangani hills. The hills run for roughly sixty or seventy kilometres, forming the western side of the Elgeyo Escarpment. The roads are mostly dirt which meant that many of them didn't show up on my map at all. I rode slowly through this beautiful area and didn't see another white skin anywhere. In the middle of the day I sat in the cool shade of an acacia tree. It was a well-earned rest and the perfect spot to enjoy the view. Sweat had cling-filmed my shirt to my body and my leather jacket was ringed with salt stains again. The foam around my goggles had a salty metallic scent to them and dust had gathered in muddy smears along the lower rims where perspiration would always collect. My eyes were drawn out over the shimmering brown and yellow plain towards the cool greens of the distant mountains. The sense of phenomenal space was quite awesome and it was only after all these months in Africa that I was really beginning to feel inspired by them. In the first months I'd been too busy just coping with my immediate environment to really take stock of just how big the land is. I felt that I was in a place where I could yell at the top of my voice for as long as I wanted, and not a soul would hear.

Totally alone and at peace with the world, I was just wondering how far away the mountains were, when suddenly, a voice behind me made me jump. "Where are you coming from?" it said. It seemed that everywhere in the world was someone's back yard; good thing I hadn't been having a good old yell after all. The man's questions were predictable so I could reel off the usual answers without thinking too

hard. "England." "Forty-three litres." "Eight hundred ccs." "Several months." "Uganda." "Nairobi." And, "Tonight? I'll stay somewhere in the hills." But I didn't mind that people asked me questions and several times I'd wondered if I would have the interest or even courage in my own country to go and ask a total stranger these sort of questions about their life. Here, the questions weren't nosy; they were a combination of curiosity, the desire to learn and a sort of innocence.

That night an elder gave me permission to put my tent up next to his village. After the initial crowd had collected, stared, dawdled, and eventually decided that there was nothing else new to see, I was left alone. It was the perfect opportunity to be a fly on the wall. Trying hard not to be caught staring, I watched the village scene. It seemed that as I hadn't minded them watching me, they didn't appear to mind me watching them.

Many of the men in the village carried small, carved wooden stools and they carried them as if they were extensions to their bodies rather than something to sit on. One of the elders had sociably come and sat near to me on his stool, and he told me that I was right, there was much more to them than 'just' something to sit on. Each stool could be hundreds of years old and in fact each was a family heirloom that was passed from generation to generation. As he talked, he smoked a cigarette which he had clasped between forefinger and thumb so that the smoke wisped up between his yellowed fingers. He was obviously right handed, and each long glowing draw was conducted with amazing elegance and appreciation. He told me that the stool is the shrine of the family's soul and that each is decorated with the family name and design. When the head of the family died, this symbol of authority would be passed to the next in line as an indication to all, the village and the tribe, that power and responsibility were in new hands. A sort of African coat of arms I thought.

The old man's knowledgeable calm impressed me, as did his clothing. He made me feel positively scruffy. I'd watched him come out of the low doorway of his mud and straw hut. He was immaculately clean with spotless dark trousers and a gleaming white creaseless shirt.

I asked him if the village had a witch doctor. He replied, "Not this village, but the area certainly has a doctor, we must have one." He told me that, besides knowing vast amounts about the herbs and medicines of the land, the doctor was for many a spiritual leader and advisor. I also knew that some were dangerous. They know which of the hundreds of Africa's plants are poisonous and how long their poison would take to work. Historically, if you wanted to bump someone off then, for a fee, the Doctor would either arrange it or give you the poison to do it. The favourite method was to dip the little finger in the poison and then, whilst serving a drink, dip the finger discreetly in the liquid... 'Doctoring the drink?' But this man's doctor was also the teller of tales. I read before coming to Africa that in the days when few could read, word of mouth had been the way that traditions and history were passed on. The storytellers had almost photographic memories for these historical tales. The witch doctors were often seers too.

One such seer dreamt of strangers coming out of the great waters to the east like yellow frogs. He dreamt that they would ride beasts with wings like butterflies and they would have magic sticks that would send out fire. The seer prophesied that some time would pass and then these strangers would arrive in great snakes whose skins would repel spears and arrows. The strangers would destroy them all. This story had been told for three generations before the explorers, slave traders and colonialists had started to arrive. The great snake part of the prophecy had come true with the building of the railway from the port of Mombassa.

I slept surrounded by the village noises until the heat of the early sun got me up and on the move. My deep green tent was perfect for hiding away in corners but its dark colour sure did attract the heat. It only had one entrance so I could never get a through draft and on wet days, it was too low to sit up in. I nick-named it 'The Space Capsule' because I had to slide in feet first. It wasn't ideal but it kept me dry and when I'd repaired the splits my friend the cat had made in Greece, it kept the mosquitoes out very well. I'd had a few nights where the mossies had been so enthusiastic they'd been pinging off the inner lining as if flying full tilt at the tent would enable them to power through the fabric to get at the 80-kilo meal inside. It was very satisfying to know that these vicious little bloodsuckers were well and truly thwarted! But, I'd have to layer on the repellent in the morning before getting out in case there were any patient, hungry and determined types still around. There usually were.

On a whim and for no better reason than there was no real reason why not to do it, I headed north. Time wasn't a problem, the bike was behaving really well, my water bottles were still pretty full and the map showed a road that it marked as 'improved but liable to be impassable in bad weather'. The weather was good and the dirt roads I'd just been on were fun, but easy and this road sounded a bit more of a challenge. I was ready for that now.

'Improved' turned out to be wishful thinking and I began to wonder why I wasn't sitting underneath the mango trees drinking coffee and chatting to the other travellers at Mama Roche's. Rut after rut rattled my teeth; soft sand made the bike squirm, and the heat was intense. But the rolling bush land was beautiful and there was hardly a soul on the road. Once again I felt like I had the world to myself. By mid afternoon the heat was getting to me and in spite of a good night's sleep, my eyelids began to droop. When a trickle of sweat made it past my goggles and into my left eye, the stinging meant that I had to stop anyway – I couldn't keep my eyes open. There was still plenty of time so I decided that a doze in the shade of one of the bushes would set me right. I squatted on my heels and put my head on my arms.

I woke to find a woman standing a couple of metres away. Her large eyes looked at me from above worn out and patched old clothes. We greeted each other in Swahili. "Jambo, habari?" "Mzuri sana" "Very well." She took a pace closer and then in pretty fair English, asked if she might rest with me for a while. She came and squatted next to me and we dozed in companionable silence. Knowing that it wasn't normal for Kenyan women to be so forward, even an older one, I wondered what her story was. After a while she asked me where I'd come from that day. She'd seen me ride past her a while back. I told her the name of the village and she looked amazed.

"All that way on this? In one day! Haw! You must be a strong man. I too have come from there", she said. "But I started five days ago."

Beth had walked all the way and was going to the village at my turn around point on the road; it would take her another day to get there. I looked at my mountain of luggage and rather guiltily knew that I shouldn't offer to take her on the bike. I was sure that her extra weight up high on my bags would be bad news on this road, even though she was quite thin.

We talked on for a little while and then Beth stood, saying that it was time for her to go. We said our goodbyes and she started down the track but had only made it a few paces before stopping almost in mid stride. After a moment she turned round and came back to me. Under her cloak was a bag that was made out of an old flour sack; I hadn't noticed it before. Reaching inside, Beth pulled out two tiny hard-boiled eggs and putting them into my hands she said, "You will need your strength for such a journey." Then she turned and set off again leaving me absolutely stunned at her gesture. I'd no doubt as to the value of these two little eggs to her. A quick rummage in my tank bag turned up my pot of salt and a new bar of soap. I'd read that these were always in short supply in the more remote areas and knew that I must give something back. When I caught up with her and put them in her wrinkled hands, she bobbed a little curtsey and then cried. It seemed that things of little value back home had great value out here, but it wasn't so much the objects, but the point of the gifts that felt so important. I'd just been part of something special and found myself thinking that this was one of the things that I'd not forget when the trip was over.

Keeping to the back roads I made it to the Central Highlands again, and having persuaded myself that the views in the late afternoon light were well worth the risk of not finding a room, I ended up in trouble. But, on the way to trouble the views were spectacular. Three quarters of Kenya's land is absolutely useless for farming; it's too dry, but here the land was lush and green. Everywhere I looked, the hills were covered with life in full bloom. The climate is cool and pleasant from the altitude, and looking around me I wondered how different the scene would have been had history taken another course. It could have stayed in the hands of the locals and if it had there would have been no

163

ordered colonial farms, the remnants of which you can still see. Or the area might have changed the history of the whole world. Back in 1903 the British Government made the Jewish people an offer. They could have the Central Highlands as a Jewish homeland. Israel would have been in the heart of Africa! Was this the ultimate in colonial arrogance? To offer to a third party, land which wasn't really theirs to give? In any case, the Jewish council turned it down.

By now it was late, and the only hotels with parking yards were full. None would let me park my bike, even for a fee. I explained my problem to the manager of one of the hotels that did at least have space for me. He listened carefully and said that he quite understood why I didn't want to leave my bike on the road. "Not to worry", he told me. "When the restaurant closes you can put your bike in there."

Perfect, except for the fifteen steps that led up to the entrance of the hotel. I'd never ridden up steps before and wasn't sure I'd get the bike up there by pushing, even with help. Help was something that I didn't like to ask for. I'd been given enough so far and it was time to stand on my own two feet. So, asking people to stand aside, I revved up and went for it - made it up three steps and promptly fell off. A crowd began to collect as I took some luggage off and had another go, this time with a longer run at it. I fell again and painfully bit my tongue. Now I was angry as well as stubborn. More luggage came off, and clearing the even larger crowd who had come to watch the mad white man, I took an even longer run. This time the bike stalled just at the last step, but there was enough momentum to carry us over the top. It was only then that I saw the cleaning lady who'd started washing the reception area's green stone floor. The tyres hit the wet and over we went. The bike slid on her smooth sided panniers to the wall at the end of the corridor where her tyres kissed the paint with two dainty black marks. At the same time the foot peg had scraped a little gully across the immaculate green. Moments later the manager stormed around the corner. I expected to be thrown right back down the stairs, but instead he rushed over apologising for any damage done to the bike and insisted that I should at least have a free breakfast in the morning!

I parked the bike between the already set tables and made a discreet exit towards the sanctuary of my room. Perhaps next time I'd not be quite so stubborn and I'd ask for help.

The bike kept on getting me into funny, oddball situations that I'd never have got into without it. But, it caused me problems too. Sometimes I could well do without the hassles but at other times the bike-led adventure was a gem.

There were parking problems again the following night. I couldn't afford another mid price range hotel so ended up in a bargain basement establishment. Shared toilets, a bucket instead of a shower, cockroaches and bed-bug splatters on the wall were the main features of a hotel that I suspected hadn't seen a tourist for years, if ever. A rusty old hasp that you put your own padlock in was the only security against the dodgy looking characters that were hanging around in the yard. The yard walls were a cobbled together collection of rough branches, beaten out old oil drums and mouldy reed matting. I worried for the bike, not because anyone would steal her as a whole, but as in Moyale, I suspected that the mirrors, lights and switches would be fair game.

The night watchman came on duty soon after dark and I found him admiring the bike. He asked permission to touch it, which was probably a good sign. I told him that he could even sit on it all night if he promised to make sure that she was all there in the morning. He nodded excitedly and I gave him some money, telling him that there would be a little more and that we could go for a ride in the morning if he did his job well. He rushed off, returning quickly with a useful looking bow and a quiver of arrows. My last sight of him before going to sleep was a shadowy figure sitting side-saddle on the bike, his bow raised and an arrow on the string. His arms were doing slow sweeps across the yard. The bike was fine in the morning and when I drove him home, his wife cooked me pancakes for breakfast over the wood fire in front of their hut. In spite of the inevitable audience, life felt pretty good.

In so many places, village and town life seemed to centre on the market. They were always a hive of activity, full of noise and more often than not, good humour. By now I'd learnt enough simple Swahili to be able to bargain, and I'd also been around enough to know what the real prices of things should be. 'Tourist' price was often more than double the price the locals paid. I was quite happy to accept never paying exactly local price for things but I always felt that tourist price was a way of ripping off people who were out of their depth or were still on the western 'must be there yesterday' rush. Bargaining without full use of the local lingo was hard, but I was getting there and in many places I found people who spoke English to a degree and then, with my bit of Swahili, the whole business would become fun. My normal shopping list on Jersey would take me about half an hour to fill in a supermarket. In Africa, it would take me two days just to find and bargain for the basics. Sometimes it was a real chore but other times I felt on form and the whole business could get very funny.

The market this day was the type where the local ladies had turned out in their best and brightest wraparound clothes. They'd laid equally bright blankets on the ground on top of which they had lovingly displayed whatever they were selling. I could have bought anything from fresh bewhiskered river fish to bunches of bananas whose fingers were at least ten unblemished inches long. The ladies all seemed to be fat and jolly, though all on closer inspection had shrewdly aware eyes. Every one seemed to be called Mama, and the day's business felt like it was a traditional game that just had to be played. I wandered, feasting my eyes on the displays until there was a lady whose papayas seemed perfect in colour and softness. I'd become a real fan of papaya so couldn't resist trying my luck. Fortunately I had on my best market clothes. Everything was clean, but patched and faded – far from the wealthy tourist look. Squatting, backside on my heels, I watched Mama's rolls of fat jiggle as she both finished dealing with her customer, and watched me out of the corner of her eye.

Papaya not only tastes good but it's a medicinal fruit too. Eaten very ripe with lemon juice, it helps stop diarrhoea. When over-ripe, it makes a good poultice to draw out infection from a wound, and down on the coast they use it on sea urchin spines. Step on one of these and they pierce the skin – the area can become infected very quickly. The white sap of a young papaya mixed with paraffin lamp oil works wonders. The chemical reaction between the two forms a rubbery skin that keeps dirt out of the wound, but that's only the bonus. The other chemical reaction actually dissolves the spines in the wound so there's no messy digging around to get them out.

Back with Mama and my stomach, the game was on. "Mama, how much do you want for this papaya?" I asked. She looked me up and down and then looking me straight in the eye told me a price that would have caused an outrage in anyone other than a tourist. I grinned at her and asked her if this was a special papaya. "Is it full of gold?" Paying her compliments about its girth and colour and telling her what a wonderful farm she must have to be able to produce such fine fruit, I told her that I couldn't possibly pay more than what I knew was a little less than the local price. Bargaining always felt as if it started with drawing out the battle lines. We dickered back and forth, both enjoying the game. The crowd that gathered to watch the show seemed to be enjoying it too, and were enthusiastically giving us both advice. The gap between us narrowed, very slowly.

"Mama, look at my clothes, I'm not one of these rich tourists. Your clothes are finer than mine yet you still want this crazy price." She looked me up and down again, as did the crowd. The price came down a little more – we'd been at it for twenty minutes. Our claims became more and more outrageous as the minutes clicked by and we both struggled to keep a straight face. "I have ten children, a lazy husband and two cows to feed, I could only let you have it for this", she said giving me a price still much higher than she had charged her last customer. Inspiration clinched it for me. "Mama, I have ten hungry wives and one child to feed and you still want me to pay that?" There was a moment's silence. Then she, laughing along with everyone else, told me to "Just take it. You are too thin and will need much strength for ten wives!" I had the feeling that she'd be dining out on the tale for weeks. We'd grinned at each other and Swahili'd goodbyes - after I'd paid the local price.

Chapter Ten

"Thinking Time"

'The World is not the way it seems.'

Ted Simon.

Back at Mama Roche's, some travellers' 'couple of days of R&R' turned into a couple of months. One long-haired hippie from Australia, who travelled almost everywhere bare-foot, had planted a garden around his tent and had tamed the local chameleons to feed from his fingers. He was the only person I'd ever met who could catch flies by reaching up and grabbing them out of the air as they flew by. The chameleons were getting fat.

Determined to see some wild life, I linked up with two Israeli guys, two Aussie girls and an American called John. Together we hired a 4x4 and set off to tour the Masai Mara National Park. Motorbikes aren't allowed in the parks – no 'meals on wheels' for the local inhabitants – none without a can opener that is.

Much to my surprise, I really enjoyed being on four wheels for a change. I no longer sat for hour after hour listening to imagined danger noises from the bike's engine, and could enjoy the scenery to the sides as well as the usual pothole view to the front. It was also an amazing sense of freedom not to have to climb into all the bike gear every day. Asking for directions was simple without the deadening bulk of my helmet muffling whatever reply I might get, and my gloveless hands started to develop a tan. It was also very nice not to have to pick the bike up several times a day.

However, I was in no danger of getting bored. We broke down twice and had to have parts flown in. Once we camped on top of an ants' nest after pitching the tents in the dark. This, much to the amusement of our Masai guide, had us hopping and bopping around the bush by torchlight. Hours later, we could only laugh too. Our luck was amazing with the wildlife, and we got closer than I'd dreamed possible to cheetahs and lions. Elephants strolled past us in the bush and grunting hippos trampled the grass around our tents at night. We saw hundreds of buffalo run and the amazingly graceful giraffe and antelope glide and skip their way across the plains.

The 'Mara' seemed rather an odd set up really. The park's rolling landscape is a stunning almost treeless collection of camouflage colours. The skies were heavy with a layer of almost purple rain clouds, under which the sun would sneak in the early morning and in the late afternoon. This light was a photographer's dream. In fact, the park was packed with them, not to mention the crowds of game spotters like us. We took to exploring the bush surrounding the park in an attempt to take photos that didn't have the wheels of someone else's 4x4 or safari-striped mini-bus in them. Even then it wasn't easy, but we did see a lot of game and I felt privileged to be there. The animals seemed bored with the constant presence of camera-clicking visitors but not, I suspected, so bored that a quick 'take away' wouldn't have been of interest, should some foolish tourist get over enthusiastic about close-ups.

The Masai themselves were an interestingly odd set up too. They seemed to be a proud people, and handsome. That word is almost outmoded now but it fits these people, men and women, quite perfectly. The men wear very little clothing and scarlet is their favourite colour. Their cloaks were always this vivid red, but each of the warriors would have his own way of wearing it. The women were equally flamboyant. Their clothes seemed to be mainly made out of leather, and their legs, arms and necks were coiled with brass loops. Some had dressed especially for we tourists and though that made it feel a bit fake, it really didn't matter. It was well worth seeing the clothes of a wedding party without having to hang around for months waiting on the off chance for an unlikely invite to such a celebration. The women had added brilliantly-coloured beaded bands to their wrists and ankles. They wore matching 'sporrans' (for want of a better word) over their leather kilts, and around their necks they'd clipped dinner plate size necklaces made out of thousands of tiny beads that had been strung and woven together in amazingly vibrant geometric designs.

I got the feeling that the Masai are struggling with the modern world. Traditionally they are nomadic, cattle-loving warrior people, but colonialism started to change their lifestyle and tourism seemed to be continuing the change. They still hang onto many of their customs, though I wondered how long some would survive. The men are still circumcised and their initiation to manhood is carried out as of old, in age groups rather than as individuals. Tradition says that when they eventually become warriors they have to kill a lion single-handed to prove their manhood. The local lions didn't seem too worried about that anymore.

I'm not normally squeamish, but was quite happy not to be invited to a Masai dinner party. The tribe eat very little game meat and almost never kill their cattle. But they do harvest them for food. Small taps are fitted into the jugular vein of a cow to make blood letting easy. The blood that's drawn is then mixed with milk, either fresh or curdled. Sometimes a small amount of cattle urine is also added to the mix to increase its potency. Nope, not for me thank you.

Eventually, heavy rain turned us north to the arid region around Lake Turkana. The 4x4 took us effortlessly over roads that the bike and I would have had to work hard on. The air here was balmy and the Jade Sea really was a fabulous milky, blue-green shade of jade. We all chanced a swim with the hope that the crocodiles were full of fish and not a bit interested in us. That night, we camped not far from the lakeshore and John and I sat out under the stars for hours. The night was so warm we were quite comfortable to sit in just shorts. It was so still, so clear and so unaffected by man-made light, that there was the constant feeling that we could reach up and touch any one of the magnificent array that was spread across the darkness. I counted five shooting stars.

The next day, John kept his shirt but lost his underwear. We were walking through the lakeshore village of Loiyangalani, rubber-necking as all good tourists should do. John had washed his socks and underwear before we'd set off and as the air in the desert was so lacking in moisture, he decided that if he hung them on his rucksack they would dry very quickly. After a while we realised that we were being followed. A wizened old man was hard on our heels and seemed fascinated with the washing. He was particularly interested in the underwear. John, thinking that the man may well have never seen a pair of western underwear before, stopped to show his Y fronts to him. The old man took them from John and thinking that they were a gift, gave him a beaming grin of thanks, and left. For once, it was John's turn to be speechless, and that didn't happen often.

The spectacular looking Samburu people who inhabit the land between the highlands and the lake are related in customs and looks to the Rendile to the east. So, I was partly prepared for the ochre coloured braided hair and beads of the men, but not for the magnificent beaded jewellery of the women. The Samburu live in their beads and though they are also related to the Masai, they seemed to be a very different people in many ways. The young men made me think of peacocks. They were tall and arrogant with their bright red blanket capes thrown over their shoulders, worn with the panache of high fashion models. Many of their spears were trimmed below their long blades with fluffy black ostrich feathers. Their ear lobes were looped with holes to carry ornaments and cylindrical snuffboxes. Besides their spears, the only thing they seemed to carry were wooden headrests so that they could lie down without wrecking their amazing orange-red hair plaits. We stopped in several of their villages because one of the Israelis had discovered that the tribesmen would pick up semi-precious stones from the desert and were very happy to trade or sell them. While Gabby traded in stones, the rest of us bought jewellery. It was simple stuff, but colourful and really well made with whatever came to hand. At first the women treated us with reserve, then with friendly good humour and finally lots of laughter.

Back once again at Mama's, the six of us parted ways knowing that we had just seen some of Kenya at its best. The trip had been a complete success though the 4x4 looked a little the worse for wear. Although I'd enjoyed riding on four wheels for a change, now I couldn't wait to get back on the bike; being inside a car had made me appreciate the way my senses seemed to work so much harder when I wasn't sheltered inside a metal box. I was also keen to get back to a style of travelling that didn't need any more group decisions. A travelling group of six relative strangers was sometimes hard going.

171

On a whim, I invited John to head south across Tanzania with me. I'd enjoyed his mad sense of humour on the safari and he'd been pondering what to do with his last few weeks in Africa. Of course I'd only ridden once with the bike fully loaded, and with a passenger. John was about double the height and weight of little Teddy in Adis Ababa, but by now I'd got rid of the top box that had caused a lot of the handling problems. I'd also disposed of a lot more gear. In the end, it hadn't been hard to do. I'd traded clothes that hardly got worn, for carvings which I then posted home, and had eaten my way through the food supply until there was only two days' food for two left. The word had also got around that if anyone needed a spare part for a BMW R80 GS, then Sam was the man. In the end I'd managed to trade, sell or give away a lot of the spare parts I'd so enthusiastically bought. It had been harder to get rid of them, but the bike was going really well. A set of rear brake shoes can easily last the life of a BMW and I had carried a spare set from England! In all, I jettisoned 15 kilo's and helped a lot of other bikers. I also decided to leave behind the extra fuel and water containers, losing another 20 kilos. The main fuel tank's forty-three litres should be enough and the leak in the water tank had just become a frustrating problem.

One of the second hand shops in Nairobi supplied a bright yellow helmet for John. It wasn't exactly stylish but hopefully it was functional. The law in Kenya states that 'a helmet must be worn at all times when moving on a motorcycle'. But, it doesn't state which part of the body it has to be worn on so the local bucks buzz around with well-protected elbows. The other travellers at Mama's organised a tough canvas jacket and a pair of gloves as the rest of John's bike gear.

By nine on the day of our departure, the Nairobi rush hour had done its worst and we were ready to go. With six foot three of John, his rucksack and my gear on board, there wasn't a lot of bike to be seen and for the first time I really began to wonder if this was such a good idea after all. We wobbled the first few metres with John bravely saying nothing. Our friends came to wave us off at the gates to Mama's only to end up lifting us off the ground. I hadn't even made it onto the road without dropping us onto the deck.

"Just go for it", John advised, so I did. Before we knew it, we were out of the city and free. It didn't take long to adapt my riding style to deal with all the extra weight and the road was good - the tyres hummed and the day began to warm up. The traffic eased and the factories disappeared behind us. In front of us loomed the green slopes and snowy top of Kilimanjaro, the tallest mountain in Africa. It was incredible to think that this enormous hunk of rock hadn't been discovered by the 'civilised' world until 1848, less than a hundred and fifty years ago. The phrase 'A young history spread across an ancient land' slipped into mind.

The Spectrum guide to Kenya states that, 'Driving in Kenya is for the fatalistic and suicidal. Too many drivers there have a blatant disregard for speed limits or traffic laws. Besides a good map, essential equipment for visitors who wish to drive is a large supply of sedatives!' I'd survived without sedatives, but perhaps I'd become a touch more fatalistic.

We waved goodbye to Kenya and to the official who seemed to think that our leaving his country was a personal affront. The sandy metres of no man's land were bordered by rusting barbed wire and rows of market stalls, most of which were piled with carvings for sale to the bus-loads of tourists on their way from the parks of Kenya to the Serengeti National Park in Tanzania.

The queue for immigration was a line made up of clean, neatly clad holidaymakers. Our dusty bike clothes and fly-splattered helmets made the sweating official raise an eyebrow when it was our turn. I was conscious of the gap that the other tourists were leaving around us as if we were carriers of some sort of disease. But I couldn't help a grin with the thought that should any of them decide to talk to us they might find out that our disease was no worse than a large dose of bad influence. I relished my freedom as the officer asked me how long we were visiting Tanzania. The plan was just two weeks for the ride, but I enjoyed the looks around us as we casually asked for a couple of months. As I walked away I told myself not to be a travel snob; I was lucky.

The Customs office was another ball game. It was 'third degree' time and this made me feel that I was paying a sort of penance for my behaviour next door. The bike's papers were shuffled and re-shuffled, and I started to get worried as a conversation over the paperwork was held with stern looks being flung in my direction. One of the officers disappeared out of the back door with some of my forms and I wondered if they'd ever be seen again. This was becoming a re-run of a story a biker at Mama's had told me. He'd been crossing into Zaire from the north and the official had hidden his yellow fever certificate under the table with no real attempt at stealth. The official had then innocently asked where the form was.

You don't cross many borders in Africa without it, so my friend was sweating. After considerable coming and going the official had told him that, as he'd obviously lost his form, for a fee of fifty dollars he had a friend who could make him a new one. With no choice, the fifty dollars was handed over and he was allowed to get on his way, with of course, his original certificate. The official would probably drink a beer or two extra that night and would be able to feed his family for another few weeks. There had been lots of stories floating around about the situation in Zaire. One of them was that officials throughout the country hadn't been paid for months. Corruption had been bad there for years, now it was rife and becoming more extreme.

Much of Africa's bribery was perhaps another bizarre sort of 'Robin Hood' way of spreading the wealth. Was it so bad? It was the oil that made the 'system' work. But that didn't mean that I had to like it and I suppose, rather selfishly, I still didn't want to have to pay a bribe to anyone. Especially if I'd done nothing wrong. All in, it was pure corruption and that the Collins English dictionary describes as 'morally wrong'. Morally wrong? To whom? Me, a stranger and visitor to these lands? Had I the right to judge the system, a fully established system at that? Perhaps I should be just looking at the bribery as a sort of road tax. I hadn't paid any of that so far either. I think what bothered me was the lack of regulation and the indiscriminate way the coercion was carried out. I thought about what Babu the truck driver had said back in Isiolo. It seemed that often, lots of little people got hurt to line a few individuals' pockets. I'd heard a story in Kenya that in fact the policeman on the checkpoint who took the bribe would keep very little of it for himself. Most would go to his boss and his boss's boss and so on. The more money a boss got, the more powerful he would become, and the more money he would get. I'd also been told that in some countries a policeman would have bought his position and would have a weekly 'standing order' to pay to keep his job.

But the Tanzanians did nothing so obvious as that Zaire official. They just used subtle threat and innuendo to make me realise that nothing and nobody were going anywhere until some money had been handed under the table. Faced with this it made sense to try the stupid tourist bit and to pretend that this tourist had no idea what the problem was. By now I was really happy that I'd not completed the currency importation forms correctly. All tourists were supposed to state exactly how many travellers cheques and how much cash they were bringing into the country. This had been quite normal at border crossings but somehow all the US dollars that were stuffed up the frame on the bike seemed to get forgotten each time. This was my 'insurance', my bank and my emergency money. I was sure now that if they'd known about my 'bank' money, their veiled requests would have been a lot more enthusiastic. Eventually they almost threw me out of the office in disgust but my money was still in my pocket, the frame-stash was untouched and my paperwork was in order. After a moment of satisfaction at having 'won', the experience left me feeling rather flat. Almost as if I was in the wrong.

John had been keeping an eye on the bike and luggage while all this was going on. Having answered the usual run of 'Where are you coming from' questions for me, he'd been getting rather worried at how long I'd been. "Let's just go", I said, and we made a speedy departure. "Welcome to Tanzania", I shouted to him as I yelled the story over my shoulder into the slipstream. It was another first for me and another lesson learned. Language and cultural barriers could be used to one's advantage with a little thought and time. Playing the respectful but ignorant tourist had come quite naturally, but the bad taste in my mouth was still there.

With this border crossing there didn't seem to be much of a difference in the landscape from one side to the other. Low scrubby  bush land surrounded us and there didn't appear to be anything new to look at, until we saw what appeared to be a series of logs suspended from the tallest trees. This was definitely worth stopping for. As we walked closer we could see a stream of bees flying in and out of the logs - they were beehives. Then we saw the hut that was tucked away in the bush and the tall Masai who was watching us. But this was a Masai with a difference. Unlike his Kenyan cousins who took pride in their vivid red robes, this man was dressed in indigo. The rest of him was little different though. He had the same type of spear, same hairstyle and from what we could see, the same sort of jewellery. His hut was built in the same way too. Further down the road we saw more Masai dressed in similar shades of purple. Perhaps this was one of the changes that had come about over the years as a result of the colonialists dividing up the land to suit themselves. In many cases they hadn't paid any attention to the local peoples' historical and tribal borders. The Masai tribe had been split by one of these lines on an early map. How much else in their lives had been changed by this particular line?

The main road swung us east and as it did so we found ourselves riding through giant sisal plantations. For many years this crop, the raw material for rope, had been Tanzania's main export. But times change and I pondered on when I'd last used string made from sisal, and couldn't remember. The blue-green spiky plants stretched away from us in orderly lines towards Mt. Kilimanjaro. The mountain-top snow gleamed in the azure blue sky as we cruised on, debating whether to attempt climbing up to it. At the town of Moshi, which is the main kick off point for such expeditions, I was quietly delighted that it was going to be far too expensive for either of us to have a go. The cost of guides, permits and equipment soon added up. An adventurous nutter called Christian Gallissian had actually ridden a trials bike up the mountain but I didn't think that the BMW qualified as suitable, so didn't worry about that challenge either. We settled for the night in a quiet little lodging house and enjoyed the mountain instead from the bougainvillea and hibiscus-clad balcony. While cooking our dinner on the camping stove, the snow up above shone orange, red and finally a deep cool purple before the cicadas began to sing in the trees and the mountain turned into a black shadow. The border hassles slipped into another time and we fell asleep to the sounds of African voices talking quietly in the room next door.

Rain on the tin roof woke us in the morning. The world in the early light was a hundred shades of grey and didn't look at all inviting to two wheelers. Whilst pulling on my rain gear I pondered the advantages of glass and metal boxes on four wheels. The map said that the next section of road was dirt and under construction. The locals looked at the bike, the sky, us and shook their heads. When we asked when the rain would stop, they just shrugged. I had a mental re-run of the road south from the border with Ethiopia, and this time it would be two-up. We decided to risk it before the rain made the road any worse. In the event, it was fine, and I learnt a little more. The tyres coped and John sat like a veteran pillion rider, even enjoying the soggy view, or so he said. But I breathed a little sigh of relief as we hit the asphalt road to the Usambara mountains. With a series of hairpin bends, this took us up through the cloud and into bright sunshine.

The hillsides were a mass of cultivation and the local farmers had planted just about every inch of land regardless of whether it was level or not. A tea plantation sprawled, neatly groomed, and hugging the higher slopes beside us. We rode through the trees and onto the murram (red earth) roads of the bustling little town of Lushoto. Sticking to our budget we chose one of the small local hotels to stay in. Riding up the steep, heavily rutted track to the 'Kilimani', I wondered what the ride back down the track would be like if the rain ventured up this high. The hotel rooms were around an enclosed courtyard and were incredibly clean. The water in the showers was horribly cold but

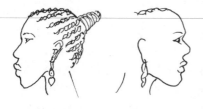

the four ladies who owned and ran the place were a delight. They happily rearranged the furniture in their front room, which was also the entrance, so that I could get the bike through into the yard. They didn't seem to mind that she was covered in filth, and the mud had the good grace to stay firmly plastered onto the bike.

We'd made our way up into the mountains because several people had told us about a spectacular viewpoint. Each had said, "Don't miss it". We'd only walked a few hundred metres out of town when a small boy quietly adopted us. With hardly a word, he just assumed that we'd need to be shown the way. He led us along the winding track through some shady deep green woods. The tall trees were strung with lianas whilst down at our level, banana trees lived in apparent peace alongside sweet smelling herbs and small bushes. Many of the trees were eucalyptus or evergreens and their scents mingled marvellously with those from the herbs to make the walk a delightful assault on the senses. The tallest yucca trees I've ever seen jutted out of the undergrowth, and we seemed to be passing through gecko land as our way was literally lined with these rather cute, scampering lizards. I particularly like them because there's no finer meal for them than a mosquito! Armies of red or black ants marched forcefully across the narrowing trail in thin, dark 'motorway' lines; I wondered, in scale to us, just how fast they were moving and how long they could keep up their insistent pace. The young lad led us on past mountain houses that clung precariously to the steep slopes in places where not a lot could grow, while around them every inch of flatter land was cultivated.

After an hour or so of walking we found it. At a jumble of rocks the world suddenly seemed to fall away at our feet. We felt as if it was almost possible to see from one side of Tanzania to another. I've always felt uncomfortable with great heights but beat part of the problem by making myself learn to rock climb at fourteen. If other people could do it then, I reasoned, so could I. Even so, I was still careful not to look straight down. The world stretched out before us. The main road cut a red slash across the beautiful savannah and the clouds overhead cast their ever-moving, ever-changing shadows across the multi-coloured plains. Sitting looking at this view, I realised that Africa had slowly changed me in a way I hadn't been aware of. Colour now really lived for me wherever I seemed to look. I'd never really been aware of nature's ability to produce so many colours or so conscious of its ability to make even the most outrageous ones match and blend.

Hawks hung effortlessly on the thermals and updraughts. Their lazy, elegant flight was a pleasure to watch, particularly as we were watching them from above. From the rim we could see that the rains had been falling in a band just along the bottom of the mountains. If the road had been built only two kilometres further away, the day's riding could have been in the dry.

Recently the local hawks had been learning new tricks. A couple of hang-gliding Wazungu with a nicely bizarre but potentially achievable idea had been in town. Fledgling hawks had been trained to fly with the two hang-gliders. They would set out from the viewpoint with the hawks sitting on the glider cross bars. When they had all flown below a certain altitude, the birds would take off in search of the hot rising air of a thermal current. They would circle in the current until the guys flew over and had gained enough height to fly on again. The hawks would then come to rest on the bars once more, until the gliders had gone too low the next time. Apparently the team had even done a night flight using the day's stored heat from the land, and fluorescent ribbons on the hawks' legs. It all worked, according to the story.

We slept that night next to bedside trays of lime green condoms. Perhaps the ladies were following some sort of government instruction that was an attempt to cut down the spread of Aids. I couldn't resist slipping one in my pocket as a souvenir and good luck charm. Next morning the tin roof told us that the rains had followed us up the mountain. Thinking again about the dirt track down from the hotel and knowing that I was almost certain to fall off, the urge was just to get on with it, to get it out of the way. I'd try to do as little damage as possible to both the bike and myself when the inevitable happened. After a breakfast of an incredibly pale omelette which looked as if someone had stolen the yolk, and toast that tasted of the charcoal brazier over which it had been literally blackened, the ladies all came and stood in the rain to say goodbye. Their smiles told us that we would be welcome anytime and that they wished us a good journey. At least, that's what we thought they said, as there was hardly a word of any language in common between us. They spoke little Swahili, just the language of the mountains. We'd had some great 'conversations' with them too. Smiles, gestures, drawings in the air and a genuine feeling of goodwill had always seemed to work. John wisely elected to walk down the track while I did the falling off in front of an open-mouthed audience of ten - the neighbours had come to watch too.

Down on the edge of the plains it was still raining and the road was grim. We waddled off through the greasy ruts but John was his usual implacable self all the way to the next stretch of asphalt. I was exhausted by that time and we were both muddy and soaked so decided to book into the first hotel we could find with safe parking for the bike. Then I discovered something. Three hours of mud and an hour of hairpin bends ago, I had left my passport and travellers' cheques under my pillow in the ladies hotel. I couldn't believe I'd been so dumb. Another three-hour ride in the mud was daunting but I had to go back, and quickly. Maybe the four ladies were as honest as they'd seemed. But the prospect of riding back was too much so I decided to try my luck at hitching and stood out in the rain with the mud washing off my waterproofs. No more than five minutes later, a jeep stopped. The driver was going my way and my luck was in, he was going straight to Lushoto. Better still, he was only going to be there for half an hour and then he was coming back.

One of the ladies saw me slipping my way up the dreaded slope and rushed back inside. Moments later all four of them were there, each with a different version on their face of 'look what we found, yes we are honest, how did you manage to leave them behind and aren't you lucky it was us?' I hugged them, and gave them ten times the price of our room to try and say thanks.

Back at the hotel, John was still shaking his head. Buying me a beer, he said, "Sam, for sure you've got someone looking out for you." On the up side was the fact that I'd actually been able to see the world along the muddy roadside and from two angles too. The first time, all concentration had been on just keeping the bike upright and moving in roughly the right direction, though I did take the time to curse at how painful some of the heavy raindrops had been on my face. The open face helmet was definitely cooler than a full-face version but some of those drops had really hit with a stinging thump. African rain wasn't much fun on two wheels, but at least it was warm rain.

We talked about a story we'd heard at Mama's. A tourist had been up on the Kenyan east coast island of Lamu. This guy was on his first ever trip away from home and by all accounts was decidedly green. He made even me with my occasional stupidity feel like an old pro. He took life up on the island as if he were at home. He would wander everywhere with his Rolex watch, his Nikon camera and a good chunk of money in his pocket. He dressed in nice western clothes and gave money to children. One night he got drunk in a bar with some friends and then set off to walk the two and a half unlit kilometres back to his hotel. On the way he apparently became tired and sat down to rest. He woke up in the morning, still on the track, wearing only his underwear and T-shirt. Next to him squatted a man in a loincloth and an old shirt. It turned out that this man and his friend had found him, but had been unable to move or wake him up. So, they had stripped him of anything he had of value and the friend had taken the things to his hut. He had slept guarding them all night while the squatting man stayed to make sure nothing happened to the tourist. They walked to the friend's hut and there everything was. Nothing was missing. The tourist gave them a big handshake and fifty dollars each. This was more than half a year's wages for them. On hearing this story, I thought 'good for him'. The men probably hadn't expected anything at all, but the thank-you 'gift' felt like it was exactly the right thing to do. I kept on hearing stories about people who had so little, yet were so honest and would give so much of themselves to help someone in trouble.

181

Perhaps, unlike the media's apparent view of the world, most people are in fact inherently good. We hear so much of the bad things that a few people do; we easily forget all the every day fine things that most of the other people do. Now, months away from reading my last newspaper and equally long away from hearing radio news, I was free enough to think about such things. When you spend hour upon hour astride a motorcycle, with a helmet on and a strong slipstream to snatch away any attempt at conversation, you have a lot of thinking time (in between the potholes anyway). Nearly everyone I'd met on the trip so far had been great. Perhaps to begin with I'd been so cautious that I'd steered clear of anyone who looked even remotely dodgy and now maybe my senses did the steering automatically. It was time to start looking for them, but how to recognise them? Should the customs officers' behaviour class them as dishonest, or should I just accept that in true African style, they were just making a living?

This thinking time was one of the things I'd started to really love about being on the bike. It was my time when, mostly I was in control, and as a rule interruptions were few. In a way the bike was making me remote from people, but this time to myself allowed me to keep my sanity and perspective in a world that I did not know, and was having to constantly re-learn. As soon as I got off the bike, I would automatically be back in the incredible vibrancy of African life. I almost always had the energy to deal with it, to experience it with a sort of freshness and to learn from it. Instead of the solitary hours making me into some sort of two-wheeled hermit, they actually made me want to go out and meet and talk to people. The bike was working well in more ways than one.

Just before the capital city of Dar Es Salaam, the main road swings west again and cuts through the Mikumi National Park. Obeying the signs we slowed right down. A running antelope would do a lot of damage to the bike and of course, the overloaded BMW could do a lot of damage to it. Our first sight of game was a rounded grey hump that seemed to be swaying through the treetops. An elephant, and to the left as we watched, in strolled a group of giraffe. Their long tongues were hooking around the tender green shoots at the treetops. For those few moments, the road was traffic free, leaving us sitting in near silence to watch these amazing beasts: right place, right time again.

I'd read about 'upside down trees' – baobabs – and was determined to see some. They were an early entry on my top one hundred list of things to see on the trip. Tanzania was supposed to be one of the places to see them at their best. We didn't even have to hunt them out. In the south we rode round a hilly corner and straight into a baobab forest. With not a leaf in sight it was easy to understand the local story about these trees. Fat grey trunks were topped by root-like branches that made them look exactly as if the gods had been angry one stormy night and had ripped the trees from the ground only to thrust them back, roots to the air. To me, they looked like an army of Tolkien's fairy tale trees marching silently across the valley. The locals say that a spirit inhabits each tree and that offerings must be made. Fourteen days' notice must be given to it if the tree needs to be cut down. The spirit should have time to find a new tree to live in.

With the ride across Tanzania coming to an end far too quickly, we knew that we'd had no more than a taste of what the country had to offer, but the bike had given us the freedom to make the most of it. This far into the trip I'd already accepted that there was no chance of seeing all there was to see in each country; the best plan was to be selective and that way to leave time to really look at things. Just as importantly, this left time for the unexpected. The theory had worked in Uganda and was still working, but I knew that we were missing a lot. Tanzania is not only home to Africa's highest point but it's lowest as well. Lake Tanganyika holds that record at 358m below sea level. It's a major part of the Rift Valley. In an early massive upheaval of the land, the river that flowed through was cut to form the lake. It holds one sixth of the world's fresh water, and is supposed to be full of fish that exist nowhere else in the world. They are reputed to have descended from the original couple of species. One has remained unchanged since before the time of the dinosaurs, while the other evolved to form very individual looking types of fish, each with their own little niche in the lake's food chain. There are probably species of fish no one has ever seen, and statistics say that there are enough of them to provide a sustainable food source for all the surrounding nations. It was a beautiful place I'd have to save for another time.

In the south of the country the rainy season had all but finished and the land was lush with a riot of colour. Plants stood strong and green, and trails of flowers hung from the trees and bushes. The road changed from potholes to immaculate asphalt that was a little touch of heaven to ride on. The locals told us that foreign aid money had been put to good use and slowly the roads around the country were being rebuilt. The economy of Tanzania didn't have a chance to improve without the ability to move people and goods around quickly. The bus drivers were loving it and John and I steered well clear of them as they came hurtling past us in one direction or another. 'Foot to the floor' seemed to be the only way to drive their loads of people, goats, chickens, bundles of sugar cane, snotty-nosed children, and an occasional numbed, uncomfortable backpacker. We decided that these grossly overloaded buses looked like hell on wheels but that, in the end, it probably did beat walking. Stickers on the front of one said 'God is with me'. John commented that he hoped that his bus back to Kenya was that one. I didn't envy him the task of curling his six foot three frame into one of the cramped seats for the long hours back to the border. He wrote to me several months later saying that his bus had crashed going down a hill. The brakes had failed and the only way the driver could stop was to grind the bus into the hillside until friction and a large rock had eventually done their job. He also told me that riding on the bike with me was at least marginally safer than the bus. Bearing in mind what happened to us next, I was impressed; as you know from chapter one, the accident saga of the accident and jail was about to roll.

Chapter Eleven
"The Chief's Second Wife"
'He is free who lives as he chooses.'

My diary entry for the first day after being set free by the Mbeya court read, 'Mental block! Can't remember! I must have been excited at being a free man!' With the events of the last days I wasn't surprised that I'd lost this day. Even ordinarily, sometimes there was so much going on that my diary didn't get written for days. Occasionally, the pages in my journal would say that there had actually been a day of my life, but somehow I would have completely forgotten what had happened. It's a really odd feeling to 'lose' a whole day, but without a regular daily pattern days would sometimes disappear or blend into one another. This was when diary discipline was so important. My diary was the perfect way to record quirky observations that otherwise would be forgotten. In a way it was also a comfort in that while writing it I made a point of taking time and quiet space to reflect on the good as well as the harder things that happened.

The entry for the following day said 'Quality time with Joseph'. He'd shown us a part of the city where young lads sat in the dust by an oily and rubbish-strewn truck yard, to carve rubber bushes (vibration spacers) out of old truck tyres. Other boys made their living by scouring the roads for shredded lumps of rubber to sell to the carvers. No doubt the truck drivers themselves would trade wrecked rubber for new bushes. This for me was typical Africa. So much that we at home would discard, here would be reshaped into something useful. I'd been riding for some time with several rubber bushes missing – some had vibrated off in northern Kenya. I liked the novelty of having hand made replacements, so bought several, and some spares.

Joseph invited us to his house for lunch. His wife served up a traditional Tanzanian meal – baked Matoke covered in peanut sauce for starters. Matoke is a type of green banana that I'd come across first in Uganda. It's really rather disgusting raw, but baked or steamed is only mildly horrible. It's a stomach filling opaque stodge that even when cooked, is pretty unpalatable. But the main course was a delightful beef stew with chunks of avocado dropped in at the last minute. This was served with Ugali (Oogali) which is another pretty tasteless, stodgy stomach filler, but it works well with a good savoury gravy. To round off a great meal, she'd found some excellent oranges for dessert. To their surprise we happily ate the dishes local style with our fingers and they seemed really pleased that we would want to do this. Joseph's wife told us that she'd never met muzungus who were so willing to fit in with the local ways. We were just happy to have the opportunity to do so at all, and we'd both long since given up eating with a knife and fork anyway.

Saturday night was party night in the town. One of the hotels had invited a band from Dar Es Salaam and we arrived to find a bare, high-ceilinged room that was echoing with the sounds of taped music. Before long the band started to play and the room livened up. People flocked onto the floor and began to move with wild, uninhibited rhythm. The band was playing in the enthusiastic and fast Zaire style. My feet tapped involuntarily to the drums as I talked to an aid worker – there were only half a dozen sweating white faces mixed in amongst at least a hundred sweating black faces. Pauline, a pretty very dark-skinned girl from Dar who was staying at the St. Joseph, came over and asked for a dance. She was a friendly bubbly girl who I thought was rather cute, so of course I said yes. We danced just about every other dance together that night, but Pauline had more energy than me. I was knackered and if it hadn't been for all the beer that was slipping down, would have been dehydrated too. But I needed this. A night of drinking and dancing finally dispelled the last remaining tension of that eventful week.

John's bus was due to leave at six thirty in the morning. He woke at six fifteen having overslept, and we only just made it in time to find that the bus wasn't there. Eventually we discovered that it had broken down and that it might be there 'sometime' that day. We knew what that meant. On Africa time it could be that day possibly, but just as likely it might be the end of the day, or the day after tomorrow. John's flight date was getting close so we scrabbled around trying to find another bus. We were lucky, though of course seat number two had been booked a long time before. John curled himself into his seat and as the bus set off, he gave me a gritted teeth smile and a laconic wave. I didn't envy him the long uncomfortable journey back to the Kenyan border, and a 'God is with us' sticker was conspicuously missing.

Joseph had turned up to wave goodbye and ever helpful, was able to get a refund on John's original ticket. He then told me that he'd had news that his mother was dying and said it would take him three days to get to her village in the forest. I thought about it for a moment and offered to take him on the bike. It would probably only take us a day and this would be another way of thanking him for all his help. I'd already bought him a cow, but this seemed like a more personal thank you.

When the time came to leave, Joseph was waiting for me wearing a denim jacket that he'd scrounged from somewhere and John's old yellow helmet, which had collected no new scratches in the accident. I'd told Joseph that he had to have decent kit for protection, or the trip wouldn't be on. After the last week he knew exactly what I was talking about. We hit the road and after two hours of riding, a rough sign indicated a narrow track into scrubby trees. "The ride will now be on foot paths", Joseph said. Worrying about being able to find my way out again, it seemed a good idea to take note of some visual landmarks as we went. It was a good job I did because different paths criss-crossed all the time. Fortunately, our path was in a pretty straight line so it was possible to get a rough compass bearing to follow as well. Also, the rains had long gone which made things easier.

So far my route through Africa had only ever run through forests whilst on asphalt. But here, for a while the trees closed in tight around our path, sometimes making it dark enough for the headlight to be needed. It was really pleasant to ride through such a peaceful environment. The scents were richly musty and every so often, a solitary shaft of light would hit us for a blinding moment or two – this was really nature's cathedral. The ride was slow but smooth until we came to an old tree that had fallen across the path. For those on foot it wasn't a major problem, and there was a smooth patch where hundreds of people and their bundles had brushed over the top of it, but for us it was a big hassle. With a great deal of effort and some enthusiastic use of Joseph's very sharp machete, we eventually managed to pull it out of the way. I hoped that there wouldn't be too many more of these; dealing with this one had eaten a lot of time.

There were two more and though not so large, the sky was almost dark by the time we got to the village. Joseph was the oldest son and his family had been very worried he wouldn't make it in time. While he went straight in to see his mother I felt a bit like a spare part and didn't know quite what to do. Eventually Joseph came out with a sad expression on his face; the news wasn't good, but at least we had made it. He explained to his family who I was and what I was doing there. After handshakes and lots of grins all round they showed us a hut to spend the night in. We ate and then I retreated to the bed to read by candlelight - it felt better to leave the family to themselves. Even here it seemed that the extended clan would only get together for weddings and funerals. Some hadn't seen each other for years.

By morning time the old lady had died. She'd been 63, and had lived more than a decade longer than the average life expectancy for a Tanzanian woman. Joseph had told me the day before that he thought she'd had a good life and that her children, grandchildren and great grandchildren, numbered over fifty. The day started with wails of grief, the fires weren't lit and a long line of friends and neighbours began to arrive. I took this as my cue and slipped away with a quiet goodbye to my friend and able helper, Captain Joseph.

Back on the road to the border again, a bum rest was needed. I had a strange feeling that something wasn't right so checked my gear and the bike, but all seemed OK. As I was having a drink of water, a voice from behind said, "Where are you coming from?" A simply dressed young man was standing there watching me with his head slightly tilted to one side. I explained the story and he relaxed. He'd been sitting in the shadows of a roadside bush when I arrived and had been watching ever since.

"Is something wrong?" he asked. For some reason it felt quite OK to tell him about the really odd feeling that was still niggling at me. I'd wondered at first if it had been sixth sense telling me that someone was watching, but as the feeling was still there and we were now talking, it couldn't be that. It felt as if there was something unfinished or something had been forgotten.

I asked him where he was from and Domu talked about his village; it seemed to be quite a long way almost due north from where we were. "It is very remote", he said, "We virtually never see outsiders there." It wasn't far from the edge of the dry interior lands of Tanzania and it seemed that he had set out to find out what went on in the outside world. He was very excited, though trying hard not to show that he was nervous. I recognised his feelings exactly. He'd learned English in mission school, a Scandinavian one I suspected, as his words were accented in a delightfully bizarre way. This reminded me of the first time I'd met a man of Pakistani descent who had been brought up in Glasgow.

As he talked about home, his eyes shone and I realised that my odd mood had gone. Perhaps this village was reachable. Domu knew what a map was but didn't understand it, so there in the dust of the roadside he drew a series of instructions, mostly using town names and then land marks. I copied them carefully into my notebook. He also told me that no one had ever been to the village in a vehicle and that he wasn't sure if it could be done on the bike, but it seemed like a great idea to try. I had enough food and water, and the bike felt amazingly light without either John or Joseph aboard, so pointing her north I set off. I didn't have any doubts about making it, which was odd really as I should have done, and normally would have. Henry David Thoreau wrote 'Go confidently in the direction of your dreams, live the life you have imagined.' Looking back, this was just about the first time on the trip that I was going anywhere with complete confidence. It just felt like the right thing to be doing. Maybe the odd sensation had been the desire to leave Tanzania on the buzz of a high of success and not with the edgy feeling of needing to escape the events of the road to Mbeya.

189

A roadside bus stop hotel housed me for the night in a bare room with a single bed and cockroaches for company. I set off again in the very early morning, happy to have just my own company once more. The landscape had dried out and the previous day had been very warm. Plenty of drink stops combated the heat, the road disappeared and then eventually the sandy track became too soft to ride. If it had been possible to ride in a straight line then perhaps I could have gone further, but the track twisted and curved through the bush. I'd made it over rocky paths and at one stage had followed a dried up riverbed. At this point I could have turned around, but decided to risk hiding the bike in the thorn bushes (with luck I wouldn't pick up any thorns in the tyres). After brushing away the tyre and footmarks (probably quite uselessly, but it made me feel better), I carried on down the track on foot. From Domu's drawings it looked as if there was a two-day walk left to do but at least the land was flatter now. Perhaps naively, I still felt total confidence in what I was doing. Fit, healthy and with plenty of food and water, this trip could be done. I stopped to rest in the hottest three hours of the day and in the afternoon the trail meandered me onwards, passing landmark after landmark that were always roughly where they were supposed to be. That night, sleeping under a thorn bush, there were just the sounds of the wind and the silence of a full moon for company. I didn't see or hear another living thing at all, but my boots did get a thorough shaking out in the morning. I'd read that snakes and scorpions like empty footwear.

By the end of the next day doubt was easing into my mind – the village wasn't where it should have been. My water supply was nearing the point of no return – if I didn't turn back soon, I wouldn't be able to make it back at all. Perhaps I was being stupid but I gave myself another couple of kilometres to find the village. If unlucky, I could still make it back OK. But then, after only another half a kilometre, a straggly bunch of goats let their herder know that there was a stranger around. The startled boy ran off up the track and by the time I'd followed him to the rough-fenced village, the people were expecting me. A group of old men sat outside the largest hut on rough benches, and one kitchen style chair — a badge of rank. All eyes followed me suspiciously as I moved cautiously across towards them. Squatting down to the level of the men on the lower seats, I tried my Swahili. Not an eyelid blinked and not a facial expression changed. English didn't work, nor did my lousy French and my few words of German (tried with the thought that as this had once been a German colony then maybe one of these older men might understand me) didn't work either. Not a blink. Resorting to sign language started to get me somewhere. I tried to convey to the man who was obviously the chief, that I was harmless and would it be possible to stay for a week to learn about his village? I explained about meeting Domu and gave the presents of salt, sugar and soap that I had brought with me. Then I had a strong urge to pinch myself. This really was me, in a village, in the middle of Africa. Months ago, I'd been selling shoes in a completely different world.

Suddenly there were smiles and then hand shakes. The men moved along to make room for me to sit and the other village folk carried on about their business, though they all still had at least one eye on me as they went.

I sat and watched life go by. My parents at one time had probably been in a similar situation to this, but a considerable amount less was known in those days about life in the villages. I'd had television documentaries and the National Geographic magazine to learn from. They'd had books whose chapters had titles such as 'Heathen Practices', 'Cannibalism and Secret Societies' and 'Getting to know the Black Man'. The chapter called 'The Native Love Feast' had not lived up to its title.

The men around me carried on talking between themselves and it seemed that one in particular was the main storyteller. He told his stories by talking and by making gestures with hands that looked as hard as leather, as did his feet. His face was lined by creases that bent and flexed as his expressions dramatically changed with each turn in the story. He appeared to be telling the tale of a hunt from days gone by. I was sure that the story had been told many times before, but attention was complete and every so often one or another of the men would excitedly join in for a moment or two. There were satisfied expressions all around as the tale came to an end.

I found myself being part of the evening's entertainment for the village whilst putting up my little two-man tent. The chief was most impressed and was not too dignified to climb in and lie down. However, he didn't seem so impressed with the lack of headroom.

Fires were lit and it appeared that a party had been planned; a goat had been killed and was being roasted over the coals. The women of the village had been busy cooking cassava, which was yet another pretty tasteless stodge; this one made from a white centred root. They were also cooking a sort of spinach vegetable, which I later found out was the leaves from the top of the cassava plant itself. In a village like this, nothing would be wasted. At last, just after ten we all sat down to eat, the women on mats, the men on chunks of wood and the chief on his kitchen chair. The sleepy eyed younger children ate and were speedily banished to bed, but the men stayed talking until well after midnight, and I was extremely happy when they did finally head for their huts. By then I was almost at falling over stage.

The village came awake shortly after five thirty, leaving me feeling that my eyes had only just closed, but not wanting to miss anything I slid out of the tent to watch. The women were bent over fires making the breakfast porridge, the boys had long gone with the goats and the cattle, and a baby was wailing somewhere. The younger men were up and were already repairing tools or tucking new thatch onto hut roofs but the older men were nowhere to be seen. Scrawny chickens pecked and clucked their way between the huts looking for morsels that were invisible to me. The cocks looked as if they had sucked in their waistlines and were strutting around with measured, stiff legged paces as if regally surveying their domain.

Finally the older men emerged and the maize meal porridge was slopped with all the grace of a school dinner lady into pottery or wooden bowls. As we ate with our fingers, I dreamt of a little sugar or cinnamon or chocolate, or anything to give it some flavour. As a novice,

I managed to keep everyone amused with my decidedly inept attempts at scooping. Very messy, and not a job for the bearded!

Sitting with the Mzees outside the chief's hut again, the conversations gently flowed once more. The storytellers gave the feeling that some of their tales were being told in my honour and even though I didn't understand everything, I understood enough to grasp the tale of the great drought when all the game went away and the spring almost dried up. I saw the battle between them and the village next door, and was there when the chief killed a lion as a young man. All told with words, mime and drawings on the beaten earth of the village floor. The days slipped by.

I'd read that many of the more remote village Africans still revere the elephant and the lion as kings of the forest and savannah. They feel that these beasts are in no way inferior to man, and that people are only one of the species permitted to walk the face of the earth. The lion and the elephant are regarded as competing equals with humans in a constant battle to survive. They too had to live and to eat, but also had equal chances to die and be eaten. The stories constantly showed this respect, but also a certain resignation towards the reality of life.

Story telling is an art that belongs to an elder, a priest or as with the village in Kenya, a doctor. In East Africa the storyteller is rarely a professional, as they often are in Northern Africa. Some of the stories are told and re-told for hundreds of years and they nearly always have obvious foundations in fact. In many of the myths and legends, the hero doesn't win, but the tale always has a point. Unfairness in life is normal and it's also accepted that wrongs may never be put right, but honour and respect are important. To me it was a new way of looking at things, and I could see how much the ethos fitted in with the reality of life in the African outback.

Towards the end of my week I almost upset the apple cart. Each day, the women would collect under a tree in the centre of the village. They would sit there through the hottest hours, fixing clothes and making jewellery out of beads and seeds. Every so often the jewellery would be lugged to the main road to be sold in order to buy such necessities as salt and medicine. The villagers grew, bred or made just about everything else they needed. Some of the other women would

 sort tiny pebbles from uncooked rice grains that they had spread across their brightly coloured cloths. The original hand winnowing on woven grass mats allowed too many of these perfectly colour matched tiny stones to get in with the grains. I'd already discovered that these could easily break a tooth if missed. Some of the women would use the time to sit; legs spread out flat in front of them, and do each other's hair. Babies were fed and played with, and thieving chickens shooed away. The men's shade always had a grown up seriousness to it, even when a funny story was being told, but the women's lunchtime shade was often riotous. I'd seen enough of village life by now to realise that nothing much happened without the women controlling it. They were however, very careful to defer to the senior men, and the chief's wishes were always speedily carried out. But it didn't alter the fact that growing the food, cooking it, fetching water, caring for the sick and just about everything else seemed to be done by the women.

My pre-trip research had taught me that in this part of the world baby girls are valued just as much as boys. It was very rare for a newborn girl to be secretly killed, as I'd read happened in China for example. Here they are regarded as not only an important part of the work force but as bringers of wealth into a family. A man with daughters who were attractive and 'well trained' could become a rich man. His daughters would draw a large bride price. For a family with both sons and daughters, a daughter would often have to get married, and bring in a good bride price for a son to be able to get married. The bride price would usually be cattle.

Wanting to see more of what went on from their point of view, I asked the chief if it would be possible to join the women under their tree at midday. I'm sure that he thought he'd not understood me at first but by now seemed to have accepted that this muzungu was decidedly

194

odd. After thinking about it for a few moments, he called the head woman over. From what I'd seen so far, she was the real queen bee around here and had an excellent sense of humour. But she lost that completely when the chief told her what the weird white man wanted – she refused. The men were scandalised and the chief was shouting. I was very sorry I'd asked now, but the deed was done and at the chief's insistence the head lady came to get me when the sun was high.

The other women watched me come over and said nothing as I sat down cross-legged with them. The chief's bemused eyes were on the back of my neck. As the sun moved overhead and I did nothing offensive, the women, who were of all ages but mostly below forty I guessed, carried on with their usual tasks. As the atmosphere relaxed a little, I chanced a question to the head lady about the beadwork she was doing. The ice thawed a little and with more questions I stumbled across a delightful discovery. This super woman not only knew some Swahili from trading at the road but she also knew a little French from the mission station that had been near her home village. Now I could talk, and with hand language the conversation flowed. It must have sounded and looked very funny, but it worked and the ice thawed some more. Laughter began to ring out again. The older men were watching intently but some were too proud to do more than look through the corners of their eyes. I never did find out why Domu appeared to be the only child who had gone to the 'Scandinavian' mission. No one else in the village had learned any English.

For a while, the younger women had been casting glances in my direction, accompanied by comments, giggles and then laughter. One of the more forward girls asked a question of the head lady who thought about it for a moment and then asked if I was married. I told her that I wasn't. When she relayed this to the girls, there were lots more giggles and elbow nudging. The back of my neck tingled a little and I hoped that they wouldn't realise that I was blushing. Then again, would they have even recognised what a blush was on me anyway? As a couple of the girls saucily gave me the eye, I wondered what sort of eye the chief and his men were giving me.

The next question amazed me. "How many children do you have?" When my, "None" was translated back, there was silence and then whispered remarks which eventually turned into giggles again. The head lady nearly baulked at asking me the final question, but steeled herself and came over. I wondered what was coming. She leant over and poking me in the testicles asked, "Something wrong?" The women shrieked with laughter and two were laying on the floor with tears running down their faces. The chief and his men were now standing up and were craning their necks to see what was going on, even the proud ones. They didn't come over though.

Later that night, the head lady had obviously been made to tell the chief what had been going on. After the meal, he took me to one side and I was stumped when it clicked that he was telling me that I obviously needed a woman and that he had decided that it would be right for me to have his second wife for the night! What amazing concern and to me, bizarre generosity. But it left me frantically searching for a way to get out of the offer without offending him or anyone else, particularly his second wife who was standing close by. I knew almost nothing about their customs and habits and they had all been so kind to me, but I really didn't want to sleep with his wife – who in fact was pretty and rather fun. With a flash of a brainwave I told him that in my country it's not allowed to sleep with a woman unless you'd known her and her family for some considerable time – I thought they might understand that. I didn't chance any comments about marriage fearing that there was another can of worms, and knowing that things in sign language should definitely be kept as simple as possible. I must have been momentarily inspired because he seemed to understand and showed no signs whatsoever of having taken offence.

With the new day, I felt that it was time to start heading for Malawi before I really dropped myself in it and spoiled everything. To keep out of the way I asked the boys to take me out herding the goats with them. No one in the village seemed to think that this was any more odd than my other strange requests. The boys start herding at a very early age. When they have proved themselves with the goats and are older, they herd the cattle. They make their own food as they move. One of the boys carried a pouch that contained a glowing ember so they could make fire whenever they wanted. Each carried a small catapult and they were deadly with them. Small birds hardly stood a chance. Lunch would often be any birds' eggs that they'd found, which were munched raw. The birds they caught were charred, feathers and all, over small fires. The blackened corpses smelt awful as they were cooking and tasted terrible but the boys loved them. Now even ugali, matoke and cassava sounded good.

That night I used my intended early departure as an excuse to go to bed straight after dinner. I fell asleep listening to the villagers quietly talking and laughing. The fire popped and crackled. Somewhere in the bush an animal was howling and every so often a goat would bleat, a dog would bark or one of the cows would low gently in the darkness at the fringes of the village. Mosquitoes buzzed around the outside of the tent's mosquito-netting doorway, and I slept deeply.

The usual dawn start to the day was perfect to get me on the track in the cool. After eating porridge with everyone and shaking hands until my arm ached, I gave away the rest of my salt and soap to the head lady, and my best T-shirt plus an envelope containing some shillings (board, lodging and many thanks) to the chief. He clasped me on the upper arm and told me to greet Domu if I saw him; the head woman gave me a wink, one of the girls a giggle, and one of the boys set off with me across the bush. It felt decidedly odd to be leaving. These kind people had welcomed a very strange person, and had shared their lives. I knew that I'd had a unique experience. The week had been a real bonus but I knew that to stay longer would be tempting fate. Mr Thoreau would have been happy though; I'd lived the dream, and this time done it with confidence.

Trudging across the sand, I started to think about the bike and wondered if she'd be still in one piece when I got to her.

Chapter Twelve

"Brain Damaged Racing Pigs"

*'I wish I could bring Stonehenge to Nyasaland (Malawi) to show that
there was a time when Britain had a savage culture.'*

Hastings Banda

The village lad turned out to be Domu's younger brother and he stayed with me until we got to the bike. Wonderfully, the ground around it was undisturbed, and there was nothing missing. In a way, I was quite glad when the lad curled up in his blanket and fell asleep on the sand next to the bike. I'd seen lice in his hair and really hadn't wanted to end up with any unwanted hitchhikers in the tent.

Next day, I retraced my steps, and as ever it seemed quicker than the outward journey. Weeks before, an Australian had told me that he made a point of never going back the same way unless he absolutely had to. "Blahdy waste a toime mate", he'd said. But by now I'd retraced my route several times on different occasions, and never found it boring or repetitive. Quite apart from the fact that one often had a very different view when facing the other way, even sights you'd already seen could look quite different the second time around – the passage of time and experience put them in a different light. And of course, some things I overlooked altogether on the outward journey. This time for example, the roadside jewellery sellers' wares had a very different meaning. I was delighted to recognise bracelets that had obviously come from the village I'd just visited. It was a nice feeling to see them, and on the way up I'd hardly even noticed the stalls.

It was a pleasant cruise down from the city of Mbeya to the Malawi border. The road was quite high up, so the temperatures were cool and the surrounding hilly countryside was green and fertile. Most of the buildings were dilapidated but the people looked healthy and life was obviously a lot easier in many ways than it was for my friends in the village. Trundling along watching the view, and listening to the rhythmic ticking of the bike's valves over the gentle rumbling from the exhaust, I realised that all the feelings that something wasn't right had disappeared.

For me, Tanzania had given far more ups than downs, and it had given me a set of experiences I'd never forget. The country and its people had dramatically changed me in the few weeks it had taken to travel through.

The main road doesn't actually go to the border but swings eastwards towards another group of towns and villages, leaving an offshoot to run south. Buses stop at the junction and there wait a mass of young boys with bicycles. These constitute the border taxi service. I sat and watched them hustling hard to get passengers. Heavy competition seemed to make them walk a fine line between losing a customer because they were charging too much, and ending up with a hard, well-loaded ride for very little. One lad set off on his black Chinese bicycle with a Mama who looked at least eighteen stone. She, her child and two large brightly coloured bundles, were all piled on the rack behind him. He had to lean over the handlebars just to stop the front wheel from lifting off the ground. His mates were all jeering and cat calling as the overloaded bicycle wobbled down the hill on almost flattened tyres. Mama sat with a regal expression on her face as if being cheered was quite normal.

My usual early start to the day meant that it was possible to be arriving at the border just as it opened for business. This was something that I'd really grown to like. Whatever happened at the border, there would be plenty of time. The plan made me feel a lot less vulnerable, especially when on my own.

Towards the bottom of the hill, the black market moneychangers tried to swamp me. All the borders in East Africa had been the same. The banks did a poor trade, but with those who had cash dollars the black marketeers did a bustling trade. The black market rate at this border was, with a bit of bargaining, almost double that of the banks. I knew what the two rates should have been because there were always other travellers to ask. Now twenty pairs of hands were thrusting money at me, while twenty voices insisted that theirs was the best rate. However, by now I had a well-worn system. I'd learned to pick three lads and to send the rest away. The three guys picked would help to get rid of the others. Then I had peace to listen to each of the three one at a time, and make my choice. If there wasn't a real difference between them, the one who had the friendliest face or who had cleared space around me the most enthusiastically got the deal. Sometimes the initial crowd of dealers were so keen that it became hard to keep the bike upright. That was scary, not for fear of falling off (there'd been plenty of practice at doing that), but for fear of the bike going over on one of them. The other thing that made me nervous about doing 'business' in the middle of a crowd was that all the argy bargy increased the chances that I'd do something stupid. So far, by using the three-guy system, I'd never been ripped off, and nearly always got a reasonable rate. In the end it was often only pennies that were being quibbled about, though in some countries the black rate itself had been enormous.

Passing through the Tanzanian side of the border was far less hassle than up on the northern side, but my papers were scrutinised thoroughly and it was obvious that there would have been trouble if they'd not been in order. My first sight on the Malawian side was a Norwegian having a haircut. He winced as his long blond hanks fell to the ground; the scissors that were doing the work didn't look too sharp. President Banda had made a series of laws that seemed to be aimed at keeping standards in Malawi high, and hippies out! Men were allowed hair no longer than their ears – if you wanted to enter, you had a haircut. Girls were not allowed to wear shorts or trousers, which seemed a little strange, but as I had short hair and am happy to see girls in skirts, it didn't worry me. With an officially approved haircut, the border crossing was a two and a half hour breeze. The officials all spoke English and though they asked pointed questions, my answers seemed OK and my manners didn't seem to upset anyone. As usual my best biking togs (well, cleanest and least patched) had been dug out and donned. A little bit of respect went a long way.

After dropping me down out of the hills, the asphalt road led me to Lake Malawi. This long strip of fresh water, once called Lake Nyasa, lies almost at the tail end of the Rift Valley. Malawi runs along its western and southern sides. It's a thin country, just a hundred and sixty kilometres at its widest point. It is eight hundred and forty kilometres long though, and it's home to one of the most densely packed populations on the continent. Fortunately it has some of the most fertile soil in southern Africa, and at least half is suitable for cultivation – a very high percentage after all the dry lands of Tanzania and Kenya. But here the landscape was mustard and sage coloured again. By crossing the borderline I'd officially ridden into Southern Africa, and the south was in the midst of a drought. It would be almost six months before I saw rain again. The land's dry colours combined with the deep clear blue of the lake to make me think of the Greek coastline in summer.

My first target was the old Scottish mission station of Livingstonia. The mission is set high up on the edge of the Nyika plateau and I'd heard scare stories from other bikers about the road up. The description usually included the words 'tortuous, hairpins, sand and gravel', but the view out over Lake Malawi was reputedly magnificent. The track didn't look too bad to begin with but as it began to climb, the gravel and ruts got deeper, the sand softer, the road suddenly got steeper and the bends became tight hairpins. Each steep bumpy corner seemed to have a different surface to be dealt with. Cars and trucks had to do three or more point turns to get round most of them, and this churning of the ground didn't make life any easier for me. Short of getting off the bike and walking up to look at them first, there was no way to plan the corners. The walking up bit wasn't possible though because there was hardly anywhere level or solid enough to park the bike. The technique in the end was to get the bike in as good a line as possible and then keep fingers crossed. By bend ten (out of the twenty-one) I knew that doing the road wasn't a good idea. But I wasn't going to be beaten and the view that eventually greeted me from the top lived up to its reputation. I breathed a sigh of relief and bumped over the ruts that were the main road through the mission. Red brick colonial houses were set amongst avenues of evergreens that looked suspiciously as if someone had tried to create a touch of home away from home. At the rim of the plateau, there was a solitary brick and gabled house with a million dollar view. In its garden a familiar looking tent shared that view. The Australian girls, Dominique and Kathy from the Kenya safari, had backpacked in to the guesthouse the day before. The evening whizzed by with an orgy of tall tales of the road and we stuffed ourselves with the most amazing scotch pancakes. The locals make them and sell them to grateful travellers. Now this was a little touch of home.

A group of us hired a lad called Gresham to show us the local waterfalls. He was about thirteen and had one of those cheeky, beaming white smiles that so many of the kids seemed to have. He stood out though because his eyes sparkled with life, whereas too many of the other children seemed to lack this zing of character. Their eyes, particularly with tourists, appeared to have a dullness to them as if determined not to let any of us in. At first, this made their smiles seem superficial but I couldn't help wondering whether hunger had stolen their 'zing'.

The falls were hundreds of feet high and tucked away behind them was a cave that once had hidden the villagers from marauding tribesmen. They could see out but no one could see them. On the morning of our trip, Gresham didn't appear, so rather than waste more of our day we hired another lad and set off. Just as we were doing so, the tardy Gresham turned up, his mental clock was on Africa time and he hadn't got a watch of course. We told him what had happened and asked if he wanted to sort it out with John or split the fee with him. He thought for a second and then serious-faced said, "No, I wasn't here on time so it's fair that John must do it." I couldn't help but be impressed.

The rough scramble to the falls and back made me realise how unfit I'd become over the past months. I'd thought that it had been the sand on the track that had been making me puff but now knew the truth – I'd got flabby. I'd made an effort to get fit before leaving home, it had felt great and it had probably helped me through some of the difficult sections. But all these months of sitting on the bike had taken their toll. A lot more walking was called for, the bike could make life just too easy. It was only midday when we got back from the falls, and as it wasn't raining, I decided to face the ride back down the precipitous hill. If the road got wet it probably wasn't going to be rideable at all. Some of the drops over the edge were sheer and the thought of slipping over one was to say the least, a bit of a worry. I loaded up quickly, and nervously rode to the first bend. Adrenaline buzzed. Standing on the back brake almost all the way down, gravity did its job with rarely a need to open the throttle, and we made it. I stood at the bottom and shook. Every time I tried something new on the bike, I realised how much I didn't know about riding. More than half way down the length of Africa, this was a sobering thought and a healthy reminder - it stopped me becoming complacent.

My good first impressions of Malawi had been bang on - for me this country was a holiday. Just about everyone along the way was friendly and helpful. The locally brewed Carlsberg was excellent and very cheap, and the fuel was the cheapest it had been since Egypt, but much better quality. I cruised down the side of Lake Malawi spending a few days here and a few days there, in this fishing village, that little market town or on yet another clean, white sandy beach. My Michelin map told me that I was passing towns with wonderful sounding names like Chilumba, Rumphi and Mzuzu, which had to be pronounced MmmZuzu. Not once did I feel in danger. Camping next to one fishing village where there were log canoes drawn up along the shore, and one of the fishermen saw my interest. He simply gave me his paddle and pointed out onto the lake. The canoe weighed a ton and it was only possible to push it off the sand with some help. Once on the water, it took on a life of its own and wallowed in a decidedly unstable fashion. It took me three soakings before even getting into the thing, and then I found that it was obviously related to 'that' trolley in the supermarket at home, the one with the left hand pull. It kept the fishermen entertained – they watched grinning as I paddled around in hopeless circles. Eventually I got the hang of it and left the beach, with its long spindly rows of fish drying racks, well behind me. The water was clear as glass and gently warm to the touch. Beneath the canoe swam hundreds of tiny fish, their colours covering pretty much the whole spectrum of a rainbow. I was torn between the view, controlling the canoe and watching the fish, but there was plenty of time, so did it all.

A name on the map caught my eye – the port of Monkey Bay. It really did have monkeys so I had to go. To get there with the best chance of an adventure, somehow I had to load the bike onto a passenger ferry. The ferry looked as if it belonged in a Humphrey Bogart movie. Every inch of its panelling was battered, and layer upon layer of white paint failed to hide the dribbling rust blisters.

We all woke up late on the day of the ferry's departure - Dom, Kathy, a group of travelling friends and I had been camping under the trees on a beautiful stretch of pebbles called Chicale beach. There weren't any houses down there, just a few children. The night before, we'd bought three-foot long Chambo fish and barbecued them down at the waterline. The night was dark with not a trace of moon, and just a few yards from our faces glowing in the firelight, you couldn't see a thing. The night was ours, the Carlsberg flowed and the warm waters lapped at our feet. Whilst stories and advice were swapped, we somehow managed to cook the meaty fish to perfection, and it wasn't until the early hours before people started drifting off to their sleeping bags. As the ferry wasn't leaving until late the next day, it didn't matter a jot. We might not have been on 'Africa time' ourselves, but were getting close.

At three in the afternoon, I headed for the dock. On the trail to the village, two dust-covered men were hard at work with a primitive but very functional lathe. Two wigwam-shaped trestles supported a smooth, polished log. Onto one end of the log a lump of wood had been fastened, and it was fast turning into a bowl. The two-man operation ran with efficient smoothness. The younger of the men had a long strip of rubber looped over the other end of the log. With rhythmic sweeps of his arms he pulled on the rubber, which in turn spun the log. The older of the men cut gently into the revolving lump. Curls of dark wood floated down onto the pile below. When they stopped to rest, both were sweating hard with shining streaks running down through the wood dust on their faces. When I asked the elder about his tools he told me that like the lathe they were self-made. He'd bought some broken truck springs, and had black-smithed them into his long handled chisels. They'd even modified the other end of their lathe to hold a stone on which to sharpen the chisels. For a penny they sharpened my Swiss army knife for me before I moved on.

Down at the dock, 'Africa time' was functioning really well and the next couple of hours passed slowly - the ship was late. To make it worse, the Port Captain was now saying that he wasn't going to let me put the bike on the ferry. "It's a passenger ferry", he snapped bluntly. "Not a vehicle ferry." This was a different tune to the one he'd been singing the day before, and I suspected that he wanted his palm greasing. One of the local guys told me to wait until the ship arrived and then to try to talk to its Captain. In the end I wasn't worried. If it was possible to get on board then terrific, if not then I could just ride on down the coast. Eventually the ship turned up and with the help of Samson, the guy I'd been talking to, I made it through the crowds of shoving people who were laden with baskets, sacks, bundles of bananas and live chickens. The chickens, hanging upside down by their ankles, looked stoic. The Captain was a small, very dark-skinned, pot-bellied man, immaculately dressed in pale blue jeans, a pale blue T-shirt and to my surprise a heavy gold Rolex watch completed his outfit. While I explained my predicament he looked totally bemused as if to say, 'What on earth are you asking me for?' He said that he was quite happy for me to bring the bike on board, but that I would have to find my own helpers. He ended up by saying "Mister, you gonna need 'em!"

I rode onto the jetty and weaved a path through the crowds. My backpacking friends helped to unload the gear and with one of the girls standing guard over it, six of us started our 'snakes and ladders' trip through the boat with the bike. Down the ramp, over a load of grain sacks, around a stack of oil drums, up ten very steep iron steps, over a half-metre watertight bulk head, down a corridor and over a group of the pipes that protruded at knee height into the gangway. Finally we made it, a railing with a lake view for the bike. We grabbed all of our gear and staked out a patch of the after deck for the voyage. If it rained, then we'd get wet. But that was definitely preferable to the worn out, claustrophobic chaos down below – shades of Sudan.

Even though the bike was already onboard, its ticket still had to be paid for and an avaricious smile greeted me at the ticket counter. "Come into my office", the official said with a wiggling finger hooked in my direction. The bike and luggage by now weighed two hundred and ninety kilos, a far cry less than my original thoroughly overloaded state. The official took me by the arm and winked with a theatrically conspiratorial manner saying, "Let us put your motorcycle on the manifest as just one hundred and thirty kilos, you pay the full amount and then we can split the difference!" I was delighted at the request, but I'll leave it up to you to work out what actually happened.

Finally, as darkness fell the ferry moved out of the bay. There wasn't any ticker tape but there should have been. Passionate goodbyes were being flung back and forth from the portholes to the jetty – it made me think that these people never expected to see each other again. I started to wonder about the ship's safety record, particularly as just outside the harbour we hit the first of the swells and the ship loudly creaked and groaned its complaints. The engines sounded good though and they throbbed us out into the darkness.

The sun was out again the next day and thankfully the swell had lessened overnight. Sunbathing on deck, once again it felt like I was in Greece, the only thing that was missing was a salty tang in the air. It wasn't until darkness was falling that we made our first stop. The bay in front of the town of Nkhotakota was too shallow to get the ferry into so everything had to be moved by canoe. The swell had risen again; this time to a couple of metres but not a thing was lost overboard. Bicycles, sacks of flour, sugar, lengths of wood and bundled-up babies all made it safely to shore. Some of the passengers' faces held expressions of sheer terror as they tried to time their jumps from the ferry into the crazily roller coasting canoes below. I'd read a magazine article (probably one from a pre-trip visit to the Doc's for one of many jabs) that had said most Africans can't swim. Even many who live on the lakeshores can't. The wildness of the swell must have been quite nightmarish to them.

The ferry arrived in Monkey Bay seven hours late and on one engine. Fortunately, the water had calmed and there was hardly a ripple in the bay. We let the mad rush of pushing, shoving humanity get off the ferry before trying to get the bike ashore. Knowing the route through the boat and having less clutter to deal with made it a relatively easy task. The big surprise was how hot and humid it was just these few kilometres further south. Little streams of sweat ran down my face as I strapped gear back onto the bike. The metal pontoon dock had been collecting heat all day and was now quite happily reflecting it straight back up at me. I was so keen to get a slipstream going that I just jumped the bike down the half-metre step from the jetty. It didn't seem to mind and by the time I'd found the track to the fishing village of Cape McClear, the sweat had gone, but my old friends the corrugations had started. Now I knew what to do; open the throttle, and skip across the top of the ruts. I still didn't like doing it but knew that it could be done and with luck they wouldn't last for long. Experience had also taught me that these ruts are not caused only by nature; overloaded heavy trucks grinding along in all weathers do most of the damage.

At Cape McClear there were signs for 'Hostel Top Quite' or 'Top Quiet' depending on who had written them. Scrunching up the sand and into an enclosure that looked as if it were a sandy stable yard with about twenty stalls/rooms around it, there was a blue and white BMW R100GS parked next to a small green tent. The English owners, Ashley and Donna, had shipped to South Africa and were on their way north. A lasting friendship started there.

These two had set off just before I had and had been some of the unfortunates that had got caught up in the chaos in Algeria all those months ago. They'd had to turn around and think again. They'd also had tremendous problems with their bike and all in, had had a much rougher trip than me. Ashley and Donna were the only other bikers I met who'd had less experience riding a bike than me when they'd set off. Ashley's way of travelling seemed to be to amble along sorting things out as they happened, by not panicking and then by gently, optimistically, getting on with it. Donna humoured Ashley's ways, thought things out a bit more and made sure things did actually happen. They seemed to be a perfect travelling team and were both incredibly positive. Of course at this stage, I didn't know that Ashley and Donna were going to be very much involved in saving my life.

The two of them were travelling with almost no luggage. 'Minimalist' would be a good way to describe it. They had one pannier, a small rucksack and that was it. Where the second pannier would normally live they had a twenty-litre jerry-can strapped on. This gave them forty-six litres or about six hundred kilometres of range. This was very good, but there was a price to pay. For example, they had a cooking pot but no cooker. Ashley's first job of the day was to scout up enough firewood to get breakfast on the go. Sometimes when camping near villages this must have been particularly difficult. My first morning saw me with the tea on, while they cooked the maize meal porridge or mealie meal as they had learned to call it in South Africa. Whilst tucking into our stodgy, stomach filling and very cheap breakfast, Patchit arrived.

Patchit, who was really called Patrick but he always let the word slip out as 'Patchit', to my imagination just had to be a descendant of the marauding Zulus of Zwangendaba. This Zulu chief had led his men north from Zululand in search of a land to make their own after he'd quarrelled with the great chief Shaka. They had found Lake Nyasa, and stayed – the locals had never had a chance. Patchit was tall, dark and had the proud manner I'd always imagined a Zulu would have. He was also an entrepreneur. After greeting us with a friendly grin, he said that he could organise canoe trips across to the nearby island, could supply and even cook fish or goat in the form of a barbecue and without a blink also let us know that should we need any ganja (marijuana) then he was our man! Top Quiet did not provide room service, let alone tent service, but who needed either with Patchit around?!

We took him up on his offer of the dugout to the island, not realising that he and his partner in crime 'One eyed Esky' were included in the price as paddlers. That left us perfectly free to do what we wanted, when we wanted. It wasn't so much the island that made the day, as getting there and getting back. We sunbathed fingers trailing in the crystal water, held lazy conversations over chilled Carlsbergs, and swam too. I was delighted to find that when swimming with bread in my hands, hundreds of the tiny brightly coloured fish would come to feed. Ashley told me that from above it looked like I was holding two giant flowers under water. Apparently ten percent of the fish that are found in tropical aquariums come from Lake Malawi.

Patchit's goat barbecue sounded like a real treat. None of us had been eating much meat while on the road as we'd seen the flies far too often to feel comfortable. Temptation had got the better of me a couple of times, but the meat had been so tough that my jaws had ached and even floss had a hard time with the sinew removal business. But freshly killed barbecued goat sounded mouth wateringly excellent. The goat, poor thing, saw it coming. He took one look at Patchit, who was hiding his machete behind his back, and legged it off through the sandy village. It never had a chance, and half an hour later it was hanging from 'TQ's' veranda post as stripped as it would ever be. Skinned and gutted, but its head still on, tongue lolling out from between yellowed teeth. We all felt as if we'd been involved in the murder of the beast, but as the first delicious scents of cooking meat wafted around us, it was easy to forget.

For a couple of days there was a bad taste to Top Quiet. Four white South African men arrived in a Land Rover. Hell-bent on partying, they announced their arrival by roaring round the compound spraying dust, sand and grit in all directions, including over us. They cowed the black hostel owner into giving them a room and proceeded to get even drunker. These obnoxious gits were the first South Africans I'd met anywhere near their home environment, and their behaviour towards the village people made me wonder if I'd enjoy South Africa at all. Their most commonly used words seemed to be 'Bledy Blecks' and 'Dambt Kaffirs'. I'd heard the word Kaffir before and knew that quite a few white South Africans used it in a derogatory rather flippant way to refer to the country's dark skinned people. The word itself actually comes from the Arab word Kafir, which quite simply means Infidel. That of course applies to all of us, in Arab eyes. To these ignorant men the word was one of hatred and disgust. I disliked their behaviour intensely and was suddenly glad that my trip hadn't started in the south. I could imagine that these sorts of actions, amongst other things, encouraged the continuing tense situation down there. I wondered if my life had been sheltered, I'd never seen such virulent animosity from one human being towards another before. When they left, T.Q subsided into a sort of stunned calm which felt like the stillness that a particularly nasty storm will leave behind.

It would have been easy to stay in this tranquil place, but after a few more days, I could feel the road calling. It suddenly seemed like the right time to go.

Lilongwe is set high up in the mountains, and it's cool by day and cold by night for much of the year. It's the capital city of Malawi, and with wide shady streets and very friendly people it was the nicest city I'd been to so far. It was also the first city since Europe where it was possible, in one form or another, to find just about anything I needed. The supermarkets made me feel like a kid let loose in a toy store at Christmas. They even had choices, but life was made rather confusing by having at least four different types of soap, sardines or soup to choose from. I was out of practice and it also felt odd not to have to bargain for everything. Lilongwe was my first mail pick up point for a long time as well, so a hefty stack was waiting for me at the post office and it felt like Christmas again.

The city market though was decidedly African. As the market in Adis Ababa had been, this one was also split into sections. The sounds rather than the sights had drawn us into the first section. The sounds were those of a tin can symphony. About forty tinsmiths sat hammering away on whatever each was making, which mostly seemed to be watering cans. In some places they were already stacked ten high along the perimeter wall and I wondered what would happen if the drought ended and the demand for watering cans slumped. One of the tinsmiths worked in aluminium. He was making saucepans out of discarded car number plates. They looked excellent and for once, travelling by bike instead of by Land Rover seemed the wrong way round. I'd have bought several sets if it had been possible to carry them.

The next section of the market was the 'Halfords' department. The men sold collections of nuts, bolts, mirrors, car panels, door handles, bumpers, bicycle bells, inner tubes - in fact just about everything that could be stripped off whatever it was that had finally given up the ghost and would no longer move. Next was 'Woolworths', and then the shoe repairer who was carefully stitching everything by hand. His glue looked as if it had been concocted by the Witch Doctor, who had his rather mysterious sacking cloth 'cave' of a stall festooned with bird skeletons, snakeskins, shrivelled up roots and collections of raw quartz. There was no sign of the great man himself but my imagination connected the scent of burning herbs that wafted around us with some sort of extreme rite that must be going on inside; an ingrown toenail cure perhaps.

We didn't linger in the butcher's section which had its usual collection of flies, scrawny cats and dogs hanging around. Tucked to one side in the shade of an overhang was a large basket of chickens, which at first glance looked like some sort of giant earth bound sea anemone. The woven sugar cane basket was oval in shape and about a meter and a half across. It contained more than thirty chickens that had wriggled their heads out through the spaces in the weave of the basket. The heads swivelled and clucked in waving, jerking relative freedom whilst their bodies remained packed sardine-like inside their prison. At least they were in the shade.

Wherever we went the air was full of the scents of barbecuing skewers of meat, the deep-frying of large doughnuts that were called mandazis and surprisingly, the scent of popcorn too. The air around the open drains wasn't so pleasant though.

A large concreted area with a rusty corrugated iron roof housed an amazing fruit and vegetable section. The displays were the best I had seen in Africa. Each vendor had carefully washed his or her wares and had laid them out in rows of almost mathematical precision, or in little four-fruit pyramid stacks. The visual effect seemed to be taken for granted by the locals but for us, the variety, the condition and the displays of goods had the desired effect. We bargained, and we bought. A three-course feast for four cost just one US dollar forty cents.

After a few days I had itchy feet once more, and when the bike's much needed service was finished it was time to go. Part of me couldn't understand this constant need to be on the move all the time, particularly when there were such marvellous places to stay. This time home had been the small campsite that was tagged onto the side of the Golf Club. Hot showers, level ground, uniformed security guards, a ten minute walk from the city centre and a very reasonable club bar (that didn't seem to mind our scruffy appearance), made it a good home. The club's caddies with their bizarre collection of typical check clothing were colourful jokers, and real opportunists. Their eyes seemed permanently open for the main chance and I had the feeling that when they were around, things should be strapped down.

But, in spite of the delights of Lilongwe, the itchy feet part of me said, 'see what's coming next', and 'get on with the trip while everything is still going well'. It was much stronger than the sedentary part of me, so I kept moving. Perhaps in fact, moving on was becoming a habit. Goodbyes were hard with Ashley and Donna but I set off for the Zambian border. The mountains dropped me down into scrubby savannah again and the border crossing took only an hour. With the whole of the rest of the day to play with, the road to Lusaka (even if it was as bad as I'd heard) wasn't going to be a problem. It would have been possible to make it in one run, but things always seemed to go wrong when I gave myself a time limit, so I decided to take it easy.

Seconds later, a black pig hurtled out of the bush and raced across the road in front of me! If I'd been riding any faster the pig would have hit me. It was large enough to badly damage the bike, and would definitely have knocked me off. I had an odd tingling feeling.

The forests and the bush along the roadsides had been burnt black in preparation for the hoped-for rains. Traditionally, vast areas were burnt when the rain was due. The idea was that fresh new growth

would have freedom to shoot up without dead wood and grasses to slow things up. The sooty remains also act as fertiliser. But on this occasion someone had got it wrong and as the rains hadn't come, the denuded land had already started to blow away on the wind. On this side of

the mountains the world really was in the midst of a severe drought and even the great Luangwa River only had a stream trickling along its bed. At the suspension bridge over the river, the soldiers on a roadblock stopped me. They asked all of the usual questions, but in a very lackadaisical fashion. The heat and dryness of the air had obviously got to them, and they allowed me to go with a yawn. I rode on, tensely aware of racing black pigs that just had to be brain damaged, for they continued to madly rush out from nowhere to play chicken with my front wheel. I had visions of little clusters of them sitting camouflaged in the blackened bush patiently waiting for vehicles to come before one would dive out to the snorting cheers of his mates. Perhaps the heat was getting to me too.

In Lusaka I was due to meet friends of a missionary called Ken. Ken lived and worked on a mission station in Botswana. Athough he was in the latter years of his career, he still rode his 1,000cc Suzuki road bike and sidecar around south-western Africa. We'd heard about each other just before my journey began and he'd offered up some very sound advice about riding in Africa. We'd been in touch by phone when I was in Lilongwe and he arranged for me to stay with his friends prior to our meeting up at Victoria Falls. His choice of meeting place was a surprise as it was a long way from his mission but as he said, "Any excuse for a ride". The night's stay in Lusaka was perfect as the house was inside a secure compound, and when riding through the city the next day it looked as if I'd have been hard pushed to find a cheap hotel with parking for the bike. There was also an edgy air about the city that didn't sit well. Ken's friends made me very welcome and in the evening even took me out for a meal in the town. 'Mr Pete's' looked like a dingy hole in the wall from the outside. It was rather more like a dilapidated old warehouse but the inside was a whole different ball game. The white T-shirted waiters served me with the best steak so far in Africa; in the morning I had the worst stomach so far in Africa!

At seven thirty in the morning, Lusaka was still half-asleep and the traffic pretty calm. This turned out to be a good thing because the road signs were either not there, or were pointing in the wrong direction. It took me a while to ask my way out of town and one man had said, "Do you have a map?" I did of course, and he took it from me, turned it upside down, then sideways and eventually said, "Yes, but where is Zambia?" The map had Zambia on one side and the city itself on the other!

Finally out of the town, I found myself riding through a series of road works. Great sandy, rutted detours looped off into the bush, and getting stuck behind a truck was a dangerous chore. These rattling old beasts threw up a mixture of dust, grit and pebbles and to get past, I had to sit in the worst of it. It never occurred to me to ride two miles behind and to stay at the truck's speed. Instead, each truck was a challenge that had to be overcome and when at last I passed each one, I'd be on a high that would stay with me for ages. The road was in an awful state from years of neglect and heavy use. There was more hole than asphalt, but the kilometres flew past whilst playing a game of trying to link the remaining ribbons of tar together so that I didn't have to thump down into the holes. It was like playing space invaders, but live! As the adrenaline buzzed I decided to make the day into an endurance test. How long was it possible to ride like this without stopping? It was a silly mood really, but it was fun and it got me to the Zambian side of Victoria Falls, the town of Livingstone, by 1p.m. It had taken just five and a half hours to ride the four hundred and fifty kilometres of sand and hole.

Chapter Thirteen
"Fluorescent Green Dreams"
'Grey skies are just clouds passing over'

Old English Proverb

Livingstone's streets reminded me of an out-back Australian town. There were the same wooden buildings with porches and verandas. Everything was weathered by the sun, and any wood that didn't have paint on it had bleached, warped and dried into a pale grey that changed only slightly in shade from one building to the next. With the sun immediately overhead, anything with the potential to reflect did so with hot glaring enthusiasm. I'd expected to see spray from Victoria Falls towering over Livingston, but the air was so dry that any mist was instantly sucked away.

Pulling onto the town's camping site was another disappointment. The ground was a dirty coloured sand, with little clusters of litter caught in the few straggly bushes; other than their spindly effort, there was hardly any shade. It was almost as if the trees had no energy to grow leaves and this, at five US dollars a night, was the most expensive camping site I'd had so far in Africa. With the arrangements to meet Ken made for this very spot, there was no choice but to stay.

To make matters worse there didn't seem to be any security measures, the toilets were filthy and there wasn't another soul on the site. Even the few birds that were hanging around lethargically pecking at ants were straggly. The ants themselves seemed to be moving with a lack of their customary enthusiasm. If the birds had had more energy they'd have been fat, but then again perhaps the ants were moving at a carefully judged speed with just enough of a margin for safety. I'd never know and at that moment, it didn't seem worth spending the energy thinking about it. The adrenaline buzz had gone, and I was back down to earth with an exhausted flop.

But this was Victoria Falls, 'Mosi Oa Tunya', 'The Smoke that Thunders'. After locking up anything that would have been a pain to lose, I went down a path through the trees, and there they were. The

215

falls were breathtaking! Did Queen Victoria ever manage to imagine what they really looked like from the etchings and paintings she must have been shown? Probably not, in which case, she missed out. If they were this good in a drought, what would they be like in the rainy season? The chasm below me thundered with the noise of the millions of gallons of water that were plunging into its depths. The lethargy had gone and suddenly I felt absolutely privileged.

There were plenty of paths around the top of the falls and one of them took me right to the water's edge. From that point it looked as if there would be a way to get right out into the middle of the falls. Thanks to the drought the water level was low enough to be able to hop from rock to rock. Out there the air was moist, the sun was only warm, and the falling water was sucking a breeze. The noise of the rest of the world was drowned by the constant stormy roar of a thousand rushing tons hitting the bubbling froth and slick rocks below.

As the afternoon came to a close, I sat upriver under an overhanging fig tree watching life float by. Coffee coloured and very scrawny monkeys were playing in the shallows at the edge of the Zambezi. I hadn't realised that monkeys would do anything with water, other than drink it. But every so often, one of them would find something of interest on the riverbed, and would stop to examine it. Inevitably one of the others would splash across to see what had been found. I began to realise that each of them had their own character. One was the investigative type and there was hardly a moment when he wasn't examining something or other. One had to be the centre of attraction and constantly played the fool, and there was one who sat quietly to one side and watched the world with me. Suddenly the peaceful play erupted. The fool had grabbed something shiny from the investigative fellow and laughing and chattering to everyone, scampered into a nearby tree where he sat taunting. Finally the investigator was goaded into racing up the tree too, and the fool, with a laughing air of disdain, dropped whatever it was back into the river before leaping to another tree.

As the cloudless sky began to change into a rich orange-red, the forest on the other side of the river hardened into a silhouette. Within moments, the dark green forest had turned into a black, palm-tree-topped line that seemed to be suspended in a world of red sky and red Zambezi. From behind me, the deep mellow rhythm of wooden drums floated through the calm warm air. As the reds mellowed into dusky shades of purple I wondered if Livingstone, so many years before, might have sat on this very spot and marvelled at the world that he too had found himself in. Then the mosquitoes found me, which meant a quick run for the shelter of my tent. I'd stupidly run out of mossie repellent, but consoled myself with the thought that Livingstone wouldn't have had any of that either.

Blue-balled monkeys joined me for breakfast next morning. The males really did have blue testicles, a bright powder blue that worked in perfect contrast with their grey bodies and scarlet penises. To begin with they just spied on me. The bravest sat a couple of metres away, while the rest stared shamelessly at me from the trees and bushes. I stared back but it didn't make a jot of difference, my breakfast bananas and bread had caught their eyes. One minute I was boiling water for my coffee, and the next minute, still sitting cross-legged on the sand, I turned to get my powdered milk and my breakfast disappeared up into the trees. I swear that they were laughing at me as they threw a piece of crust in my direction! Another lesson had been learned the hard way and it'd left me with maize meal porridge for breakfast, again. They didn't seem so interested in that.

By the time the tent was down and all my gear was packed, Ken had arrived. He turned out to be a small, stocky, very friendly man with a never-ending source of conversation. This was probably very useful when out fulfilling the evangelist side of his job description.

"Let's go for a coffee", he'd said leading me in the direction of the Rainbow Lodge Hotel. The sign in the entrance hall said that the cheapest room was a hundred and eighty dollars a night and suddenly, the campsite's five dollars seemed extremely reasonable. Bet the toilets were clean though, and I'd bet that the guests hadn't had such charming company for breakfast either. Fortunately the coffee was reasonably priced and it felt really rather special to be sitting in those sleek surroundings, supping cappuccino from a china cup.

Ken took me out onto the 1,500 tons of iron suspension bridge that straddles the gorge in front of the falls. As we stood and stared down into rapids that he said were called the 'boiling pot', he explained that the bridge itself had been made in Darlington in 1904, and had been reassembled over the deep gorge using really ingenious methods.

I later read that the engineers had to build a 400-foot steel tower over the centre of the rapids. Then, using a rocket, they shot a cable from one side to the other. This was tensioned on both sides and was strong enough to carry a five-ton shuttle that would move the sections of the bridge into place. During its use, the 870-foot cable stretched a full eight inches. (Descriptions of the plan included such phrases as 'spandrel-braced arch bridge', 'skewbacks', 'saddles' and 'annular projection' – double Dutch to me).

Leaving me to deal with the border crossing into Zimbabwe, Ken walked across the bridge, and with no bike to deal with at customs he had plenty of time to get to the National Park on the 'Zim' side of the falls. By the time I got there, he'd arranged for one of the wardens to watch the bike and my gear while we went to see the falls from this, the more famous angle.

This border crossing had been quite different from all the others. I'd gone from the cash-strapped, worn out Zambia, to a more stable area where tourist dollars flowed far more easily and it showed immediately. The stern and suspicious Zambian officials were abrupt to everyone. The Zimbabwe officials were abrupt to everyone except tourists, and their offices were neat, even showing signs of recent paint, and their uniforms were clean and smart. In spite of the usual border-crossing bustle of the travel-worn, the nervous and those with something to hide, the officials worked with crisp good humour. It suddenly felt refreshing to leave behind the tense air of Zambia. One of the 'Zim' customs officials gave me a good going over though. Not out of suspicion, but just pure enthusiasm. He'd been fascinated and even asked to sit on the bike. One minute he'd been just another officer who could give me hassle and the next, an enthusiastic man who'd wanted to 'know'. I enjoyed his curiosity.

Once inside the National Park with Ken, the pathways took us past the statue of Livingstone and on through the dense foliage to a series of viewing platforms. Here again, even though the Zambezi was running at about half strength the falls weren't a disappointment. In fact I wondered if the views of the plunging waters were better without the usual drenching from the spray that the sign posts and guide books warned about. The famous rainbows still hung magically in the spray that there was, and it would have been easy to spend hours watching these shimmering misty colours. The overwhelming sense of immense power that the falls engendered was absolutely magnetic. But it wasn't only the raw power that made such an impression on me, it was the history and the pure natural beauty of the falls that made the attraction so strong. I knew then that if there were to be only one place in Africa that I could come back to, it would be here.

The town of Victoria Falls was basically there for tourists rather than the surrounding bush farms. Cafés, bars, restaurants, hotels and T-shirt shops lined the streets. We also found a large, western looking photographic shop. My camera bag now contained films from Kenya, Tanzania, Malawi and Zambia and I'd been getting worried that the constant heat might be damaging them. The samples of work in the shop window looked as good as my developer's at home and a lot tourists seemed to be having their films developed at the Falls, so this would perhaps make it a good bet for mine.

In the meantime Ken and I got into trouble with the police. Being a bit of a wheeler-dealer, he'd managed to get us rooms at a very large discount in the Zambezi Lodge Hotel which was just a few kilometres down the road. I got the feeling that Ken was probably rather good at his 'arranger' job. He'd left his bike there in the morning and had come to me by bus. For the return journey he positioned himself on top of my luggage, and a copper caught us leaving the town. I suspected that this was the first country I'd been to in Africa where the law had said that a helmet on the head was mandatory. Ken of course didn't have a helmet on and the policeman insisted that he couldn't ride without one. Ken set out to be good, but a kilometre down the road and out of sight of the town, he was back on the bike. Moments later we were safely into the Zambezi Lodge's compound, with no one the wiser. After the Tanzanian episode it had felt decidedly odd to be doing it, but my missionary friend seemed to enjoy having the wind in his hair. It was this side of the man that obviously had a lot to do with his still burning around on two or three wheels.

In the evening he treated us both to a braai. In southern Africa a barbecue isn't a barbecue at all, but it's a braai. That night I stuffed myself with spicy, juicy Boerewors (sausages), antelope, crocodile and ostrich steaks and to be healthy, a little salad. In the morning the hotel laid on a splendid buffet spread for breakfast and the two of us ate until bursting. I hadn't eaten as much meat as this, or as well, since leaving home. The new day bode well, until arriving at the camera shop. All my films were grey – every single one was ruined. This was a hard lesson to learn; I should have made the time and put a test film in first.

But there were still my paintings. I'd painted a few watercolours on the way down. Before starting the trip, the weight and space of the equipment had nearly made me throw them out, but now I was doubly glad I'd decided to keep them. The paintings, though not particularly good, would at least give me a series of images. In a way, because of the time taken to complete each one, they were more valuable. Each had its own collection of memories.

Before riding out of Victoria, Ken took me to the railway station where he graphically described how life had been there in the early days. With a dollop of imagination it wasn't hard to visualise the scene. In fact, all those years before he and his wife Ada had stepped out into an alien world of heat, wrought iron walkways, bougainvillea, black faces and solar helmets just like this one must have been in those days. The train had brought them straight off the boat from England. It was their first time over the borders of the British Isles, and having seen photographs and read books of those times, what a tense moment it must have been for them. He later wrote, 'It was the last few years of a typical colonial era. Half a century is quite a chunk of anyone's life and I'm glad I have lived long enough to realise that it was history. One does not think about it like that at the time.'

Before leaving for his mission in Botswana, Ken wanted to show me the area around Zimbabwe's second city Bulawayo. In spite of the help from tourist dollars, the economy wasn't good in Zimbabwe as a whole and one of the signs that things were hard was the lack of traffic. Heading south, we passed on average just six cars an hour and rolling down the excellent roads through the drought stricken countryside was a sobering experience. The cattle had cropped vast acres until the land was lucky if it even had a crew cut of stubbly straw on it. Villagers were out on the roadsides collecting the straw that their cattle hadn't been able to get to, and the cattle themselves looked thin and miserable. Few would survive if the drought didn't break soon.

As we rode, Ken pointed out sections of the old Bulawayo road. In the early days of motorcars something had to be done to get them across the bush in all weathers, but money was short then too so there had been no chance of laying asphalt roads. They couldn't even afford to lay a car-width run of asphalt, so they developed the strip system – two thin lines of tar at wheel distance apart. If another car came towards you you'd have to thump two wheels onto the dirt, leaving just two up. He said that the system had worked really well as in those days there weren't many cars and they weren't very fast. "Anyway", he said. "When you met a neighbour, you'd always stop for a chat so slowing right down wasn't an inconvenience. If you lost concentration though, you were quickly in trouble."

I liked Bulawayo straight away. The clean streets in the centre were 'motorway' width, there were traffic lights that people took notice of and the drivers drove as if they hadn't just bought their licences on the black market. The buildings were mainly old colonial, many of them dating back to the days of Cecil Rhodes. Rhodes was a man who had once stated that his, only religion was 'the expansion of the British Empire'. In fact when Zimbabwe was Rhodesia (named after this icon of imperialism) it was Rhodes who ordered the streets to be so wide. 'They must be wide enough to turn a wagon and full span of oxen in one go', he'd apparently said. They had certainly come into their own with modern day wagons as the traffic flowed smoothly and easily. Africa seemed to be dotted with examples of these grandiose thinkers, though not all of their ideas were so welcome.

In the middle of the city stood an oasis of green grass, palm trees and flowering shrubs. The recycling of the city's partially treated wastewater was at work to try to keep the well-tended parks and gardens alive. It was well worth the effort but I did wonder how many thirsty locals actually understood the concept of recycled water. Next to the park was the camping site. It was shady and lush – wastewater was at work here too. This was with the thought that tourist dollars were much needed and that everything should be done to keep them flowing in. For me, it was the most beautiful and best-tended campsite in Africa. The showers worked too and even the toilets weren't blocked, though long drop toilets with no need to flush away a gallon of water with each visit would have had my conscience sitting more comfortably – especially as locals told me that the city had just one month of water left in the reservoir.

The city made a good base to visit the Matopos National Park where the bush and rounded boulders are home to rhinos, elephant, San bushman paintings and Rhodes' tomb. It's also the scene of the massacre of Wilson's Patrol; now that was an ill-fated, misguided patrol if ever there was one. There were thirty-three soldiers in the Shangani River Patrol. They were hot-footing it after King Lobengula – 'the Elephant king' as his people were supposed to have called him after his enormous bulk. Legend has it that he was so big that the earth shook when he walked which I suspect, wasn't very often. Anyway, Rhodes and his bunch had been after Lobengula and his fearless Ndebele warriors for months. What was becoming Rhodesia had been the king's land and quite naturally he wanted to hang onto it. Lots of dirty tricks were played on him and eventually they got him on the run. The patrol ended up going after him because of a false report that he'd attacked Fort Victoria. The report was so false that it made no mention that the Ndebele warriors these 33 soldiers were after, numbered over thirty thousand. Well, they had no chance, though apparently they did take over three hundred warriors with them.

Ken and I also trudged the stone walls of the ancient city of Khami. We managed to beat the coach tours to the ruins too. For a precious hour we had the amazingly solid, maze-like walls to ourselves. As we wandered it dawned on me that I hadn't seen anything as structurally old as this since Ethiopia.

Funnily enough I didn't mind the intrusive nature of the coach tours because the point was that the people were out seeing something for themselves. Looking at the average age of the 'coachies', these folks were being just as adventurous as I but in their own manageable way. Perhaps they were less likely to experience so much 'real' life, but with luck they'd go home inspired by the wildlife and history they'd seen. And, because they'd seen it, the wildlife was more likely to survive and the historical sites to be preserved. Besides that, only the most insensitive were going to leave unaware that there really are an awful lot of people in this world who are a heck of a lot worse off than they were. TV reports can show what's real, but sitting at home never made me feel as if it actually was. I suppose that if all the senses aren't working then an alien scene doesn't have so much meaning. For example, the coach visitors might not have actually touched poverty, but they'd have smelt it. With sight, sound and smell at work, the images would have been unforgettable. I wondered if they had also seen that, though almost unbelievably poor the people really were human beings and individuals. Maybe they'd even seen that these folks had some of the same set of dreams that the rest of us harbour: security, health and happiness, a dry comfortable place to sleep, and food in the stomach. For me, once, these people had been little more than a fleeting collection of images. Perhaps I'd thought, 'Poor things' and then thought, 'Oh no, it's going to rain again', as the weather forecast came on. Mark Twain once wrote, 'Travel is fatal to prejudice, bigotry and narrow mindedness.' As I watched the 'coachies' explore, I realised that Africa was continuing to change the way I both saw and thought about things.

Back in the bustle of the new city we shopped for supplies. One of my favourite foods was tuna fish. You could get it just about anywhere, it was safe protein and it went with everything. Tuna sandwiches, tuna pasta, pasta and tuna, tuna and potatoes, tuna, onions and potatoes, tuna, packet soup mix and potatoes, tuna salad, and sometimes as a treat, tuna curry. Like Monty Python's spam, the versions seemed endless and could be mixed with whatever was available locally. When I was a kid in Africa, the stalls all seemed to stock oval or oblong tins of sardines in a tomato sauce, but perhaps this was a West African thing. Mostly it seemed to be tuna in the East. I'd not minded that at all, partly I suppose because we'd eaten an awful lot of sardines, but I was eating so much tuna now, I was afraid they were becoming an endangered species!

Later that day I made a commitment to the future. When I'd started the trip I'd had no idea how I was going to do. Would I like riding the bike? How would I do if it broke down and how would my money last? I'd also had no idea how long it would take me to ride the length of Africa. This far south, the pre-trip worry, 'would I die?' seemed decidedly over dramatic, especially when compared to the life expectancy of a tuna!

Over the weeks, answers to those questions emerged. Yes, riding the bike was fun; in fact I loved it and it had been the perfect way to get close to Africa. The BMW had been mechanically fantastic, and hardly anything had gone wrong. There had been a faulty speedometer from new which I'd been able to sort out in Nairobi. There'd been just one puncture, which had been a fizzle of air with no dramatics, and of course there'd been the electrical problem on the road south from Ethiopia. I'd learned a lot more about the bike and was still learning every day. In fact it even developed a personality. It was a girl, she just felt that way and I even discovered a few traits that fitted in with some of the girls in my past life. For example, if I didn't treat her well, then she'd always do something rotten to me. She'd got me a little too close to Africa from time to time, but I'd lived through all my falls; there'd been twenty-one hard ones by now and I'd lost count of the more gentle tumbles. Each one had taught me something and I never made the same mistake twice, either with the road, or with the bike. Over the months the bike went from being 'it' to 'she' to 'Libby'. With her name, (short for Liberty because that was what she gave me every day) she developed even more personality. Fresh out of Jersey, I'd never have believed that two-thirds of the way down Africa, I'd be talking to her!

So, I was still alive, enjoying myself and the money was lasting well. It had taken eight months to get to Bulawayo, and probably another two would comfortably get me to Cape Town. If that was the case then there'd be more than enough money to ship to Australia and surely there I'd be able to earn enough to make it back overland to Europe. This thought had been slipping into my mind with increasing regularity. Stopping the trip seemed more and more distasteful. Having worked in Australia before, combined with the idea of being there with Libby, made the notion magnetic.

With all of these thoughts and more in mind, I signed on a faxed dotted line for a ship to get across the Indian Ocean. I was nervous of creating a deadline time-wise, but knew that to go on a cargo ship with passenger space; the booking had to be made well in advance. The idea of leaving Africa the slow way appealed far more than a quick flight in any case. The clincher was that the shipping company happened to have an empty berth at exactly the time I'd estimated to be ready to go. The money went down the wires and the commitment was made. I had exactly two and a half months to make it to Cape Town and then up to the docks in Durban. It felt a very strange thing to have done. Partly it was the commitment to the future, but perhaps too it was the fact that after all the months of watching the pennies, I'd just spent a giant amount of money in one hit. The dreaded time limit would be OK (so I thought) and the dream would live on after Africa. My last months on the continent would now not be invaded by thoughts of the return to 'real life'.

Ken needed to get back to work, so we set off for Botswana. As we rode through the heat I contemplated that this was going to be my thirteenth country. I'd become a little superstitious over the months and wondered if there was trouble ahead. At the border, the officials were officious but could have been worse, and being with Ken saved a lot of time as he'd done the crossing many times before. He knew exactly where to go. At some of the crossings on the way down, finding the right offices had been a major part of the hassle.

My first impression of Botswana was that it was filthy. The drought was of course raging here too, but instead of the tidy roads of Zimbabwe, these were rubbish strewn. Bottles, tin cans and carrier bags lined the road to make the country the ugliest I'd been to. The towns we went through were almost European in style and the vast selection of goods on display went with the immaculate asphalt road to tell the story of the diamond fields that had been discovered within Botswana's borders. The country, once known as Bechuanaland, had been a protectorate of Britain since the early days of colonialism in southern Africa. In more recent years not a lot had got done there without fingers in the pie from South Africa, but now with independence, the wealth had radiated out at (for Africa) a rapid rate. The general living standards seemed good, but the transition from Third World to Second World had taken place so quickly that no one had had time to teach the locals that if they weren't careful with their new found wealth, their country would turn into one giant rubbish tip. Some of the more enterprising people had retained the typical 'make a use of it' attitude, and had done so in innovative style. Their houses were constructed of soft drink cans that had been filled with sand and then used as bricks. They looked uniquely practical and surprisingly attractive.

We arrived at the mission station in the dark. I didn't like to ride in the dark at all but Ken assured me that with the roads being so good, it wasn't a problem. I hung out at the base for a couple of days as Ken seemed to enjoy having company. It gave the chance to explore the area and take the opportunity to use his workshop to give Libby a full service. Over the years Ken had done most of his own servicing so was a good man to have around in the background in case something went wrong. It was really nice to be doing a service on the bike in an environment where there was no need to worry about what grit a puff of wind might be carrying, or having to deal with the risk of losing a nut or a washer in the dust. All went well, until I dropped the oil out of the final drive. The magnet that was set into the drain bolt was full of slivers of metal. It hadn't felt as if anything was wrong, and there'd never been metal on the magnet before so I knew that I had a problem brewing. Ken told me not to worry, that it was probably just a warning or wearing-in sign and that anyway, there wasn't a lot to do about it where we were. I decided to take his advice and be positive.

This was also the perfect opportunity to visit the hospital in town. From about a week after Lusaka, there'd been blood in my stool when I'd been to the toilet. The visits to the toilet were getting more and more frequent and I wasn't feeling very well at all. I felt tired, shivered a bit at night and felt weak after every visit to the loo. After a five-hour wait in outpatients, a Glasgow trained doctor listened to my story, pushed a gloved finger up my backside, told me that it wasn't piles and gave me a prescription for antibiotics. The steak at Mr Pete's had been a villain. I took my assaulted body down to the chemist and popped the first pill. Having committed myself to Australia, there was no time to get laid up with a bug.

By now I'd decided not to stay longer in Botswana; there was more of friendly, pretty Zimbabwe to see and there would, with a bit of luck, be mail waiting for me in the capital city Harare. Plus, I rather liked the idea of seeing some more game. Friends had advised that the Mana Pools Park in the north was the place to go, particularly to see elephants. By now these had become my favourite animals. For some reason, the time spent on trip research had included very little on Botswana, so I didn't know that in fact one of Africa's greatest concentrations of these amazing animals was just to the north of where I was with Ken.

I was back in Bulawayo before dark in spite of stopping on the way. I'd spent an hour collecting all the bottles and cans from over a kilometre of Botswanan roadside. The idea was that perhaps the big pile of them with a very apt sign stuck into the top of the heap might make one or two people think. Meanwhile the weather had changed, no rain but it had turned cold. For the first time in months, my fingers were numb as I rode. There was no reason to stay in the city for more than a night so the morning saw me riding south to the ruined city of

Zimbabwe, which gave the country its name. An ancient civilisation had once lived in a city that radiated around a large outcrop of rock. On to and into this rock, a fortress city had been built. Steep, narrow

staircase entrances made the city's heart easy to defend. Archaeologists have shown that at one time the plains below were covered with life. Soldiers, farmers, artisans and shopkeepers had lived their lives in this city of international trade. Jewellery from the Swahili coast, Arab coins and more importantly, ancient pottery from as far away as China had been dug up – China ruled the waves at one time, even as far as Africa. For me the site was another of those places that, like the Greek ruins at Delphi, had presence. It felt cold here too though, and for the first time in Africa my sleeping bag didn't seem to hold the heat in and the cold out. When the sun came up in the morning, moving on was the only way to get warm. This time the monkeys in the surrounding trees didn't get a free breakfast though.

Guidebooks said that the Chimanimani Mountains were well worth a visit and I'd been told that they weren't being so hard hit by the drought. I made a run for it in the warming sunshine and riding through the baobab trees, towards lunchtime, I finally shook off the chill.

The mountains have an air of mystery about them. They form much of Zimbabwe's eastern border with Mozambique and for generations they'd hidden smuggling trails between the two countries. An abundance of water and secret caves along the trails had encouraged their use. Yet again the road was in excellent condition and I settled down to cruise the twists and turns in happy mood. Small wood and straw villages that seemed to be only inhabited by women, children and goats, sat just back from the road. There were dogs too. They had fangs the size of Dracula's best and were intent on using them. In most countries, dogs hadn't had the energy to chase me, had been too sick to have a go, or had learned that a motorcyclist's boots make for poor chewing. These creatures, which looked so mongrelised and inbred that they seemed to form a pedigree of their own, fitted none of these categories. In fact their main aim in life seemed to be to rip passing motorcyclists to shreds. Every village had a few, but I developed a master plan to combat them. I started to play games with the beasts as they ran alongside trailing foamy drool behind them. I'd slow down until just going faster than they were, let them nearly catch up and then lean down and bark furiously at them. It worked every time. They'd screech to an amazed and bewildered halt, and I'd leave 'em looking dumbfounded in the dust. A few villagers looked a bit dumbfounded too.

Children stood by the roadside selling some sort of strange looking fruit and on stopping to buy some, it turned out to be the furry-skinned pod of the baobab tree. When I broke one open, it was lined with seeds that were coated with creamy coloured fuzz that tasted exactly like cream of tartar. I cruised on, planting baobab trees along the way until a sharp corner crept up on me when I should have been watching the road. Fighting to reduce my speed on some loose gravel I nearly came a cropper and had just managed to pull the bike upright when the front wheel thumped straight into a deep pothole. It was 10cm deep, with hard asphalt edges and I hit it at 70 km/h. But to my surprise, neither front wheel nor tyre showed any sign of damage. I didn't know how I'd made it out of that one. My bowels started to rumble though, and I only just made it into the bushes before a second close disaster; fortunately I had my toilet paper handy. In fact toilet paper had been readily available in the shops and on the stalls almost all the way down, which had surprised me. I wondered who, besides tourists and the wealthy, bought the stuff. I'd never seen anyone even buy any except tourists. No complaints though – I'd not got into the habit of some travellers who deftly use a bottle of water for rinsing. I mostly needed to drink all that I could carry anyway.

Now my cruise onwards was more cautious. The road had sheer craggy drops to one side and the rare potholes got the respect they deserved. My original idea had been to stay for a couple of days in the mountains, but by late afternoon the shivers had started again. Perhaps the cold ride into Bulawayo had given me a chill. I wasn't going to deal well with another cold night so regretfully headed back to the plains. Over the next hour we dropped from deep greens to the now almost uniform shade of beige that seemed to cover so much of the country. Back on level ground I pulled over into the first lay-by for a drink and to see what the time was. When just swinging my leg over the saddle, there was a loud pop and the front end of the bike sank a few centimetres. I was feeling pretty ill by now: my thoughts weren't clear, my bones felt tired, my bowels were still rumbling and even though down on the warmer plains again, the shivering was worse. To make the day even better, the rubber seal on my foot pump had perished, and that made using it an inefficient chore. I stood feeling pretty sorry for myself for a few moments and then thought sod it. No one else was going to fix the tyre so out came my new inner tube and the pump. The bead (rubber tyre on the rim of the wheel) broke nicely with the 'G' clamp I was now carrying for the task, and out came the tube that a six-centimetre split had wrecked. The split deserved a few moments of contemplation; how odd it was to make it through all those curves and sheer drops. It was strange that the tyre had waited until I got to the bottom, and that the wheel had stopped turning before it had popped. I tingled for a moment and then, putting the tingle down to flu, got on with changing the tube. At least the work was warming me up but with the pump not working properly the rubber wouldn't pop back out onto the rim all the way round. I struggled for an hour and a half with it before deciding to ride on the wobbly wheel, but to take it very slowly. It wasn't far to go to get to the city of Mutare and there was supposed to be a camping site that was easy to locate. I'd find it, put the tent up and flop. The tyre could be dealt with the next day – I was knackered.

Riding almost in a daze through the city and then on up through Christmas Pass got me to the camping site. It was almost deserted so I could choose a spot with an uninterrupted view of the valley. From somewhere came the energy to open a can of beans, heat them up and to make a cup of tea. I made a pathetic attempt at brushing my teeth, took my antibiotic from Botswana, my anti malaria tablet and then curled into my sleeping bag fully clothed. I shivered myself to sleep but at least my bowels weren't playing games any more; not funny to deal with when you are stuck inside a sleeping bag and then still have to face the tent fastenings!

It's amazing what a cup of tea and a good warm kip can do. I woke up in the morning busting for a pee and ran for it. A hearty breakfast of maize meal porridge, with a luxurious spoon full of cocoa powder and an extra one of sugar, plus a couple of mugs of coffee to wash it down, started the day on a high. The sun was shining, there'd been no cockerel to wake me up at an unearthly hour, the shivers had gone, there was no sign of a runny nose and there'd been a shop in the town where it should be possible to get a foot pump. Life wasn't so bad after all.

Sadly, the shop didn't have a pump and neither did anywhere else. I'd been to the petrol stations to try to use their pumps, but none of them worked. No worries though, there was still my emergency card to play. The 'card' was a couple of pressurised gas cylinders from England that I'd packed for just such an emergency. Back at the tent, I let out what air there was in the tyre, re-soaped the rims and screwed the cylinder on. Almost instantly there was an enormous bang! The tyre popped off the side of the rim, spitting out pieces of the brand new tube that had gone in the day before. The noise echoed around the valley walls, BANG! Bannng, bang, bang, bang… I wondered how many poor folks there were diving for cover in their villages down below. There was nothing to show what had gone wrong, but whatever it was, a new tube was ruined, and there was only a patched one left. The whole process started again, but this time I took the tyre off the rim as well. While messing around, I thought that I might as well have another look to see if there was any sign of what had caused the original puncture.

I remember the following 'tingle' very well. On the inside was a four-centimetre split across the bottom of the 'U' of the tyre. The pothole must have put it there and I'd suddenly no doubt that 'something' hadn't wanted me to ride the bike without finding it. The split must have been pinching the tube each time it went round and I knew that I'd been very lucky. With the split in the tyre there could have been a blow out at speed, and then everything might have been over.

It was quite a sobering moment. I made a coffee and sat looking out over the valley, my mind wandering over all the things that had happened on the trip, especially all the things I'd got away with and almost certainly shouldn't have. Why hadn't my inexpert usage of the bike caused problems? It had been bizarre to make it through Ethiopia. Why hadn't the militia shot first and asked questions after as was normal for them? Why hadn't the bullets from the roadblock hit us? Why had we missed the ambush of the bus? Why had I so often missed darting animals? Why hadn't my foot been ripped off on the road from Marsabit? Why had I never broken anything when falling off? Why had I not killed the man in Tanzania and in fact, why had John been in the truck and able to save him? Why had I not ended up in prison the three times I'd come close to it? I carried on running through my list of good fortune, never having really thought about it before. I'd always been just too busy getting on with life.

Someone on the trip had told me that bikers have guardian angels. Perhaps this was true; it would certainly explain all my lucky escapes. No one I thought, could possibly have this sort of run of luck without help, could they? I told myself not to be so bloody silly. I'd just got flu, coincidences happen all the time and I was as always, just a lucky traveller. Angels indeed!

By the end of the afternoon I was feeling a bit grim again so went to sit in the toilet block. This time not because of the squits but because it was the warmest place I could find. The other campers gave me a few very odd looks but I didn't care – I was past caring about anything except being warm and stopping the shivering that was getting so bad it was exhausting. The tiles on the wall next to the boiler room were bliss – I loved those tiles. Eventually, too tired to stay up and with a bug that was obviously still at work in spite of the antibiotics, bed was the place to be and an early night wouldn't do any harm. Shivering myself to sleep again made me wonder if it was time to take a rest day. At least my spare tyre was on and strangely enough, it had gone on all the way this time.

In the morning, the sun was up, the skies were clear, and the days saved by not staying in the mountains, made sense – emergency extra time. There was of course a time limit now, and they could be very handy. Not feeling too bad, I decided to move on, but the ride to Harare ended up being done in a dream. I don't remember the last half of the day and don't remember finding the camping site. I do remember being disappointed that there weren't any other overlanding vehicles on the site – I really needed some company. There were some backpackers in the morning though, and we chatted off and on over the next days. I felt too sick to move on for the first couple of mornings. But, telling myself not to be a wimp, I set off to visit the post office, to buy food, to change money on the black market and even to explore the street stalls that had such excellent carvings on display. For the first hour or two there always seemed enough energy to do my excursions. I went because I didn't want to miss out on anything, and I'd met too many travellers who'd sat around all day whinging about having this or that bug; often it'd been the main topic of conversation. But by midday I was usually feeling grim. Mr Pete's had given me a tenacious bug and the antibiotics didn't really seem to be helping. As I got worse, my powers of reasoning became fuzzy around the edges. An aching body and a sore neck told me that there was probably some flu to go with my stomach problems. Eating vitamin C tablets and paracetamol seemed to keep me going, but my 'mountain saving days' slipped on by.

Then to my surprise one day, Ashley and Donna turned up. They should have been half way up Tanzania by then. They told me their tale of woe; they were lucky to be alive. They too had braved the road up to Livingstonia and had enjoyed the view and the scotch pancakes. On the way down, a rut or some gravel had whipped the front wheel from under them, and they and their bike had gone over the edge of the road. The three of them had only been saved by the trees and bushes that were growing out of the sheer fall. These had managed to slow them down and fortunately the two of them had been wearing good gear; both had survived with just bruises and shock. The bike however had hundreds of dollars worth of damage. Up there they were a long way from a BMW garage, or in fact anyone who might have been able to help them. They had actually hitchhiked with their wrecked bike back to Harare. 'Only in Africa', I'd thought to myself.

A long-time BMW rider and fan runs a garage in Harare. Robbie Rushforth said that he could put them to rights, and that it would only take spare parts and time. Fortunately no major components had been broken beyond repair. For me it was good news; I now had friends for company. Some of the backpackers on the site had said, "Hmmm, you might have malaria", but I'd ignored the idea because I'd had malaria before and remembered what it felt like. I'd also been reliably taking the disgusting tasting anti-malarial tablets and except for a week, had had plenty of mossie repellent. Sitting around with long sleeves on at night meant that the mossies had hardly had a taste of me the whole way down. Nope, it was flu and a stomach bug.

Ashley and Donna could see the difference in me though, and on telling them about how much I was sweating at night, they made me go to a doctor. The doctor that had been recommended by the tourist office said, with a little sideways wiggle of his head but without taking blood tests, "Oh no Mister, you are not having malaria, I'm thinking you are carrying some virus, you must be taking these antibiotics and everything will be being absolutely fine." So I went home to my tent, popped the new antibiotics and three days later was not feeling 'absolutely fine'. My nights were filled with psychedelic fluorescent green nightmares. In the mornings, though always feeling a little better for what sleep there'd been, my sleeping bag was drenched with sweat. Ashley and Donna made me go to another doctor and this one said, "You definitely have malaria. Take these tablets and if you don't notice a difference in the morning, I'm putting you in hospital." Malaria was at that time the world's biggest killer disease. I'd been lucky that Ashley and Donna had survived their accident and had found me. It seemed the Angels had been looking after us all. Ridiculous thought, but kind of nice...

Chapter Fourteen

"Angel on Overtime"

'Never ride faster than your Angel can fly'

Peggy Tamsky

It had taken two weeks before I'd felt ready to move on, but my plans during the recovery time had changed. A lot of people had told me what a fantastic country Namibia was. They'd given me some pretty graphic descriptions of amazing canyons, desert elephants, some of the world's tallest sand dunes, and tribes in the north that almost nobody ever saw. They told of Bushmen in the Kalahari who talk with a language made up of clicks and who lived a nomadic life in what most of us would call a desert waste.

The Bushmen believe that all belongs to all, and to no one, and that the stars were formerly animals or people. Bushmen also believe that ancestors can appear as snakes, and therefore treat them with even more respect than the rest of the animal kingdom. These little people would thank an animal for the gift of its life before they killed it to eat, so much respect have they for their surroundings. I was told that the Bushmen knew what roots contained water, which plants could be eaten and of course, where water could be found when to the rest of us, there was none. I'd seen a picture of a Bushman, large rounded fat-storing buttocks thrust into the air, with his lips sucking on a giant straw that was made of some sort of hollow plant stem. The straw disappeared into a patch of arid, dry looking ground. They were also one of the races that the original colonialists to southern Africa had hounded almost out of existence. There were tales of hundreds of kilometres of sandy beach where diamonds washed ashore with the changing tides. Nice idea, but of course the whole lot had been fenced and guarded for years. Who could resist these tales - Namibia sounded interesting.

My original plan had been to ride South Africa's backbone through the gold and diamond fields, across the Cape vineyards and then down into Cape Town. From there the plan was to go up the east coast following the 'Garden route', and then finally to Durban and my cargo boat for Australia. But a bit of mental coin tossing had landed on Namibia's side, and it felt absolutely right. Most of the roads had been well travelled since Kenya and it would be good to get off that beaten track for a while. Namibia sounded exactly the place to do just that. But first, getting there would mean a long loop back up into Zambia and a night at Victoria Falls. Of course the idea of being at the falls again was great and that helped convince me. From there I'd have to cut across to the Caprivi Strip. This is a thin finger of Namibian land that runs between war-torn Angola and Botswana. Its scrubby desert bush and the track across was reputedly very hard work for two wheels. Soft sand and thorn bushes were supposed to be there a plenty, as were smugglers and wild animals. The build-up stories were a bit scary but nothing ventured, nothing gained. Namibia seemed like it was going to be a worthwhile reward for some rough kilometres. My time commitment had me worried though - with the new plan things would be stretched a bit.

The convalescent weeks in Harare had been interesting. When feeling better I'd begun to explore more and had noticed more of the city's quirks. As I was too tired to ride the bike, getting anywhere had mostly been done in 'emergency taxis '. These were beat up car versions of Kenya's matatus. The name had come from their emergence into common use in the days of the independence troubles and even though that emergency was over, the system had carried on. They were always a cheerfully crowded mesh of life on four wheels that technically should have been on the scrap heap. But, to determined Zimbabwean hands, they still got from A to B with reasonable reliability. The taxis would run set routes, so to get one just involved getting out onto a route and flagging one down. Then would come the difficult bit; getting in! The drivers always seemed to believe that their cars had rubber sides and unbreakable suspension. But, the taxis were cheap and gave me a chance to get close to people in a way that riding the bike didn't. Mind you, sometimes that wasn't so nice. Children always seemed to have snotty noses that never got wiped. Their slimy nose dribbles never seemed to be noticed by anyone except for me, and flies who would crawl enthusiastically around any damp orifice they could find.

Dribbling noses seemed to be their most popular spots and whenever a car stopped, we'd be swarmed. Sometimes backpackers were on a winner but having seen this I wouldn't have swapped places with one. The bike gave me too much freedom and normally my main contact with flies was to head butt them at speed, or to provide them with goggle space on which to commit gory suicide.

Many of the local schools demanded that the children wore uniform, and the style of these looked as if they were straight out of the nineteen forties. The girls wore thick pinafore dresses and gingham check blouses. The boys looked like cub scouts with shorts, bush shirts and peaked caps. The paved walkways in the city centre were home to a collection of street bands that had shoppers' feet tapping, and street café sunbathers entertained. The sounds were almost magically produced from drums made out of old oil barrels, home made guitars, maracas and an assortment of native instruments. Strolling puppeteers would make their characters dance with incredibly lifelike movements and we found a cinema with completely up to date facilities that was showing just released movies. We watched 'The Hand That Rocks the Cradle' for a dollar just four weeks after it had been released in Europe. That had felt like a little time warp and for a couple of hours we'd been mentally out of Africa. In spite of all this, the streets were a bit of a risk for the unwary and there were, as with every big city, plenty of 'no go' streets.

For weeks I'd regretted not having a lamp to use inside the tent. I hadn't dared to use a candle but beside the safety point of view, knew that normally it would have made it too hot inside. My torch had been eating batteries and when sick I'd often had to lie in the dark with nothing to do. It had been the same when in places where the mosquitoes had been so bad that being inside the tent with the zip firmly closed had been the only way to escape. Of course the tent didn't allow me to escape from the demented noises that frustrated mosquitoes make, but at least the noise hadn't itched! Some survival books say that the natural way to escape these loathed insects is to have a smoky fire. It'd only taken one try and the subsequent smoky stench that clung to both me and my clothes for days had turned me off that idea. In a back street Asian shop I found a small electric lamp (for just five dollars) that would run off the bike's battery. My living standards had immediately taken a big leap upwards.

But the week wasn't all good news. I'd run out of money and with the black market offering fifty per cent more than the bank it was mad not to change on the street. In my fuzzy state the decision to do it had been an embarrassing mistake. I'd been ripped off, almost as if the guy had sensed my weakened condition. Fortunately the temptation to change a big lump sum hadn't been strong. The only consolation at the time was that it could have been worse, but then it clicked that this was exactly the same amount of money that the Tanzanian army gave Joseph as his yearly pension.

There'd also been news of Mike and Sally - Ashley and Donna had briefly bumped into them and then Stephan from Switzerland arrived on the site with an update. He'd travelled with them for a while and told me that they'd earned some money in Kenya, and had got their finances sorted out in England. They were now planning to head for South America from South Africa. He said that they were well and that their bike was doing a good job. It was great to hear about them, though it was Stephan who worried me. He'd set himself the target of making it from Switzerland to Cape Town on just one set of tyres. His rear tyre was down to the cloth and he'd been lining the inside of it with old inner tubes. The thought of that had given me the shivers again – suddenly I'd been very glad to be riding in a completely different direction! Stephan was an accident waiting to happen.

The days ticked by terribly fast and I knew that now I was quite a bit behind schedule. After all the past months this was a totally alien feeling but the thought of the cargo ship spurred me on, perhaps too soon. I hit the road and ran for the border with Zambia. I had a twinge of regret while scooting past the edge of the Mana Pools Park, but I was sure that Namibia would be worth it. After four hours on the road my backside was the sorest it'd been the whole trip; losing two stone over the previous weeks had left me with a thin bum. By nightfall I was exhausted. If there'd been any common sense around I'd have called it a day and stopped for a holiday, but the next morning saw me up and on the run again. It was great to be back on the bike. The break from riding made me appreciate how special the sounds and the changing smells were. It had made me miss the surreal momentary feeling that when on the bike I was the one sitting still and that it was the world that was rushing past me. I'd missed the changing scenery and the feeling that around every corner was a potential new adventure.

On my second night out, I bush-camped in a perfect spot. The sun went down in a blaze of orange that seemed to change to pitch darkness with a click of the fingers. I woke in the early hours to find that the sky was orange again – the bush was on fire. Dense smoke was streaming in my direction and small animals were scurrying past, oblivious to my presence. The flames were no more than twenty feet away by the time I had stuffed everything into boxes and had the tent strapped onto the bike. It was stupid; I should have just run with the animals but the bike started first time and for once I didn't drop it in the sand. I watched the flames in my mirrors all the way to the border. I was alive and knowing how lucky I'd been, was back on a roll. Even the road to Victoria Falls had been improved since I'd originally ridden south.

Going back into Zambia had given me a chance to see something that I'd just not noticed on my original speedy flit through. The currency was the 'Kwacha' and the notes had pictures of President Kaunda's face on them. What I hadn't noticed was that the lowest denomination note had the president's image with a typically correct serious expression. On the next value up there was a very slightly more humorous expression, on the next came a happy smile and by the highest denomination, Kaunda had been given a delightfully large cheesy grin. Brilliant, note designers with humour – or were they?

My arrival at the Livingstone camping site was on a tired high again. After cooking a large meal and drinking litres of tea, I went to sit in my spot on the banks of the Zambezi. Kingfishers darted around me and with recent rains up-river the falls lived up to their nickname – 'Smoke that Thunders'. The Zim tourist office statistics said that in the rainy season over five million litres would go over the edge per minute. As the sun had gone down it set the sky alight with orange-red and the forest darkened into its now familiar silhouette. But the glowing red waters of the river had a surprise in store for me – a group of ripples turned into the rounded shape of a head. The hippo yawned a giant yawn, and with a series of lazy, laughing grunts, it slid back into the gently swirling red. As I realised I'd been holding my breath, the breeze changed direction and the deep rhythmic melody from a xylophone band playing in the Rainbow Lodge had come floating with it. This time I had plenty of mossie repellent and I sat enjoying the sounds in the mellow warmth of the night. Nothing and no one bothered me. It was moments like these that I'd come to Africa for.

A feathered alarm clock woke me early in the morning and I was on the way by seven. The map said that the minor road to the border with Namibia was 'in poor condition'. It hadn't been wrong; the road was eighty percent hole and twenty percent crumbling asphalt. A purely dirt road would have been a lot simpler to ride but it was far easier for me than it was for the cars and trucks. At least I only had two wheels to manoeuvre through the holes. One or another of a car's four wheels was bound to hit something, so they could only travel at half my speed and in half my comfort. I could have gone faster too, but decided to save strength, and the bike.

After a while I was waved to a halt at a roadblock, a foot and mouth disease checkpoint. The overalled wellington booted soldiers sprayed the bike and my hands were washed in chemicals, but the soles of my boots were missed. There'd been this sort of situation so many times before in Africa. The good intention was there but the training and therefore the understanding was not. It made me realise yet again how lucky I was to be able to live in a first world country.

The swift, muddy coloured river just before the border had no bridge, but a pontoon ferry that was tugged back and forth by a rope. This was a first for me and though the pontoon seemed rickety we all made it across with ease.

The small collection of border huts kept life simple and the officials knew what to do. They showed no sign of wanting to play games,

240

but this was the first time that my face and name were checked against wanted posters. According to these, there were a lot of white-skinned villains around. The bald, bullet headed officer, who instead of having three chins had three fat rings around the back of his neck, took his time. 'These whities all look the same', was an irresistible thought that slipped into my mind before riding up the pale sand road into Namibia.

The town of Katima Mullilo sprawled somewhat lethargically in the dust along the roadside. The beat up old fuel station had petrol so it made sense to fill up straight away – this could be my last chance for about three hundred kilometres and it would have been nuts to go back in the morning to find that they'd none left. There were now just seven weeks to make it to Durban and that would have been a stupid delay. The petrol attendant told me that the best places to find someone to ride across the desert with would be the petrol station itself or the hotel. So I rode down to the 'other' Zambezi Lodge where there was a camping site along the river's edge, a swimming pool and a bar. Free bush camping would have been possible, but with all the stories that were floating around about the border area it was an additional risk that didn't seem worthwhile. Another thought that made sense was that the bar would be a good place to hunt out someone to ride with. I'd learnt enough about Africa by this time to know that deserts shouldn't be ridden alone if there was a choice. Unless perhaps you were very good, and my riding style still couldn't be described as being that.

No luck in the bar that night or the next four nights and the traffic at the petrol station seemed only to be moving locally or back into Zambia. The drivers gave me conflicting reports about the track and some told me that under no circumstances should it be done solo. There were too many dangerous people, the road was very bad in long sections and if I broke down, it could be days before anyone found me. Others said that it was very hard going, but with having made it this far down through Africa then I ought to make it. Another driver advised that, except for about fifty kilometres, the going was good gravel. Now that was more like it. These fifty kilometres seemed to be the trouble zone that all the stories had in common and the sand and the gravel

241

were white. If and when eventually riding track, the glare was going to make life hard. Back on Jersey the local motocross shop had sold me a polarised lens for my goggles. I'd nearly dumped it on several occasions but had never been able to bring myself to do it. The lens was going to be very handy now but there was still no one to ride with. The hotel campsite was eating a hole in my budget, the sailing date was getting ever closer and I didn't know who to believe about the road. At the rate I was going I could have sat there for weeks, so I tossed a coin.

Heads! Go for it on my own and with care it should be OK. I had learnt a lot since February and anyway I did have my guardian angel, didn't I? I told the police what I was doing and that I'd report in on the other side. They appeared to be quite easy with the plan so I was set.

The first gentle glow of sunrise lit up the soft tail of dust that the bike was swirling up behind us as we eased out of town and headed west. The fuel and water tanks were full, I had plenty of food, the map was a good one and my compass worked. With the early sun low behind me there was no glare, and this would be a critical factor. When the sun was at its highest and then falling down directly before us the glare would be at its worst, but there were at least five hours before then. If all went well we could go a long way in that time. The only other road users were a man on a black boneshaker bicycle, and his goat that trotted along beside him as if an early morning jog was quite the thing to be doing. Neither seemed particularly bothered that it was a long way to anywhere.

The road was fine and we clicked along at seventy k's. Eighty or even ninety would have been fine too but common sense said, 'just take it easy'. At times on the way south when all had been going well it had been a temptation to push to the limits. The Paris-Dakar spirit was always dangerously bubbling away on those good days. On some of them I'd felt absolutely invincible and once or twice had scared myself silly. But this was not the time to do anything daft. Besides a lot of skill, the Paris-Dakar riders had support teams made up of mechanics that could strip down and rebuild a bust bike in moments. I had just me. A checkpoint's book showed that the last vehicle through had been two days before. How had I missed it?

The road stayed pretty good. Every so often there'd be a softer patch, but the sunlight would catch the change in texture enough for me to see it and react accordingly. One long soft patch had me opening the throttle wide and with a series of wild wiggles, the bike and I were through it. The gravel continued easily with only the soft ridges that other vehicles had thrown up from the loose surface giving cause for concern. This was space invader time again. With my reactions sharpening as each new little problem appeared in front, it was actually fun. The roads in the northern half of Africa had been far harder than this one.

By mid morning I was half way across. Two quick breaks for drinks had been enough to keep me lubricated and release the tension that was there all the time we were moving. This hadn't been mental stress but pure, 100%, every muscle working, body stress. I liked this feeling and sometimes it built so hard and so fast that I hadn't been aware of its energy drain until the end of a ride. But on this particular day it had made me feel tired during the ride. I put that down to the malaria and got on with the road, but for the first time I was wondering if I'd recovered enough to be doing the ride. It was a pity that there was no wildlife to see, but in the end my eyes were mostly on the track so I probably would have missed anything anyway. Time wise, things were going very well, but the worst section was still to come. However, I was sure now that with common sense this road wasn't going to beat me. I rode on looking forward to the buzzing high of making it to Rundu, the first town of consequence on the other side.

Movement other than swirling dust in my rear view mirror made me take a rare second look. I hadn't been checking the mirror very often as there was too much going on in front to take the time out to do it, and anyway, I didn't really expect to see anyone there. But this time there was and out of my dust cloud nosed a 4x4; I closed the throttle to let him by. Perhaps my angel had been having a snooze at that moment as I woke up four days later, in hospital.

The glaring white lights made me think to begin with that I was still out on the road. With senses just beginning to work there seemed to be something wrong, but I'd no idea what. Whilst keeping my eyes partially closed I took a sneaky look at my surroundings. For some reason it seemed important to look without anyone noticing. Well, it was pretty obvious that it was a hospital; the smell and then

the beds and screens around me told me that, but what had happened? Trying to work it out, I realised that it wasn't just my bony backside that was aching – everything seemed to be aching. I had toothache; my jaw was killing me and on trying to move my chest had said 'No', in no uncertain terms. My arm even had a cast on it. What had happened? Feeling around the rest of my body, everything seemed to be still there.

A dark face with a white cap on loomed out of the glare; it was a nurse and she'd seen me moving. "So Mister, you are awake, heh", she said. "How about some pain killa heh?"

This seemed quite a sensible idea but when I realised that it wasn't going to be in tablet form and that I was going to get a needle in the backside, it didn't seem such a good idea after all. It worked though, the aches drifted away and I slept again. Waking up the next time, the Namibian Matron was there. Through aching teeth I could ask her what had happened.

"This hospital is Rundu", she said. "You smesh your bike und dey bring you in from der bush, how you feeling?"

She didn't know the full story of what happened, but it appeared that I'd been unconscious for four days. In that time I'd been in three hospitals including a South African army bush hospital, in Angola! She laughed when I asked her where Libby was before I asked what was wrong with me. "You bike is outside, but not so pretty", she said. As for me, just loads of bruises, seventeen stitches in my face, and a broken wrist. It seemed that this traveller had just had a lucky escape and then it sunk in, I was sure to miss my boat. I couldn't help feeling frustrated when I should have been feeling, 'Brill, I'm still alive!'

Eventually the Portuguese doctor came to see me. When SW Africa had recently become an independent Namibia, many South African people had gone home. No one had known what would happen and more than a few had feared for their lives. Others had just not wanted to live under a black government. Hospital staff had gone too and now this one was manned by trained, and many partially trained Namibian nurses, plus doctors from overseas. Matron told me that there were doctors from Cuba, Portugal, and the Soviet Union as well as a couple from Namibia. A real mix and the hospital was in the throes of trying to make a go of it.

The round-faced, sallow-skinned doctor knew a little more about what had happened to me and told me that I really was lucky. The arm would mend and the surgeon had done a great job with my stitches but they had been worried when I'd taken so long to wake up. They hadn't done an x ray of my skull and neck but he told me that it wasn't necessary. I didn't feel so sure but didn't have the energy to argue. He also told me that I was lucky that I could see. My glasses had smashed and filled both eyes with splinters. Apparently two German holidaymakers had found me and they had washed out nearly all of the glass before they'd moved me. The damage to my eyes showed that if they had moved me with glass still in them, I'd have been blinded. The doctor gave me a scrap of paper that had been torn out of a notebook. Before driving on, Peter and Edith had left their names and address for me. I knew no more about them or about what had happened.

After two days I felt a little better. Matron was always amazingly kind and one day even took my blood stained clothes back to her village where she washed them. They came back cleaner than they had been for months. I also had a visitor. Clive was an aid worker in the town; his job was to make sure that the aid goods destined for Angola made it to the right places. He was also a biker and in his free time would burn around the desert on his 500 cc Honda trail bike. He brought me his company, chocolate, books to read and an invitation to convalesce in his house.

Nurses meantime had wheeled me to a phone in the entrance corridor to call my travel insurance company who said that they would monitor the situation, and just as importantly, they agreed to pay the bills. These had eventually totalled over thirty thousand dollars so without the insurance, my trip would have been over and I would have been deep in debt. I also managed to phone my mother who told me, "Yes, I realised that something was wrong but haven't worried because I knew that you weren't dying!" How had she known?

Suddenly, Clive's offer seemed like a very good idea. The nurse had been due to give me another pain killing injection and I watched her carefully as she prepared for it. She opened a new syringe packet. (Unable to get at them, my supply had stayed in the medical kit on the bike – these ones were added to the bill.) She took a new needle and was wearing rubber gloves, brilliant. She swabbed the top of the painkiller vial and then, while having a chat with another nurse she put her hand on top of some blood stained swabs from the patient next door to me who was obviously dying. Turning back to me, she had no idea why I wouldn't let her come near me with the syringe. I had to argue hard. The next day I felt that booking myself out of the hospital might well be safer. I dreaded to think what had happened to me during my days of unconsciousness. This border area had one of the highest Aids rates in Africa.

The doctor made out a prescription for painkillers and Clive, who'd kindly already moved Libby there, took me home. It felt as if I was being rather ungrateful towards the hospital; they had done their best, done it kindly and it was lucky for me that they'd been nearby but I didn't feel safe in there any more.

When first seeing Libby, it looked as if most of the damage was expensively cosmetic or could be fixed fairly easily. As we explored the bike it became clear that all the damage was conducive to having hit something and my having gone over the handlebars; my wounds fit that story too. The bike's forks were twisted, the mini fairing shattered and the speedo looked like an old can of beans that had been crushed. Both the bash bars and the centre stand had been bent into modern art. Amazingly, none of my luggage was missing and someone had even collected up all the broken bits of plastic. There was just one piece the size of a coke bottle top missing. There must have been so many opportunities for things to be stolen that it was quite a statement that nothing had been.

Clive and his wife were more people I ended up owing a lot to; they took great care of me and Clive knew of a local man living in this edge-of-the-desert town whose hobby was making things out of fibreglass. William took all the broken parts of the fairing and instrument panel, and glued them together. He then made a mould and finally shaped new parts that were in every way as good as the originals. William had a friend who was a welder. The welder straightened, cut and patched in sections until Libby, in spite of all her cuts and bruises, began to look her old self again. Clive straightened the forks himself and re-wired the front end. These friendly people fixed five hundred dollars worth of damage for just seventy. I was really happy when she fired up first time, but knew that it was going to be a long time before I'd be able to ride her again. I was also nervous; now she looked much bigger and even heavier than she had before.

While all that was going on, Peter and Edith's note had gone astray. It wasn't until almost a year later, when finding that it had gone through a hole in my jacket pocket, that I could thank them and find out what had happened. This adventurous duo had travelled the Caprivi Strip a day later than they'd planned because Edith had suddenly been feeling unwell. They'd come across a group of local men on the strip and had almost driven on by. They'd not wanted to get involved in whatever was going on in the middle of a dangerous nowhere. Very wise, but thankfully they'd caught a glimpse of Libby and realised that there had been an accident. There'd been blood pouring down my face and over my clothes – the bike was on her side by a hole in the road. Though kneeling, I was semi-conscious and disorientated.

We guessed that what had happened was that the 4x4 had shot on past me without slowing down to lessen its dust cloud as vehicles would normally do out of courtesy. I obviously hadn't slowed enough myself and in the sudden dust cloud hadn't seen the hole - which was nearly a metre deep. It looked as if I'd driven straight into it and had gone right over the handlebars. The 4x4 probably hadn't seen a thing.

On checking my wounds, Edith had seen the glass in my eyes and had used the whole of their water supply to wash the glass away. They had then given the empty canisters to the group of men in order to make room for me in their 4x4. As they'd done that a truck had appeared and they had persuaded the driver to take the bike on board. The driver knew that there was a small hospital in the next village. Bike and I were taken there, and when Peter and Edith left Libby was next to me on the hospital ward. They later showed me a video they'd taken when the bike was being unloaded by the male nurses at the hospital – a very odd thing to watch happening. The two of them had had to leave me because their flight home was just a couple of days away and they'd a long way to drive to get to it. I'm sure that I owe them my eyesight and more than likely my life too. If they hadn't been passing and stopped, the worst could have happened. I think that my angel had literally been caught napping, but had sweated to make up for it afterwards.

After several days with Clive and Jo it appeared that something wasn't right with the way I was healing. Even with the pills there was too much pain. It seemed odd that my neck hurt so much and that no X-ray of it had been done. But it was a long way to the capital city of Namibia, and Clive said Windhoek was the only place to get really good care. That was all well and good, but the bus ride down would have been a hell of a journey in my state. When Clive was talking about the airport that he was working out of, I had a brainwave. Why not try to hitch a lift on a plane? It must be possible and was definitely a better option than road transport.

Leaving Libby with Clive to put on a truck to the capital, I went to the airport and there to my delight was a MAF plane about to set off for Windhoek. This was the same company that my friend Heather in Uganda had been working for and I didn't even need to try to look pitiful. I was doing the job quite naturally.

Within the hour, I was up in the air and riding in absolute comfort to the city. The pilot did an extra smooth landing and then found a taxi. He warned the driver that there would be trouble if he went through any potholes on the way to the hospital; the taxi driver drove with extreme care and didn't hit a single bump. The driver also realised that I couldn't get out of the car on my own and had scuttled around to ease me out. He'd even wanted to go and get a wheel chair but I'd needed to stretch a bit. The nurse listened to my story and at the word Rundu; she found me a wheel chair and ordered: "You sit, you don't move!" I'd just about run out of energy by then so didn't complain and it wasn't long before the X-ray department had me retelling the tale. They rayed me from head to toe and it didn't sound like it was good news.

Twenty quiet minutes later, a white-coated Doctor walked in with a set of X-rays in his hand. Laughing, he looked at them, at me and then at the sheets again. "I don't need telling that these are yours", were his first words. "You're a bit of a mess", he said with a grin and I told the story once more. "Lucky too eh?" the Doc said. "Well, do you want the good news or the bad news first?" I opted for the bad.

It seemed that I didn't have just a bust wrist; all my ribs and my jaw were fractured too. My teeth hurt because four of them were broken. My wrist felt like it wasn't healing properly because it wasn't. Both the bones had been broken, but only one of them had been set and that hadn't been set in the right place. The other bone had fractured in two places and they were well on the way to mending themselves in the wrong positions. The good news was that my neck and skull were OK. The doctor told me that the best thing to do was to have the wrist broken again and have it all reset. If I didn't have this done there would be a lot of the use of the wrist missing. It takes six weeks for bones to heal, and including the days since the accident, three had already been eaten. At that moment I knew that I'd never make it to the ship on time. Ho Hum.

The doctor must have seen my face fall but of course didn't know the reason why. He told me that the Catholic hospital in the city was one of the best in Africa and definitely on a par with most in Europe, He said that in a strange sort of way my luck was in. "South Africa's second best orthopaedic surgeon is on an exchange in the city and I think that I can get him to do the operation." That fitted in with my crazy run of luck; it felt that now my poor old angel really was working overtime.

I booked myself into the town's only backpackers' hostel to await instructions, but was only there for a day before being admitted. The day gave the chance to arrange storage for Libby and to let Clive and Jo know what was happening. The hospital itself was absolute luxury. I had a room to myself, TV, excellent meals and over the next days I put on some much needed weight. The nurses were brilliant too and the operation went well; the surgeon put a plate and seven screws into my wrist. "You might bleep with airport metal detectors", he said with a smile. My bedside radio had bad news though. While I was lying there, Sterling was devalued by 20% against the US dollar and as just about every country anywhere seemed to set their rates against the dollar, an enormous chunk of my travel money had just disappeared. What else was going to go wrong?

The days in the hospital went by almost too fast and I ended up back on the street feeling vulnerable – a little as if I'd been thrown out into reality. A taxi went over every bump it could find and I booked myself back into the hostel. The next day they told me that no one, not even in my state, was allowed in the hostel between ten a.m. and four p.m. Not wanting to spend money for cafes there wasn't much to do except wander the streets, but it did encourage me to phone the shipping company to let them know what was happening. I'd been afraid that I might have lost my money but the news was good news. A really cute-sounding girl commiserated with me and then booked me on to a boat that would sail seven weeks later than planned. It would leave me short of time in South Africa but I couldn't complain; something else had just gone right.

As if to warn me off any hint of complacency, a mugger got me the next day. It was a silly situation too. With my right arm in a sling, I could no longer reach into my trousers to pull out my money belt. But I'd no cash left and as the belt was exactly the same shade of cream as my sling I thought I could tuck it inside for a trip to the bank, and then when inside I could take some travellers cheques out with my left hand. I'd been practising left-handed versions of my signature so thought that the plan would work, and so it did. But just two steps outside the bank, a hand reached into my sling and grabbed the belt. Instinct took over. Being an idiot I hung onto the belt cord, with my broken wrist complaining like mad. There was just enough resistance for the guy, whose face I never really saw, to give up and make a run for it. I couldn't chase after him and he left me standing aware of just how weak and vulnerable I really was. The city rushed on around me – I felt quite alone.

Then amazingly, there were Mike and Sally walking down the street towards me. A beer – painkiller cocktail, combined with their good company to see me on top of the world again. They pointed out that without doubt, I was lucky that the wipe out had happened in Namibia and not in some remote place further north where even 'Rundus' were few and far between. The two of them had managed to get work in the city and we saw quite a bit of each other over the next weeks.

Over those weeks I also saw a fair chunk of Namibia, and it lived up to my expectations. By staying at the hostel I'd met other travellers and between us we hired a mini bus to do our exploring. It was a fun time and a real bonus. It wouldn't have been possible to see it by bike without another major delay. The multi-coloured three hundred metre high sand dunes at the Soussusvlei oasis enthralled us. The 'Quiver Tree Forest' was beautiful, the desert was absolutely stunning sand and the vast Fish River Canyon purely impressive. It's the largest of its kind in Africa and the vistas demanded that we sit and stare at them – in between dealing with the five punctures we suffered that is.

Later on I teamed up with some other travellers to head north to the seal colony at Cape Cross. We'd been able to smell the colony well before getting to the estimated 80,000 lumbering, grunting,

barking lumps of doe eyed blubber. The gut-turning stink around them
was that of rotting, putrid flesh. But amazingly we got used to the
stench very quickly and were able to watch the seals antics for hours;
they even let us get within a few feet of them. The down side was that
somehow, even though we'd touched nothing except our boots on the
rocks, our clothes reeked with seal odour until we had washed them
twice. When the 4x4 was returned I suspect that the owner knew
exactly where we'd been. My boots in fact retained a whiff of Cape
Cross until they eventually fell apart years later.

Together, we also explored some of the Skeleton Coast, so
named for all the shipwrecks that lie rusting in the cold salt air of the
dunes. There are many stories about these wrecks. It must have been
desperation itself to survive a wreck only to find that you were
confronted by hundreds of kilometres of almost waterless desert. You'd
need to be a survival expert to make it. In spite of its bleakness though,
Bushmen wander this coast living off the land. They build shelters out
of whalebones and seaweed. They collect moisture from the dense fog
that rolls in from the cold sea, and eat shellfish and seal. There was
always plenty of driftwood for fires. This type of existence seemed so
far from my own that, as I stood staring out over the cold green and
white breakers, I just couldn't work out if the Bushmen would have
been happy or if it had been an endless, 'on-the-edge' struggle to
survive. Uncomplicated, uninterrupted peace, or purgatory?

My broken bones had been a high price to pay for all of this
exploring, but every cloud does have a silver lining and mine had been
not the wonderful geography, but all of the amazingly kind people that
I'd met. By this time one of the things Africa had taught me was that most
of the people in our world are kind, considerate, honest and hospitable
– most of the time. But the continent had also taught me to beware of
the 'Chameleon Factor'. These small pop-eyed lizards are all over Africa
and there are many fables about them. It would have done me well to
remember one particular tale before setting out from Harare.

'The gods made the world beautiful but when they'd finished it
had felt that something was missing, so they quickly made people.

Watching from above, the Gods decided that the people, who seemed confused, should be told something important. They picked the trusted chameleon as their messenger for the news. 'People will not die forever but will come back to life like the moon.' The chameleon, 'Mr Slow, he who moves cautiously', set off on the long walk to earth. Each step was measured, planned and certain. Obstacles were judged, considered and, one by one, dealt with in an equally certain manner. The journey progressed, but slowly. Such a long time passed that the Gods decided to send a back-up messenger, just in case. After all, the message was important and would reassure all the people they'd made. The hare, 'he who rushes', sped off without waiting to hear the full message. He arrived first of course and blurted out what he had heard. "The gods say you will die forever!" The people tore their hair, got drunk, fought each other and mayhem ruled. The gods looked down shocked, but the hare had sped off somewhere else. Finally the chameleon arrived, but it was too late. The word could not be changed once delivered.

The moral of this now very apt fable is that, 'to move in haste may lead to disaster'. Perhaps an extra recovery week in Harare and an extra day or two in Katima would have made the month completely different.

Chapter Fifteen

"The Turning Point"

Four wheels rolled me into Cape Town in the late sun of that November day. My arm was still in a cast, my ribs were sore but no longer hurt and I could now talk with my jaw doing what it was supposed to do. It was an exciting time to be arriving in South Africa; apartheid had recently been abolished and the whole country was buzzing with 'what will happen next' conversations. This was a massive turning point for everybody and everything. The next few years would be 'make or break', and those who'd escaped from South West Africa (Namibia) in a hurry were looking at their situation with irony, or leaving South Africa too.

My four wheels were actually a hitchhiked ride. The trip had so far seen me on the bike, buses, a train, an aeroplane, taxis, matatus, boats, canoes, a bicycle and I'd walked a lot too, but had never hitched anywhere. I'd always intended that the bike shouldn't be the main reason for the trip but that it should be the means to get me into adventures, and so it had. This time the situation it had landed me in encouraged the idea to hitchhike down to Cape Town. It would be another form of transport for the list and of course it could well be a cheap and simple option. And, I thought, how many people would be able to drive past a backpacker with his arm in a sling? But then the idea got simpler – the Windhoek radio station ran a service that I'd not come across before. If you phoned them with a little personal information, the day you wanted to travel and of course where you wanted to go, they would broadcast that a ride was needed. Anyone who was going in your direction and had space, would then phone in to complete the connection. Mostly the rides would be for free though some were looking for passengers to help share the cost. The distances in South Western Africa are so vast that my driver was looking for company just to keep him awake. He didn't want cabaret, just someone to talk to him. With my jaw working and weeks of stifled conversation bubbling out of me, he stayed awake and the journey down passed quickly.

The desolation of the north west of South Africa hadn't been a surprise as good old Michelin map No 955 had shown me that in fact it's just an extension of Namibia and Botswana's deserts. But as the little Volkswagen Beetle pulled ever southwards, the land began to turn green and the riverbeds began to have water in them. When you approach Cape Town from the north you drive around a long sweeping bend which opens out into a view that has Table Mountain as its focal point. It sits dominating the Cape and my first sight of it was without its fabled tablecloth, which for some reason I hadn't expected. I could see that the mountain really is flat-topped but I'd read that for much of the time white cloud shrouds the plateau. In certain weather conditions, this cloud flows down over the rim in a wispy curtain that, with a dash of imagination, is supposed to look like a tablecloth being unfurled in slow motion. As we rolled towards it, I wasn't sure if my preconceived ideas had turned my first sight of the famous mountain into a disappointment, or if in fact I should consider myself lucky to have seen it nude.

Meantime, Libby was coming into South Africa on fourteen wheels. As I couldn't ride her anyway she'd gone to get checked over properly by BMW at their head office in Johannesburg. That way there'd be peace of mind, she'd definitely be working as she should and I could pick her up from Jo'burg later when I was able to ride again. The other bonus was that she'd have safe storage until that time. The plan looked as if it would work out very nicely, especially when BMW told me that they'd have to order a speedometer from Europe as all of theirs were in kilometres and mine had been in miles. This of course was going to take time. All that was needed for the plan to work out was for me to get fit again and to be able to face riding, but I was having odd feelings about that. It wasn't a fear of riding, but more that when climbing aboard the bike for the first time, perhaps something would act as a trigger and all of a sudden memories of the accident would come back. Maybe the reason that there weren't any memories of the accident was because of the bang on the head, or perhaps it was that I'd mentally blocked it out, or possibly even that it had all happened so

255

quickly in a dust cloud that there hadn't been anything to see to remember. With luck it was the latter.

Cape Town was a surprise. Not only was it the most modern city I'd been to since Europe – it beat Lilongwe hands down for that – but there was also something peculiar about the place and it took quite a while to realise what it was. Many of the people on the streets were either white or light skinned and after all the other cities on the way down, that looked really odd. This city had a cosmopolitan air to it in spite of the world's sanctions which had technically cut it off for so many years. There was a sort of mellow but buzzing feeling to it and this contradiction in terms itself was strangely apt. Cape Town's foundations are set in visible history; skyscrapers loom crisp and modern over the old slave quarters and the piers where the East Indiamen square-rigged sailing ships would have docked. Over the next weeks the streets showed themselves to be a delightfully jumbled collection of such contradictions and they constantly surprised me. However well I felt I was getting to know the place, it always had something else in store to raise an eyebrow. The city also contained an almost unrespectable sized slice of freethinking, 'alternative' society, and they provided an excellent contrast to the larger population of more traditional thinkers. All in all, the city was fun.

Johnny, the Beetle's owner, kindly gave me door-to-door service. Most of my gear had gone with the bike, so camping wasn't in the plan. For that matter climbing in and out of the 'space capsule' probably wouldn't have been possible anyway. The door he dropped me off at was the one belonging to a backpackers hostel called quite aptly, 'The Backpack'. With apartheid gone, Lee, Toni and Geoff, rare South African travellers, had recently opened it up. They believed that tourists were going to flock to the country and the hostel already had a good reputation. A neat and traditionally styled veranda fronted cool rooms with stripped wooden floors and white-washed walls. On going in it never occurred to me to check to see if the showers and toilets worked, but it was odd to find a place to stay without making the first question, "Is there parking for my bike?" The bunkrooms were mixed, which had felt rather strange at first but by the time the girl on the bunk above stripped to knickers in front of me next morning, it didn't feel odd at all. The hostel wasn't crazily expensive but it was a lot more than I'd paid just about anywhere else in Africa. That of course reflected the standards.

I arrived in the city with lots to do. My bones needed a check-up, the four teeth were still broken, and the mid January sailing date needed confirming. Besides all of that, Namibia's four missing days were a constant niggle; an Aids test would be in order. There'd been too many signs of Aids in Uganda and Tanzania and those visual effects had been frightening. The statistics had painted an even fuller picture. In Uganda it was said that a whole generation would be gone by the end of the decade. It hadn't seemed possible; the thought was just too enormous, but you could see that it really was going to happen unless there were some pretty dramatic developments in the world of medicine. The cynical afterthought to that was, even if there are such developments, will anyone pay the price of the help?

My bones were healing well and Lee recommended her dentist, who just happened to be a BMW biker and very good at fixing dinged gnashers. For the first time in six weeks, my teeth didn't hurt and my tongue wasn't getting cut on the sharp edges, but there the good news stopped. The shipping company told me that there wasn't going to be a sailing as planned. Instead, there'd be a ship on the thirty-first of December and another in the middle of February. The thirty-first was far too early; by then the cast would only just have come off and there wouldn't have been time to see much of South Africa. The middle of February was really too late as it would be autumn in Australia by the time the ship got there. It would also be very late in the year for biking in New Zealand, even if I'd been able to earn enough money to get there. Still, booking for mid-February was the only logical option and being positive about it was the only way to be. There was a reason and if I looked hard enough, there would be plenty of bonus points for arriving late. Sure enough, the hospital told me that it wouldn't be until the middle of January before the incubation time for Aids would be up. I'd wait. Life in Cape Town was not going to be hard, but my budget would

257

be very tight. This extra month was going to hurt it, but 'no worries', things had always worked out for the best so far, so why not this time too?

With the friendly staff at the Backpack mothering me, life took on a pleasant routine. It was easy to walk into the city and the days meandered by with exploring the streets, parks and markets. For a change I was a straightforward tourist and it was fun; I hadn't really felt like one since Italy and Greece. The weather was Mediterranean which fitted the mood. The people down on Clifton beach took full advantage of the sunshine and it was a bit of a culture shock; topless bathing had been pretty much a no-no in every country I'd passed through on the way down. The women on this beach, most of whom seemed to be rich, wore bikinis that left little to the imagination. In fact the amount of gold jewellery on some of the girls had covered more skin than their bikinis did. The contrast here was the cluster or two of black people sitting self-consciously around the fringes. Now they were allowed to be on the same beach they were testing the water. Decidedly cold for everyone – in every sense of the word.

Almost everywhere accepted credit cards and if I'd had enough money, I could have bought just about anything which was a very odd feeling after so many months. A Rolls, no worries, an ocean going yacht, sure, a diamond (no point, no girl), a hand carved statue, definitely. The contrast here came in the form of barbed wire on the walls and ANC graffiti, but the telephones worked every time, the petrol stations were spotless and there was even fast food of a kind that I recognised, bought and didn't bother with again. The market food stalls kept my custom but I did have a couple of pig-out sessions on some disgustingly delicious cream cakes. The cakes had real cream, and the cake itself didn't taste like coloured cardboard as it had everywhere else on the odd occasions I'd risked one before. The cinemas showed up to date films and now the Guinness on sale was chilled to perfection. Further north it had been on sale too, though often brewed in places like Nigeria. It always looked just as it should, but had inevitably been exactly the wrong temperature. Warm Guinness is an acquired taste. It was also fun to be around other travellers. The feeling was a pleasant one and strangely happy-family-ish.

The Backpack was a really good atmosphere in which to rub shoulders with travellers from many different countries. There were so many Aussie accents around that when walking the old colonial streets with their wrought iron balconies and verandas, it would have been easy to have been wandering the back streets of Paddington in Sydney. The two cities had developed fast during much the same period so perhaps the notion shouldn't have stood out as much as it did. An 'Ach man, don't be bleddy silly' or some such sentence would bring me back to Cape Town pretty fast though.

Travellers are inevitably on the lookout for a way to earn a bit of cash, and if a laugh can be had at the same time, all the better. Not that the two usually combine in the world of black market labour. The film company didn't want me because they said that my plaster cast was a little bit too much. It made me imperfectly 'cast' for the role I'd supposed out loud and collected suitable groans. But they did want almost all of the other backpackers at the hostel. The task? An advert for insurance. Now apartheid had gone, the Australians were coming to play rugby and an insurance company wanted as many people who could speak with an Aussie accent as possible. The hype, (the Wallabies v the Springboks) was all over the press and the advert was aimed at getting in on the roll. The perks included getting fed all day, supplied with free beer through all the shoots, and wages at the end. The acting roles were easy after a few takes. They only had to behave like pissed, totally obnoxious, hooligan Aussie fans. The worse they were and the louder they were the better. 'Look Out!' 'The Australians are coming!' Who knows if it sold insurance, but it sure made a lot of travellers happy.

One of the reasons for not wanting to leave South Africa in December was that I'd discovered that I had family relations there. As a child I'd been brought up to believe that my father and I were probably the last males with our family name. In Cape Town, it appeared that that wasn't true. The early days of colonialism had got my ancestors heading for Australia, and they had set out on two different ships. On meeting Rod and Claire, the South African Manicom family unfolded before me. It seemed that one of the ships had sunk in a storm off the coast of South Africa. Some of my ancestors were amongst the survivors and they vowed that having made it to dry land they would take their chances where they were. The family prospered and to my delight they made me very welcome. To my surprise there were strong resemblances between my father and cousins in England, and my cousins in South Africa. It was interesting to see how some genes had remained strong and it was a great feeling to suddenly have 'family'.

The world's newspapers were saying a lot about the political situation, but I wanted to know what people in the country were thinking and saying. I'd been making a point of talking to everyone who might have an opinion and of course just about everybody did. Some folks parroted the papers, and some were genuinely afraid for their lives thinking that their world was about to come to an end. For the more bigoted, ignorant and angry, it probably was. Many more of all backgrounds were cautiously optimistic. Change was going to happen and so it should, but the thing that worried everybody was how fast the changes would come, and whether they would come in peace or in anger. One of my cousins told me that there had been no chance to integrate black workers into middle or higher levels of companies, even though for some time they'd known that it should be happening. He said that the few brave companies that tried had to deal with poorly educated candidates (inevitably) and tremendous pressure from police, government, customers and other businesses. Some of the company directors who had attempted change had gone to jail for their efforts. The rules had been clear.

It was surprising to find how many white South Africans had had no idea about how bad things really were for most of the non-whites. Some had quite simply turned a blind eye to the reality. Though some had seen the effects of the cruelty and had elected to ignore them because they themselves didn't have a direct part in it, other than using different toilets for example. They told me that when you are brought up with that sort of thing being the norm, you don't think about it. You do think about paying your bills, educating your children, staying well and putting something away for retirement. The newspapers had so often printed propaganda and it was always tempting to believe it. This was a perfect example of the power of the printed word and we in the outside world had known more than they had. Some people admitted to me that they really hadn't believed that the horror had been going on until very recently, and even then hadn't wanted to believe it. When they'd known that the violence and deprivation really was true, they'd been shocked. Others had known about it, had protested and been beaten or jailed. A cousin of mine suffered that fate. I was equally surprised at how many had quietly done all they could, within the 'rules'. Though, one woman told me that she had been quite aware that things were bad but that she'd felt totally helpless. She'd felt guilty because of her feelings of helplessness and as much as anything else, she'd just hadn't known what to do. A man in one of the bars said to me, "Ach man, not everybeddy is brave."

Some of the 'Cape Coloured' people talked to me about it and their comments were guarded but positive. But hardly a black person would talk. Several of those that did looked over their shoulders as if habitually knowing that they shouldn't be speaking to me at all, let alone about this subject. A few were literally seething with anger and were taking every opportunity to make their strong and sometimes understandably extreme comments. I felt small when one young guy looked at me and said, "So you are a tourist. What sort of people live in your country that they should have seen what has gone on here and done nothing really to stop it? Do you want us to make you welcome now?" I, the 'rich' and free European travelling across Africa by motorcycle, couldn't say much to that, but having learned so much more already just hoped that these angrier people were not the majority. If they were, then the country was in trouble. The human abilities to forgive, to learn and to mend would need to be strong. It seemed to me that a lot more people of all backgrounds would be hurt if they weren't. The tourist office told me that roughly 78% of the population was black, 12.5% white, 7% 'mixed colour' and 2.5% of Indian descent; not much of a balance at all.

The more I talked to people, the more it seemed that there was in fact a quiet air of optimism from the majority. People wanted peace, they wanted wrongs to be righted and ultimately, many were now accepting that everyone should have the same opportunities. Perhaps the prospects for the country were good, though almost every one of the optimists made a point of telling me that there were vast areas in the north where guns, anger, ignorance and frustration were the norm. The Cape was the peaceful province. "You'll find out some more as you head up", they told me.

From the start, everything to do with the shipping company had involved time and in fact the whole process made me really think about how I could make the best of time. Further north in Africa it had been possible to let life just unfold before me, with only heat, the rains, and visas heavily influencing any plans, but now I had the feeling that I had to make things happen. The cast was almost ready to come off my arm but with shrunken muscles, riding the bike long distance wasn't a consideration for a while. So the question was, what to do next?

Option one was to stick to the original plan of picking the bike up in Jo'burg, and option two was to spend another big chunk of money and live the dream much sooner. The chunk of money would go by arranging for Libby to be trucked down to Cape Town. By doing that, as soon as it would be possible to ride, I could explore the Cape area some more. At the same time my arm muscles would be encouraged to grow again. Under my own steam, the journey north to the port in Durban would be rather more predictable, and exciting. I was very much aware of how dependent I'd become on other people, and after months of the bike allowing me to blow with the wind, this wasn't a comfortable feeling. The only way to see anything outside the city was to go by bus or train or cadge a lift with someone. Even the experience of breaking a barrier or two by travelling on the 'black taxis' lost its shine after a while. These were South Africa's version of the matatus and the emergency wrecks, but in much better condition. The atmosphere inside them was different as well. In Kenya, a muzungu had been tolerated with squashed good humour. In South Africa my presence often made everyone feel uncomfortable. Missing my two-wheeled friend, the money was spent and time started to feel as if it were being lived rather than just lived in.

Another chunk of money went while waiting for Libby to arrive; I had the chance to explore the Garden Route. Every South African I'd met had raved about the beauty of this area. Some travellers at the Backpack planned to hire a car and needed a fifth to share the costs. We crammed ourselves into a Fiat Uno and two packed weeks passed as if they were two days. We watched whales swimming just off the coast, visited tiny fishing villages of thick white-washed stone walled houses and we ate delicious ostrich sausages. The limestone Kango caves surprised us all with their beautiful collections of stalagmites and stalactites and we travelled on an ageing steam train that called at stations with names like George and Wilderness. Surfing on the steep waves at Jeffrey's Bay looked absolutely awesome and we topped the two weeks off by spending hours looking for elephants in the Addo National Park. In fact we'd just about given up hope of seeing any when, there they were – a mother, who was throwing dust across her back, an inquisitive youngster and a baby. Hiding under his mother from the dust, the baby was trying to suckle. For me, the cost of the trip was justified by that moment alone.

Before we left, Lee had very kindly told me that I should come to stay in her house until it was OK to head to Durban. The two of us felt very relaxed together and Lee said that it was nice to have someone to wind down with every day. Mellow evenings and long walks with her beautiful dog Pax forged a good friendship. Lee was her own variety of typical African kindness and hospitality.

Finally the cast was off and with perfect timing it was Christmas. Lee, Toni and Geoff had organised a party for the backpackers and two sheep were spit roasted in the back garden. Lion and Castle beers slipped down in a sunny 26 degrees. It wasn't a complete Christmas for me though; my presents and mail from home were sitting waiting in Durban's main post office.

The New Year slipped in during a party with Lee and her friends in their house on the southern side of the Cape. The ease with which the year started had to be a good omen. I felt that I was due one after my lame duck weeks. Then at last Libby arrived. Some Australian friends — Rob and Fiona — gave me a lift out to the truck depot and there she was, filthy and scratched. She'd obviously been standing outside for a long time, but had a clean bill of health at least. Now, finally, I was faced with riding her and I procrastinated for a moment or two, using checking her over as an excuse. Then it had to be done. Swinging my leg over all the edgy thoughts instantly disappeared as if it was the most natural thing in the world to be doing. She started first time and though my wrist still felt rather weak in fact it was my left hand, the clutch hand, which seemed most out of condition. It was aching furiously by the time we all got back to the hostel. But, if that was the only problem then it was good news. All that was needed now was some practice and I couldn't wait to get on with it.

In the morning Libby wouldn't start. After five hours of searching, nothing seemed to be wrong. Perhaps a good wash and a waxing would do the trick; maybe she was annoyed at having been neglected for so long. An hour later, clean again, and talked to, she started first time. But ten kilometres away she died on me, and again there was no trace of the fault. This was the first time I'd been stuck by the roadside on my own without a clue how to fix a problem. Fortunately, in my notebook was the address of a garage that could probably help me. I'd been given the name and address of Charlie's by another biker up in Kenya. Wolf and his brother Gerald are a bit of a legend on the bikers' circuit and over the years, in spite of the sanctions meaning a lack of spares, they'd managed to keep many an overlander's wheels on the road. Wolf came straight out to me with his truck and by the next day he and his BMW specialist Mohammed had found the electrical fault. I like a bike that waits to break down until help is at hand.

The close camaraderie of the few bikers I'd met had impressed me. Several times swapped information had stopped me riding past something well worth looking at. Having our own wheels frequently allowed us to stop and explore some very off beat places. At each of these remote places, the arrival of a dusty overgrown motorcycle had been full entertainment-value for the locals. Overlanders were a complete contrast to everyday life and everyone would want to touch, to talk, and to ask questions. Sometimes it had felt as if they were hunting for a way to rub off a little adventure into their own lives. At those moments it was always frustrating not to have enough language to be able to explain that in fact in some respects we were not so different from them. In my previous life, I would have loved some adventurous soul to pass through.

The roads around Cape Town were a biker's dream. The surfaces were great, the views spectacular and the weather perfect. Revelling in the freedom of being back on the bike it was easy to spend hours riding the peninsular, and the road around Chapman's Peak lived up to its spectacular reputation. Of course, being at the bottom of Africa meant that I had to go as close to the end as was possible but if it hadn't been for the sign, Cape Agulhas could have been any section of coast anywhere. The winemaking area of Stellenbosh had been a bit of a tease though. These roads seemed to have been changed so little over the years that they gave me the sensation of riding across an island in time. Long rows of neatly groomed vines stretched out as they had for generations. Ornate Dutch style farms always seemed to be set in the most picturesque parts of the vineyards and vast, solid looking barns stored the wines. Pity that wine tasting had been so likely to add to my list of fall offs, though I did risk a few sips and climbed back on the bike with a couple of 'take aways'.

One of the biggest surprises was at 'Boulder beach'. A penguin waddled right past me as if it was quite normal to be taking a stroll in the sunshine. But this brought it home to me; I'd done it – the north coast of Africa to the south – camels to penguins!

By the middle of January the Aids incubation period had been completed and I could go for tests. In a way, this living waiting for the clock to tick round gave me time to face the fact that I might well have Aids and therefore only a few years left to live. Snuffing it was no longer so distant a thought and therefore not so easy to joke about. It wasn't happening to me, but it was. Once the test was done there were five more days to wait for the results, and they were very long. I used some of them to go to have blood tests done for more ordinary lurgies that may have been picked up on the way down. Africa's guidebooks talk in one form or another about all the nasties that can have a go at you on the way through. Giardia, dysentery, cholera, gastroenteritis, hepatitis, sunburn, heat stroke, rabies, worms, malaria, typhus, typhoid, bed bugs, lice, leeches, ticks, yellow fever, prickly heat, diphtheria, bilharzia, sleeping sickness, meningitis, 'crotch rot', 'toe rot', altitude sickness, dengue fever and good old diarrhoea. The list of nasties had been daunting before I'd started the trip, and still was.

Faced with all this, it wasn't surprising that travellers' conversations often took on a somewhat basic tone, even between people who'd just met. To some, the number of illnesses they'd had seemed to be notches on their belt as if they were proof of being hardened and battle worn. Some would describe the intimate details with travel worn modesty, but when most travellers gathered around a campfire or a few beers, graphic descriptions would flow with sound effects thrown in. In fact, some of the funniest travel stories came from the disastrous effects of one lurgie or another. Dark runs to outside long drop toilets in the middle of the night always had potential. Spiders, mosquitoes and cockroaches inhabit these unlit huts, with their mud walls, stick and straw roofs, as if they'd been built especially for them. Disaster could be doubled when in an emergency dash one couldn't spare the time for a loo roll hunt and then inside the hut, someone had already used the last of the torn-up newspapers that would, in higher-class long drops, hang from a rusty nail on a wooden corner post. The biggest and best mosquitoes always seemed to have claimed the most frequently used long drops as their right. They also had the unerring ability to see pallid exposed buttocks in the dark.

Many Africans greet each other with caring, "How was the night? Are you well?" Perhaps we'd all picked up on the habit, but more likely it was just the gruesome in all of us having the chance to pop out and play. Or, it could have been that we'd all picked up on the African sense of humour. Not that I'm saying that Africans make jokes about the 'Cairo Craps' or the 'Addis Abdabs' but their humour seemed to be of a particular refreshing type. Slipped-on banana skins always got a laugh, whoever had done the slipping. Charlie Chaplin and Buster Keaton would have gone down a bomb. The laughter was never cruel but more a spontaneous recognition of the funny side of life and the unfairness of it. In a banana skin 'incident', the laughter, (which could involve tears rolling down cheeks) had nearly always been tinged with a tone of sympathy. A sort of, 'poor you thank goodness it didn't happen to me, but you did look silly'.

The malaria I'd probably been zapped with at Vic Falls would always be in the blood, but maybe something else was lurking there too. Whilst sitting waiting to do one of the 'ordinary' tests, I'd decided that if the Aids result was positive then the only way to go, was out kicking! I'd finish the trip, and then go to live somewhere beautiful like Kenya's Mombassa coast where Aids is rife. If I was going to die, I was going to do it in a great place and somewhere I wasn't likely to be treated as a pariah. Even having decided this though, the butterflies had fluttered on the way to get the results. The ordinary blood tests were clear except for Bilharzia. This is a parasite that basically eats your liver and kidneys. As for many people there aren't any symptoms until it's too late, it was good to have found out about it early. Bilharzia is the second largest disease in the world but mostly that's because it isn't diagnosed. The cure is just a couple of giant tablets. As a child in Zaire the treatment had been a series of injections with very large needles, so these tablets were easy to deal with.

The Aids results were back and they were negative. I grinned all the way home to Lee's; it hadn't happened to me this time and the sense of relief was phenomenal. Bravado put aside, it wasn't until I was sitting outside Lee's house soaking up a view which I didn't seem to focus on, that I allowed myself to admit I had been scared, really scared. I'd been frightened on the trip on several occasions but they had been nothing in comparison to this. I'd tried to be optimistic and to think positively through the whole process, but it was obvious now that I hadn't really convinced myself. I'd attempted to face the reality of the worst outcome, but in fact I had never allowed the prospect of having Aids, and all that would have been involved, to sink in. Now I knew I was safe, I seemed to be able to allow my thoughts to go that far and knew that without doubt I had escaped a situation that really would have turned my life upside down. When I had first been thinking about doing the trip, the thought had been in my mind that my life needed a damn good shake up, but this sort of shake-up had been extreme. The experience I realised had made me grow older, and I knew that the way I put everyday things and new adventures into perspective would now have a different balance and depth.

The twenty fifth of January was my own turning point. The bones were where they should have been at last, Libby was as ready as she'd ever be, and after nearly a year of zigzagging south, it was time to head north. In the main, Cape Town had been a pleasant limbo but now it was time to go.

The day started with high winds that made the trees lean, arms waving furiously at something far away on the horizon. The world looked as if a giant magnet was teasing and tugging every living thing towards the western skyline. The wild winds pushed and shoved me from one side of my lane to another as if I had no right to be disobeying the invisible magnet's demands. As the wind grew stronger, every exposed section of road was a battle between the strong gusts, gravity and common sense. I was not going to be stopped though; I was free and I was going to stay free! We ran for the north and under me Libby was singing. She roared with the twists of the throttle and purred her way through the sheltered zones. I sang with her and shouted at the wind to go and blow on someone else. Head down, riding ever faster, my old friend adrenaline popped and buzzed. We seemed unstoppable. Then a hefty gust of wind caught me on a gravelly corner and, "Oh ****", we were over. But, at least this time I'd learned not to stick my fist out and a grassy verge had taken the sting out of the fall.

That night, falling knackered into the tent, I knew that I was living again. It felt that I'd ridden across the day leaving giant exclamations marks behind me wherever I'd been. I hadn't realised how low I'd become, how worn out and how much Africa had taken its toll. Living in Cape Town's limbo had charged my batteries and the city had spat me back out into Africa, 'travel blind' no more. Long distance travellers often seem to get to a stage where they are still 'on the road' and out there 'doing it', but with something missing. It's almost as if the need to survive becomes more important than the early days' need to taste new things, see new things, and generally put oneself into more challenging situations than mere survival requires. South Africa's air of change was obviously infectious. My turning point had come at the perfect time; there were still a lot of kilometres to do.

"Ticket to the World"

'There are no foreign lands. It is the traveller only who is foreign.'

Robert Louis Stevenson

A side road that wasn't marked on my map led me down to Rainbow Bay. One of the nice things about being an original explorer or colonialist must have been the freedom to choose your own place names. South Africa in particular is full of some beauties and I supposed that there must be a story behind each of them. Were Dordrecht, Newcastle, Hamburg and Dundee named with fond memories of home? Had there been a Simon, a Pieter and a Richard of Simonstown, Pietersburg and Richard's Bay? Was it patriotism that had named Port Edward, Port Alfred and George? Had someone from the Orkneys really settled in Orkney and there had to be a story behind a town called Koffiefontein. Who had Christiana, Chrissie and Carolina been? But Rainbow Bay, what a great address to put on your mail.

The road grew smaller, and then it dropped me into a village that was set into the tall shady trees of a coastal forest. Rainbow Bay was narrow and rocky with white sand, and while the colours may not have been a full rainbow, there was a fair selection from the spectrum. It was one of those places where you are quite happy to let time stand still. There was absolutely nothing to disturb the peace or the delightfully stunning beauty of the bay. Sun-bleached and well-rounded driftwood trees, not just logs, gave me a perfect seat to watch the world from. The sea within the bay was a smooth glassy shade of aqua marine with a turquoise fringe along the sand. But outside the rocks, the water changed into a rich deep blue that high waves were cresting with a white that any washing powder manufacturer would have paid dearly to achieve. The sky above was a clear constant shade of azure that didn't seem to change in density however far away it stretched from me. The icing on the cake was the sudden appearance of surfers out riding the waves – their brilliantly coloured gear in perfect keeping, and their movements so naturally sleek that they complemented the scene. At first sight, the peacocks that wandered the camping site seemed like a touch of overkill but after a while it seemed quite natural that these shimmering birds should be there. They appeared to think that it was quite natural that I was there, and that they were going to get fed.

I lingered far too long, watching the gorgeous surfer girls in the Miss Jeffrey's Bay beauty competition. This no doubt contributed to the feeling that the next day's ride took me into a time warp. I moved into one of those strange zones that for one reason or another are tucked away across the African continent. In this case, a line that someone drew on a map somewhere had set a lot of lives into comparative slow motion. The 'state' of Transkei, an apartheid political solution, made me feel as if I were, within minutes, riding from the first world to the third. This state had been designated a homeland for 'blacks' in the early days of apartheid determination to separate black and white. It was almost a bad dream. Litter lined the road, carrier bags flew from thorn trees as if they were some sort of bizarre, multi-coloured, third world only shrub. It was almost as if this forcible detention had taken away traditional pride in the land. In fact it wasn't very good land and the 'line' seemed to have blocked any chance of an overflow of environmental awareness from first to third. The people either no longer cared about their surroundings, or had never been taught that 'carrier bag trees' would become carrier bag forests; that these in time would suffocate what goodness there was in their 'state'. A heavily laden truck in front of me, with sagging springs on one side, bald tyres and peeling

271

paint, spewed a kilometre long trail of greasy black smoke behind it. The fumes had smothered me, coating the exposed part of my face with sooty residue. That would never have happened in South Africa which probably had the cleanest breathing trucks on the continent. Scrawny goats hopped lazily across the rocky hillsides, their herders carrying catapults so like those used by the boys in Tanzania. The asphalt road had ended smooth and slick on the South African side, to be taken up in Transkei as a collection of patches and holes. Within seconds of rolling back into 'Africa' the game of space invaders had restarted with a delightful feeling of familiarity, but this time the holes seemed to have been spaced intentionally so the game changed to sport as I slalomed my way northwards. Roadside signs pointed the way to 'Wild Coast' places - Mroxexnoxa, Mqanduli, Ngqelenl, Colly Wobbles, Coffee Bay and Port St. Johns. The former conjured up a vision of ancient Africa and the latter, the early times of colonialists, farmers, explorers and entrepreneurs alike. It felt as if I were riding through a strangely warped unreality of a real world. It was a bizarre place.

In Transkei's capital Umtata, African vibrancy with its energy and flamboyant colour was alive and kicking. But at a stop for fuel in one of the larger towns, there was a sense of fear from the boys that sold boiled sweets, chewing gum, bananas and sugar coated doughnuts from wooden trays and chipped enamel bowls. They watched me, knowing that they shouldn't approach and it was almost as if they seemed to know that my skin colour was as good a 'Keep away!' warning as the brightest reds of the birds in the forests. My smiles had almost tempted the bravest boy across, but experience and the others held him back. I rode on, sad that the natural curiosity of children towards something new had been so fearfully squashed out of these, the next decision makers of their world. How different they were from Gresham in Malawi, from the boy who'd adopted John and I in the mountains of Tanzania, or the one with the bike poster way back in Ethiopia, and of course from the character who'd hooked the umbrella onto my luggage in Egypt.

Then, in the next village, as a bony, long horned cow followed me through with resigned and baleful eyes, an excited child ran out smiling and waving at me. He'd stopped dead when I grinned and waved back, but watching him in my mirror his face was lit up with a smile again as he did a little jiggle on the spot. If things were to develop as they surely must, then were I to ride by in a few years' time, perhaps this boy would have sold me a doughnut at the petrol station. For me, he lifted the day again and instead of just doom and gloom, I started to see the beautiful things that were around me as well. The colours of the land were changing rapidly as the broken clouds above made the sun flicker across the rolling hills. The wind was still running hard and the sun was darting between the cloud breaks as if it were a giant strobe light. It seemed to fit the irrepressible energy that the new times were bringing alive in the people. Away from the factories of the first world and the wood smoky fires of the third, the air was clean and clear and the colours of the land were bright and sharp. The trees and the horizon all had crisp hard-edged lines that were just beginning to tinge with sepia as the sun carried on with its fall into the centre of southern Africa. At the border, a crew cut, clean-shaven, machine-gun toting soldier respectfully asked if I had any guns on board.

Back into South Africa, in spite of the banana trees it felt like riding into a touch of England, and as the darkness came over the sea I eased into Margate. Giant camping sites were dotted in and around the town, and to me they looked like vast luxury refugee camps for run away white folks. Instead of aid agency blue, the predominant colour was white. White caravans, camper vans and tents were parked or pitched within inches of each other and privacy didn't seem to be an issue as braais were being lit. The friendly hissing sounds of cans of beer being popped seemed to echo in a curious sort of delayed action around the site. I didn't have meat to braai or an endless supply of cans of beer to pop so with my dusty, battered bike and dusty, oily bike clothes, I felt decidedly like a square peg in a round hole. But by then, alone was OK, and anyway, my tent was green.

The days of the ride through Africa had so often felt as if I was moving through a sort of twilight zone. By being forever an outsider, the journey seemed to have floated me on or just below the surface of a hundred of Africa's worlds. My twilight zone had allowed me to suck up a little life from each of those worlds and I'd learned every time, but now sitting alone outside my tent and pretending to read, my thoughts wandered. How many of the worlds that I'd been lucky enough to taste, had I at the same time managed to scar with my foreign ways? Had I been a form of pollution or just another fact of modern life? Had I helped the local economies by buying my food, paying for hotels, buying souvenirs and my petrol? Or, had I just flaunted my comparative wealth? Would what the continent and its people had taught me ever make a difference to anyone else but me, and in fact should it? Had the simple fact of getting off my backside and getting out there to experience things in Africa been enough justification for the trip? Or, was pure, simple, fun and adventure enough of a reason to have been there?

In the morning, still feeling a little mellow, I decided to take advantage of my rediscovered freedom and took a holiday. The white sands and palm trees of the coast had got the better of me but there was also a niggling problem with Libby: she'd blown a fuse five times on the way up. There was something wrong with the indicators and they'd often not worked at all, which was a worry. Though quite aware that probably no one took a blind bit of notice when I religiously used them, the indicators were strangely comforting. If there was an accident then it wouldn't be because I hadn't been doing everything possible to prevent it. This time Libby's problem was easy to find. It was just a loose wire, and it had been shorting out. I actually felt quite pleased with myself for this bit of on-the-road problem solving. Even if it had been a lucky find and not very difficult, it was a start.

Posters advertised the film 'Sarafina'. It was a surprise to see it on show in this particular town as the film was a graphic portrayal of apartheid, and most of the holidaymakers here seemed to have gruff Boer accents. Cliché maybe, but the men appeared to have been built out of granite blocks and above their square, muscle bound shoulders most had crew cut, blond heads. They all looked disgustingly fit but also appeared to be stepping through a foreign land as if confused to be there. It was amazing to see both black and white intermingled in the cinema audience. No one walked out of the movie in disgust though there had been a few contradictory comments made while it was on. As we filed out afterwards I was surprised to see how many of these big men carried pistols in full view. It was a sobering sight. There'd been stories of people making their homes into mini fortresses, and others of normal everyday folk making their cellars into factories for manufacturing bullets and the like. In the Cape, guns may have been carried but if they had been then they were carried discreetly. Down there, houses had barbed wire but up here, many had razor wire, electric fences and enough broken bottles to start a recycling business. Each fortress house was perhaps a mini Transkei, but for whites.

Out on the street was more evidence of apartheid's habits. Several times black and white did what I ended up calling the South African waltz. Walking down the street towards each other, they would tense, and carefully watching each other would complete the opposite sides of a circle before walking on in a straight line. If they'd had hackles, they'd have been up.

Back at the camping site I greeted my neighbours as I had done the day before, but this time I was greeted back with a, "Man, come und have en beer with us." Not once did we approach a controversial topic and they taught me a lot about life on an Afrikaner farm up in the north. The family were genuinely good fun and it was hard to imagine them being active enthusiasts of apartheid. They made me so welcome that in spite of a strong itch to ask awkward questions, I held back. Fortunately the beer shop was open so buying my share of the rounds wasn't a problem, even though there were many. These folks could really drink. Much later, I weaved my way back to the tent and poured myself into my sleeping bag. For once I didn't need my earplugs.

That general feeling of bonhomie was almost spoiled over a giant breakfast. My neighbour's braai was hard at work again, almost groaning under the weight of steaks, sausages, bacon, prawns and mushrooms. Fried eggs were on the calor gas stove, and if it hadn't been for the farmer's obviously enlightened daughter I'd have fought a lonely losing battle over the top of those eggs. The trouble started when one of the campsite workers walked around the corner of the adjacent trees, gently sweeping leaves as she came. The farmer was instantly furious and hurled all sorts of foul language at her for creating dust while the breakfast was cooking. 'Kaffir', 'bitch' and 'stupid ignorant bastard' were some of the kinder words. I had to speak out even though it felt as if I was abusing all of his very generous hospitality; Boer hospitality comes traditionally with a capital 'H'.

He stopped in mid torrent and swung round to me, fists clenched, his face red with fury at the woman. It was probably only that I was white and a guest that stopped him from belting me. But once I started, it wasn't possible for me to stop; I said straight out that she owed him an apology, but that a little dust hadn't earned his outburst. I told him that I would leave and thanked him for his kindness but, putting it as politely as possible, said that he appeared to be reacting without thinking. Fortunately his teenage daughter agreed with me and put her hand on her father's arm; his face was already losing its redness. It occurred to me then that the daughter's generation (of all backgrounds) was going to have the next big battle.

The cleaning lady did apologise, in a quiet, frightened voice. Then, to my surprise the farmer seemed to have realised that he was no longer allowed to behave in this, to him, probably quite traditional manner. He apologised back. For a moment I was absolutely stunned, as were most of the other people around the breakfast trestle. I couldn't help but be impressed but was also left with the feeling that perhaps I'd been horribly pompous. The meal continued with slightly overdone eggs and to begin with, a rather subdued air. But it wasn't long before the sunshine and the good food did their job.

The streets of my last big city in Africa managed to lose me like no other had. A wrong turn somewhere led me down to the edge of Durban's harbour. Lined with palm trees and flower gardens, the Esplanade was actually a very nice introduction to the place where I would spend my last hours on the continent and in fact, my wrong turn had been a short cut to the city's youth hostel. A biker several weeks before had warned that Durban was a hard place to find cheap accommodation with parking for bikes. He'd already been there and had said that the YHA was the place to aim for. Most budget travellers seemed to steer clear of the few YHAs that were in Africa, the list of rules being the big put-off. For me they were always more expensive than my usual places anyway. The YHAs may well have been cockroach free, but I was long past the stage of being worried about that.

American John, last seen hunched in the Tanzanian bus, once told me about one of his cockroach encounters. As a Peace Corps volunteer up in Cameroon his job was to teach, which he was without doubt well qualified to do. If nothing else, his sense of humour was such that he could have kept a class of kids to attention for hours. As with all Peace Corps volunteers there often isn't a choice of accommodation with the 'job'. John's wasn't too bad but it had a serious cockroach problem; there'd been hundreds of them. These beasties will fly anywhere and are major disease carriers. John worried a bit and then tracked down where they were coming from. Actually that hadn't been hard – there'd always been a suspicious buzzing noise in the outhouse. The bug killer John bought from the market flamboyantly guaranteed doom, death and destruction. He dumped the lot down the loo and ran for cover, shutting the door and sealing the edges behind him. From inside came a furious buzzing and beating of wings, and John thought, 'Ah ha, you scum!' Then from next door came shouts of horror. What he hadn't realised was that the next-door neighbour's outhouse was connected to his and the hundreds of dying cockroaches were snuffing it all over the place next door. My Mother had once told me that in the Congo villages, babies could never be left unattended; cockroaches would happily lunch on tender young fingers and toes if they were given the chance.

Durban turned out to be amazingly multi-cultural. Being a city there were of course plenty of white folks, many of whom were descended from British immigrants. I was told that the black people were a real mix but that the largest percentage is Zulu. This area and to the north along the coastal belt was in fact their traditional homeland. There were also many Asian South Africans and they seemed to dominate middle business. Apparently, they were in the main descended from the hundreds of Indians that had been brought across to work in the fields. The cane fields had been one of the biggest employers. Neither blacks nor whites seemed to like the Asians though. A well-dressed white businessman said to me, "Indians! Bloody coolies with no manners or cheating businessmen who all scratch each other's backs. Asian bloody Mafia, that's what they are!" Perhaps they were, but if the way he'd been speaking was common then they'd probably had to be that way. As an outsider it seemed that there was a large dose of jealousy from both sides. Perhaps in fact everyone should have been applauding their talents and determination.

Rather than Cape Town's complementary contradictions, this city seemed to be a far brasher affair. As practically the largest commercial harbour on the east coast of Africa, it had that particular sort of atmosphere that goes with so many major port cities. There was a lot of grey and the architecture was a collection of styles that mostly had no connection to each other, except for the fact that they were there. The few remaining old colonial buildings seemed to be hanging on in times that appeared to have very little mercy. 'Old' was space-consuming and inefficient, but to me the palm tree lined squares that were bordered by gargoyled buildings were a necessary break from 'city'.

That all sounds a bit negative, but even after Cape Town the mass of people and the noise felt quite unnatural. For me, a city was purely a place to get things done and otherwise to be avoided. This one though was an eclectic jumble of African, Asian and European life that either rushed in the way of cities, or eased gently along in the humid, energy-sucking air that this section of coast is famous for. Small pockets of individuality thrived and I began to see that it was these that gave Durban its backbone and actually turned the jumble into a unique identity. I began to like the place.

Down on the beaches were the remains of the 'colour code', but even here the beginnings of integration were obvious. The various colour groups were starting to blend, though it was clearly still early days for complete change. Even the swimming outfits were an example of that. The white people dressed exactly as you would expect them to on a white sand beach that had great curls of surf rolling in. The guys wore long multi-coloured shorts and carried surfboards or beers. The girls were just about clad in skimpy bikinis and lounged lizard-like in the sunshine. The Asian women were dressed from neck to toe in thin baggy robes that when wet clung to their bodies so much that I wondered what the point was. In spite of their robes and regardless of age they splashed about enthusiastically in the waves. It was nice to see how relaxed they were and this was a real contrast to the demure and quiet versions of themselves that you'd normally see on the city streets. The black guys wore whatever they had and so did the girls. The guys managed shorts, cut off trousers and a few even had proper bathing trunks. The women didn't seem to care what they had on and wherever they were, there always seemed to be great hoots of laughter and water fights. They were full of life and living it to the full. One very enthusiastic fighter was a blimp-shaped woman who was dressed in a voluminous bra and an enormous white girdle; both were big enough to make quite satisfactory hammocks! She didn't care though. Fun was the name of the game and her shrieks left no doubt that she was having it.

Rod and Claire had said that I'd find more family up here and they'd arranged for me to link up with a couple of cousins called Ros and Brian. We got on together instantly and with a surprise party they introduced me to the rest of the family. It was a good opportunity as some of them were about to leave the country. Fearing the worst for their children's future, they'd made the decision to go to the States or Canada. Many people were leaving and the country was already feeling the effects of the brain drain, but after these months in South Africa I was beginning to understand why some felt they had to go. Not many blamed those emigrating and more than a few were envious of their chance to get away, even if the price was having to leave almost everything behind.

The ANC was very strong in this province of Natal, although they had made a lot of promises that they knew they were unlikely to be able to keep. I was told the story of a white businessman whose work had relocated to the other side of the city. He decided to move house so that he wouldn't have to commute so far every day. A new house was found and the plan put into motion.

Their maid had been with the family for many years and they felt that in fact she was pretty much part of the family, so they'd bought a house with a granny flat for her to live in, rent-free. That way she wouldn't have to catch the bus each day from where she was currently living in one of the townships. The family also decided to pay for her to travel across the city to see her friends and that she could have her brothers and sisters to stay with her so long as they didn't move in permanently.

As the story was being told, I thought how fair the family were being, but apparently the maid had outright refused to move and informed them that there would be trouble if they carried out their plan. The ANC had told her that in return for subscriptions and her loyalty, when they came to power the house would be hers. Of course this was of great importance to her and she obviously felt that the promise would be kept. I wondered how many similar promises had been made and how the future was going to deal with them. The ANC's promise was full of potential betrayal, but in a way was understandable. It was perhaps a combination of raw politics and survival.

The hostel was a great place to make new friends. Three of us, a lanky American guy, Raphael, a petite Israeli girl called Micael and I, decided to explore some of the nearby Drakensberg. The name means Dragon mountain and the craggy angular mountains look exactly like a dragon's back when viewed from the plains. None of us had much time left so we decided to be selective and instead of doing a rush tour of everything, we'd pick our spot. We concentrated on the Monk's Peak area. The three of us set off to trek in the baking February heat. I'd loved the idea of that phrase when writing it in my journal. 'Baking heat in February', but I'd still managed to shiver at the thought of that time of year in England. As we trudged over the rocky path my mind had wandered over what I'd been doing in February the previous year.

It seemed almost a lifetime away and I walked thinking about the cold learning rides on Jersey, and of one of my first rides on the BMW. I'd set off one frosty Sunday morning to take the bike up onto some of the clifftop paths; there was a real variety of surfaces to ride on up there. In those days I'd felt quite useless and totally unprepared. Once, I'd even looked up the definition of 'sanity' in the dictionary. 'Collins' said 'Sane – of sound mind, sensible, rational'. And, 'Insane - stupidly irresponsible'! The latter had seemed to fit the bill just a little too closely for comfort, but this particular Sunday morning all had been going well. The tracks were kind to me and having already ridden them on the little trail bike I'd learnt on had helped a lot. There hadn't been any hidden nasties and though much bigger, the BMW had been surprisingly easy to manoeuvre. By lunchtime I'd had enough though and there were too many people around to continue.

The way back up to the road was along a narrow sunken track that cut across the steeply sloping fields. It ran between two probably six-foot high banks that were topped by hedges. There wasn't actually very much of the track to see as most of it was covered with long, tussocky grass. Where the grass had already been in the sun it was pretty dry, but where it had been in the shade for the morning it was wet and in places still a little frosty. I stood up on the bike, as I'd read that you are supposed to do when riding over ruts and through puddles, and set off. But then over the brow of the hill two people appeared. They looked in their late sixties and the man was dressed in a tweed jacket, a soft checked shirt, knitted tie and a flat hunting cap. The bottoms of his cavalry twill trousers and his brown brogues were soaked from the damp grass. His partner was not dressed so appropriately for a stroll on the cliff tops. She wore a long camel coloured winter coat that was topped with a paisley scarf and a large glittering broach. On her feet were town shoes. Their two poodles were dressed in fluffy white coats and were leaping around their owners, yipping and yapping as they came down the hill towards me. I'd been going at a fair speed and hadn't expected to see anyone coming down this particular track, so had to react quickly. The bike slid on the wet grass and promptly twisted round to wedge its front wheel on one of the low banks and its rear wheel on the other. It had then of course fallen over, and down hill at that.

The couple and the dogs stopped dead in their tracks and stared at me. Fortunately I'd fallen clear and though by then was soaking wet, wasn't hurt. The man took a pace towards my embarrassed red face and said, "I say old chap, do you think you could possibly move your motorcycle to one side so that we may pass?" There was no way to move the bike on my own so I asked if he could help me, and to his credit he got stuck straight in. As he did so he called over his shoulder, "Come along Mabel, put a bit of weight in, what." If it hadn't been such a struggle at that moment, I'd have been smiling! We got the bike up, and with enthusiastic cheerleading support from the poodles, had it pointing in the right direction. With a "Cheerio old chap" from the couple, who I hoped would dine out on the story, I climbed back on the bike and started the engine. As soon as they were around the corner, I put the bike into gear. The back wheel spun on the grass, the tail of the bike did an enormous wiggle and we both ended up back almost exactly where we'd been. No damage again, but I had to laugh. Yeah, this had been good practice! Another cliff top walker gave me a hand for this lift and then kindly stayed as I gently let the clutch in. The back wheel had spun on the damp grass again but this time I'd been expecting it, so hung on tight and within seconds we were at the top. So much sweat had poured off me whilst picking the bike up in the cold that I'd wondered what it was going to be like picking it up in Africa's heat.

Natal's heat on this morning was blistering. When we found a waterfall that had a large pool under it we called a halt. Even at altitude the air was warm enough to allow us to sit and slumber in just bathing gear. After a long cooling soak, the rest of the day had been whiled away with lazy conversation in the shade of a perfect look out point. The one hundred and eighty degree view had taken in the cool craggy mountaintops, the rich greens of the hillside forests, small villages of round, straw-roofed mud brick huts and shimmering yellow valleys below them. With a change in the breeze, a shout and then the sound of laughter made it up to us for a freak moment or two, and that had changed the conversation from the sights of Africa to Africans themselves.

The people of Africa had impressed me, not so much the officials, but the ordinary people. Many along the way had appeared to have deliberately kept themselves connected with nature, and they seemed to approach the environment with a sort of respect that we in the developed world so often lack, even though we know better. The only thing that mucked up this connection was a sudden availability of things first world – like carrier bags. People in Africa hadn't seemed to 'just' exist; each day was lived with splashes of flamboyant style. There'd usually been cheerful laughter around and it never seemed to take much to set someone dancing. Perhaps, this was because life was so hard that only those with energy, determination and intuition make it through each day? But much as I respected their ability to live 'on the edge', things in my world like hospitals and dentists were aspects that I wouldn't want to leave behind.

In Uganda a Canadian girl had come up to me to ask directions for the bus station. Her right thigh was almost double the size it should have been. It was bright red and there was a dangerously nasty smell coming from under a dirty bandage. She'd been travelling through Zaire by local transport and one day the mini bus she'd been in had toppled into a ravine. One of the tubular steel seat legs had snapped and had speared her thigh, from one side to the other. Five people had died and many had been badly injured so she had been relatively lucky. She'd been travelling for a week to get to hospital and in spite of the state of her leg and my arguments, planned to travel on for another day to get to a hospital in Kenya. She'd heard too many scare stories about Uganda's in those days. In England, I might have had to wait for an hour or three in A&E but certainly not for a week and certainly not with a festering leg. For most of the people in Africa, the Canadian girl was still lucky though; she could afford the inevitable hospital bill or had insurance.

A friend had been shocked to hear tear-rolling laughter from an African over someone's death. The laughter hadn't been from lack of respect but more perhaps from awareness of the harsh reality of life and as a sort of mental protection towards yet another death. Living on the edge seemed to inspire the desire to make the most of each day and being in this positive atmosphere had been one of the best things about the continent. I'd read a saying to the effect of 'Remember your yesterdays and dream of your tomorrows, but live the day!' For sure, many priorities African people seemed to have were totally out of order in comparison to those of the developed world, but maybe our world had developed too far and left reality behind? Were we always trying to live for tomorrow?

We came down into the muggy warmth of the valleys as the sun began to turn red over the mountains, and whilst skirting one of the villages we'd seen from the look-out, there was a totally unexpected sight. A skinny, tan-coloured dog with a curly tail stood there, hackles raised, but so silently that he'd warned us something was up. We followed his stare and there on the edge of the huts was a lioness. She padded gracefully through the almost deserted village, only seen by the dog and us. He had his tail between his legs and ears flat against his head as he watched this invader of his territory. For all of us, instinct won the day and we stood still too. Soon, with a long arrogant 'So what' stare over her shoulder, she eased into the undergrowth and it was only then that the dog noticed us. He started guiltily before slinking away. As he went he looked at us with a worried expression on his face. Perhaps he was afraid that we'd report his dereliction of duty. I just admired his common sense.

Micael and I cruised back to Durban on our own. The 'Valley of a Thousand Hills' was a dream to ride on the bike. The road curled and swooped its way along the grassy contours through Zululand. As we rode I could easily imagine proud Zulu warriors coming over the hillsides in great feather-topped, shield-banging waves. The buzz of riding through the centre of such a deeply historical area was one of pure enjoyment; life was good. A bike, a girl, a view, a sunny day, a warm breeze, good health and an open road to ride; life was very good.

Slightly to the north of Durban, after passing through waving fields of sugar cane, we came to Shaka's Rock. Shaka was one of the most important of the Zulu chiefs and this jutting rock was a prominent symbol of his power. His enemies were brought to this rock, and then as the ultimate punishment, would be thrown to their deaths from it.

Legend and history say that Shaka was quite a character. He was a ruthless military genius who transformed the Zulu style of warfare into a technique that had even the famous red-jacketed British regiments beaten for a while. Traditionally the Zulus would have rushed fearlessly and  noisily at their foe, and then hurled their short-stemmed assegai spears with fingers crossed for some sort of suitable effect. Shaka trained picked men from the Zulu tribes to live only for battle. These regiments fought at close quarters in disciplined formations using their assegais to stab and slash, not throw. They were formidable and the Zulu borders had stretched dramatically as a result.

Shaka ended up going the historical way of many who live by the sword. He was assassinated, and by his brothers at that. The next famous leader was one of those brothers and Dingane turned out to be just as clever and fearless as Shaka. It was he that the Boer trekkers had to face as they headed north on their search for farming land. They were also trekking northwards in an attempt to get away from British government interference in the way they wanted to live their lives. The Boers, though much smaller in numbers than the Zulu, won the war with a combination of pure bravery, superior tactics, and guns.

My cousin Ros invited me to stay with her for the rest of my time in Durban. She'd already proved to be a great cook, a lover of good wine and had a wonderfully dry sense of humour. The trip had taught me that staying with people was the best way to find out more of what it was really like to live in a country. These rare and valued times had been some of the occasions when it was possible to do more than skate across the surface of whichever world I was in. The two of us spent long hours talking history, both family and South Africa's. We'd talked books and music, laughed a lot and while she was at work, I explored more and worked on Libby. To get her into Australia without having to pay quarantine fees, she had to be absolutely spotless. This involved literally going over her with a toothbrush and disinfectant; removing no doubt, a little soil from each country since England. The final preparation was to cover her with '3 in 1' oil. With luck this would work as some sort of protection during the passage. She was going on the manifest as 'baggage' and so it would be a free ride for her, albeit up on deck. Even covered with tarpaulins, the salt air and spray were bound to be a big problem so the more I could get oil onto the better. It was a nice job to do whilst sitting on the shady kerbstone outside Ros's house, a constant stream of everyday Durban wandering or chugging on past me as I worked. Strangely, no one took any notice of me – it was almost as if I wasn't there.

The day came to take Libby to the docks. A representative of the shipping company was going to show me where to go to deal with customs and then how to find the ship. With the practice of the past year, customs at least were a doddle, but finding the ship would not have been so easy without help. One of the brilliant things about the journey was that the bike had made me go to places a traveller wouldn't usually see. She'd taken me into office confusion, made me deal with the devious and also with the dusty remnants of old colonial systems. But she'd also taken me where good humour was the order of the day and where the frequent desire of the officials was not to cheat but to help. Almost every minute of whatever had been going on had been bonus time, though inevitably slow.

The container ship, the MSC Sabrina, lay waiting for me. Her one hundred and eight metres of jet-black hull and white superstructure were going to be my home for the next seventeen days. The crew were a mixture of Samoans, Madagascans and South East Asians. Some of them took the panniers, bags, helmet and jacket up to my cabin for me, and there wasn't a long wait before one of the Italian officers came to explain what the plan was to get Libby up onto the deck. To my relief he was a biker himself and had done this job before. He knew exactly where to fix the sling ropes that dangled from the dockside crane and moments later there she was, swinging in the breeze above my head. My pride and joy was suddenly fifty feet up, hanging on the end of a few ropes. It was a nervous moment, but I did see a potentially expensive spot on the underside of her engine that I'd missed cleaning.

An hour later she was strapped to some solid looking fixing points and was swaddled in so many layers of plastic that she appeared to be more like some sort of bizarre cocoon than a bike. The cabin looked like a mini version of a good quality motel room and there was even a towel embroidered with my name. This was a far cry from the roaches, bed bugs, fly-infested long drop toilets and the risk of head lice.

Ros and I spent the last day together. We wandered the botanical gardens and sat on the grass drinking champagne, which seemed a fine way to be leaving. I woke at six the next morning with a sore head and the feeling that for some reason the day was different. A swaying motion and the rumble of the engines below told me that we were on our way. From the deck the view held a still slumbering city in a dawn collection of mother of pearl greys. Seagulls cruised over our wake as seagulls are supposed to do, and I pondered the feeling of loss that was growing stronger as the coastline grew smaller.

The year had been superb. It was a good thing to be leaving slowly by ship; the seventeen days passage would give me time to relive the pile of memories. I knew that now I had much greater faith in human beings; Africans had taught me that. I'd been as low as I never wanted to get again, but I had survived and grown as a result. I could ride my bike without falling off all the time (well, mostly) and I'd been right, Libby really was proving to be my ticket to the world. So many of the year's high points would never have happened without her. I'd wanted adventure and had found it. I'd also found an angel who, except for the odd little snooze, had taken good care of me. After the months of this strange, hard, contradictory and wonderful continent, I really knew how it felt to be alive.

The trip had started by leaving a country in the dark and I'd been nervous. This time my ship was leaving in the dawn and I was feeling good. In front of me lay Australia and I'd already realised that my late departure was in two ways, good news. There'd been more time in Africa, and the fruit-picking season was about to roll in Oz. With Libby to get me around, I'd get work for sure. As they say in Swahili, "Hakuna Matata - No worries."

Epilogue

Australia worked well, and I earned enough money to make it back to Europe, but before taking off on the route back, via SE Asia, Asia, the Middle East and Eastern Europe, I met my partner Birgit in New Zealand.

My Guardian Angel continued to work overtime on the journey across Asia, but still had the habit of taking a nap! You can find out more in my book, 'Under Asian Skies'.

What next? The adventures continued to roll and there just didn't seem any good reason to stop – so I carried on around the rest of the world.

First stop Africa. Birgit had never been there and I leapt at the chance to travel this amazing continent again. It can be hard going but it's beautiful and almost every corner hides new adventures and discoveries. The third book in the series, which I'm completing as this second edition of 'Into Africa' goes to press, takes you from Africa and on through the vast and stunning lands of South America.

Over eight years I covered 200,000 miles and managed to visit 55 countries on seven continents. The BMW continued to work really well in spite of my abuse and the places I made her go. At the time of writing she remains my sole means of transport. She's still quite young in comparison to Birgit's 1971 BMW road bike and yes, Birgit rode her own bike. She came on the back of mine in India and Nepal, but for some reason said she felt better in charge of her own two wheels. Strange that…

sam-manicom.com

Also by Sam Manicom:

'...a unique and wonderful adventure.'
Ted Simon

'...the thing I most enjoyed about this book was the feeling that I was there
with him as he went through everything. I've travelled a bit myself in this
part of the world, and the feeling of the hustle, the smells, the people, the
smiles the bartering, Sam's account brought it all back to me. The fact he did
it on a bike only gives me hope that one day I too could be riding the road
from Quetta to Taftan myself.'
London Bikers.com

'... this fascinating adventure story by a man well and truly bitten by the
world motorcycle travel bug... What sets this book apart is the detail in the
narrative... It's the positive human relationships that make this story, from
simple welcomes along the road to meeting life long friends... This book will
undoubtedly inspire some to follow in his tracks and is essential reading for
anyone contemplating such a journey...'
Bikers Digest

'Sam's acute observations on everything from human behaviour to locations
visited, transport the reader effortlessly to places another world away.
Prolonged stays at locations along his chosen routes allowed him to
accumulate much knowledge and he doesn't hesitate to pass that on. While his
first book 'Into Africa' was detailed I felt his confidence shine through even
more with this second effort.'
DieselBike.net

Acknowledgements

So many people made this trip both possible and an amazing adventure. I hope that as you read the book you'll know that I am eternally grateful to you all for making my mad idea work.

I do need to say a special thanks to Peter and Edith, and to Ashley and Donna for keeping me alive. Also to Mike and Sally for sharing part of their trip with me.

I must also pick out Jez Cooper for his special talent. The motorcycle cartoons are his work and I'm grateful to him for drawing them for me. Thanks to Francis Matta for her help and advice with the line drawings. Thanks to Fil Schiannini and Chris Woodman for the cover. Their innovative minds and graphic skill made it work.

Many thanks to Paul Blezard – motorcycle journalist and photographer, Nikki Madan Schiannini – who I wish I'd had as a teacher when I was at school, and Peter Henshaw - motorcycle magazine editor and author. Also to Chris Scott - motorcycle adventurer, desert specialist, author and tour organiser www.adventure-motorcycling.com. The guys took my words and heaped on some very pointed but tactful criticism; Into Africa is so much better because of your help.

Bernd Tesch, author, supporter and supplier of motorcycle travel equipment to those with touring intent, and owner of the world's largest collection of motorcycle travel books, also gave me great advice about Into Africa - www.berndtesch.de

I owe thanks to my partner Birgit for working with me on the book, for her support and unstinting belief in me. Also to my family who I know dealt courageously with the more disastrous of my adventures.

Thanks to my friends who didn't laugh when I said I was going to write the book, and have supported me all the way down the line. You are special people and this trip has made me realise just how much I value you all.

And finally, a historical note. I've very carefully not specified dates within 'Into Africa', until now. The actual dates of events are not so important to me – adventure, the land and the people are. Thankfully, those things change little with passing time.

However, if you know something about recent African history then you'll have recognised that this year was a time of major change in Southern Africa. 1992 was the time when apartheid was finally being removed as a form of governing South Africa, and people were either optimistic or extremely fearful about what would happen.

This fear made many white people leave their homes forever, and some of those who stayed took on an increasingly defensive/aggressive stance.

But, the vast majority of South Africans who stayed in their land, of all colours, got on with the job of moving the country forward without full-blown civil war. Integration has obviously been hard – there were generations of mindsets to change and many promises that had been made were broken.

On the whole though, to my mind, South Africa has moved on from this time in a really positive way – I very much hope that it will continue to do so. It remains a country in Africa that is one of my favourites.

The tale of Zimbabwe is another situation altogether. This wonderful country has been wrecked by a despotic ruler. I am always amazed that western powers have not worked harder to stop the desperate straits that this country is now in, from getting even worse. But no, we seem to sit on our hands quite happily and nothing happens, except things do get worse, much worse.

As for most of the other countries from my journey, theirs are tales of typical Africa. Governments have changed, sometimes as a result of war. Bribery, corruption and disease are rife and the poor remain struggling to survive each day. No doubt they do this with hope, warm and friendly smiles, laughter and keen entrepreneurialism.

My memories of Africans are not of people with their hands out begging for help, but of people who are keen to make things happen for themselves. They do need fair treatment by those of us who are fortunate enough to live in the First World.

They also need a little respect for being the amazing people that so many of them are.

293

Motorcycle Organizations, Clubs and Parts Suppliers:

www.gsclubuk.org
BMW GS CLUB UK – Enthusiast's Club

www.ukgser.com
BMW 'GS' Enthusiast's Forum

www.bmw-club.org.uk
BMW Owners Club

www.bmridersclub.com
The alternative BMW Owners Club

www.cwmotorcycles.co.uk
Extremely helpful and experienced BMW garage

www.motobins.co.uk
BMW parts and equipment – New and Second hand

www.motorworks.co.uk
BMW parts and equipment – New and Second hand

www.james-sherlock.co.uk
BMW parts and equipment – New and Second hand

www.worldofbmw.com
Find out what's going on with BMW here

www.metalmule.com
Supplier of aluminium panniers

www.touratech.co.uk
Suppliers of an extensive selection of overlanding kit

www.traveldri-plus.co.uk
Traveldri:Waterproof bags, tents and loads more

www.dhl.co.uk
Invaluable for parts delivery

Bob Porecha Motorcycles/London Tel 0208-6598860
Very experienced 'Air-head' mechanic

www.berndtesch.de
Books, survival training, equipment and overland enthusiast

www.bmwmoa.com
    BMW Owners Of America
www.airheads.org
    Airheads Beemer Club
www.advrider.com
    The Adventure Motorcycle Forum

Publications and Travel Information:

www.horizonsunlimited.com
    The world's motorcycle travel site
www.lonelyplanet.com
    Supplier of superb travel guides
www.bradt-travelguides.com
    Some useful general info
www.jupitalia.com
    Ted Simon author of 'Jupiters Travels' and 'Riding High' and his new book – 'Dreaming of Jupiter'.
www.globetrotters.co.uk
    Travel club for independent travellers
www.wanderlust.com
    Travel magazine
www.stanfords.co.uk
    UK's best one stop shop for travel books and maps
www.backpackers.co.za
    The best Backpackers' hostel in CapeTtown
www.africaguide.com/culture/artcraft.htm
    A Cultural Discovery
www.uclh.org/about/htd.shtml
    Tropical Disease Hospital/Travel Clinic offers pre-travel advice e.g. inoculations
www.adventure-motorcycling.com
    Chris Scott desert specialist

www.maf.org
Mission Aviation Fellowship
'Stay Alive in the Desert'
  K. E. M. Melville, ISBN 0 903909 11 1

Embassies:

www.fco.gov.uk
  British Foreign and Commonwealth information
Botswana: botswana.embassyhomepage.com
Egypt: egypt.embassyhomepage.com
Ethiopia: www.ethioembassy.org.uk
Kenya: kenya.embassyhomepage.com
Namibia: namibia.embassyhomepage.com
South Africa: www.southafricahouse.com
Sudan: www.sudan-embassy.co.uk
Tanzania: www.tanzania-online.gov.uk
Uganda: uganda.embassyhomepage.com
Zambia: zambia.embassyhomepage.com
Zimbabwe: zimbabwe.embassyhomepage.com